WILSON'S SYNDROME

The Miracle of Feeling Well

E. Denis Wilson, M.D.

Third Edition

CORNERSTONE PUBLISHING COMPANY
Orlando, Florida

Wilson's SYNDROME ISBN 0-9629875-0-6
Copyright © 1991;
Second Edition Copyright © 1993;
Third Edition Copyright © 1996 all by E. Denis Wilson, MD

The publisher and author have printed this material for awareness purposes only. They do not recommend that you or your doctor base your treatment solely upon the information presented here, but that your doctor consider these points and the medical literature in this area in the exercise of his clinical, professional judgment.

Published by Cornerstone Publishing Company
4524 Curry Ford Road, Suite 211
Orlando, Florida 32812

ORDERING INFORMATION

Product	Description	Price	S&H
Wilson's Syndrome, Miracle of Feeling Well	This book	$21.95*	$4.00
Doctor's Manual for Wilson's Syndrome (Second Edition)	Fully illustrated, well-organized, Treatment Protocol in full detail	$27.00*	$3.00
Information Magazine	16-page, full-color	$4.00*	included
Single Doctor Referral	By Zip Code	$3.00	included

* volume discounts available; International rates higher

By Credit Card, simply call **800-621-7006**

By Check or Money Order, please send to:

**Wilson's Syndrome Foundation
P.O.Box 539
Summerfield, FL 34492**

Also visit our website @ http://www.wilsonssyndrome.com

TABLE OF CONTENTS

Table of Contents

Table of Contents

Dedication

To the Source of all truth and knowledge.

INTRODUCTION

Bottom Line It Works

There is sometimes a tendency for us to dismiss something out-of-hand even though we don't know anything about it. To save anyone any embarrassment, I should point out that the treatment for Wilson's Syndrome works. It works predictably and reproducibly well. There may be some debate as to <u>why</u> it works, but don't make the mistake of saying that it doesn't, because it does. The most significant aspect to this treatment is that patients often <u>remain</u> improved even after the treatment has been discontinued! This "resetting phenomenon" is what sets Wilson's Syndrome apart.

I am very pleased to report that over the last 5 years (since the first edition of this book) hundreds of other physicians have reproduced my results.

I have given presentations about Wilson's Syndrome at CME-approved Medical Conventions. Wilson's Syndrome has also been the topic of many radio shows, as well as TV, Medical Newsletters, Magazines, other Books, Textbooks, Nutritional Guides, the Internet, etc.. The word has spread quickly to the delight of thousands who suffer from it and who are now obtaining relief. In this book, is the information that is bringing predictable and reproducible help to many who were told nothing was wrong, and nothing could be done to help them. This condition has been overlooked for a long time and must not be overlooked any longer.

What Is Wilson's Syndrome?

Wilson's Syndrome is a condition that causes symptoms characteristic of decreased thyroid system function. Named Wilson's Syndrome in 1990, it is best identified by its reproducible and predictable response to a special thyroid hormone treatment protocol recently developed by

Introduction

E. Denis Wilson, MD. It is the cluster of often debilitating symptoms especially brought on by significant physical, or emotional stress that can persist even after the stress has passed (due to a maladaptive slowing of the metabolism). It is characterized by a body temperature that runs, on average, below normal and routine thyroid blood tests are often in the "normal range."

Classically, Wilson's Syndrome sufferers are going along fine in their lives, and then they go through some major stress, develop symptoms of Wilson's Syndrome and are never the same.

They often develop numerous burdensome complaints, like those listed on the cover. In this book, each symptom is characterized so thoroughly, that you'll get a good idea of what it feels like to have Wilson's Syndrome.

Wilson's Syndrome is especially brought on by stresses such as: childbirth (#1 cause), divorce, death of a loved one, job or family stress, surgery or accidents, excessive dieting, and others.

Some people are more prone to developing Wilson's Syndrome than others. Their symptoms may come on earlier in life, and tend to worsen more gradually over time, they may not even know what it feels like to be normal. It seems that those who are most prone to developing WS are those whose ancestors survived famine, such as Irish, Scot, Welsh, American Indian, Russian, etc. Most susceptible of all seem to be those who are part Irish, and part American Indian. But under severe circumstances people of any nationality can develop Wilson's Syndrome. It seems that about 80% of Wilson's Syndrome sufferers are women. In this book, Dr. Wilson gives his explanation as to why.

It's easy to predict whether or not a person has a low body temperature, based on his/her symptoms and how and when they came on. If people have a story that's just classic for Wilson's Syndrome then the chances of their temperature not averaging below 98.6 degrees is less than one in two hundred. In fact, most of them by far, will average 97.8 and lower (>92%).

How Your Low Body Temperature could be causing so many different symptoms... check it with a mercury thermometer.

The efficiency of all the chemical reactions taking place in your body vitally depends on your <u>body temperature</u>. Virtually all of these chemical reactions depend on properly functioning enzymes to take place as they should. How an enzyme functions depends on its temperature as well as its structure. When enzymes are too hot they get too loose and when they are too cold they get too tight, but when they are just the right temperature they are just the right shape and function with the most ease. When the temperature is too hot, too cold, or unsteady, the enzymes will spend less time in their optimal shape—which simply translates into having a less than optimal metabolism. So, for the body's enzymes to work at peak efficiency **the body temperature has to be just right**. Thus, the body temperature is like one critical card at the bottom that can't be moved too much without bringing down the whole house of cards. And in this way, low body temperatures are more than enough to explain numerous burdensome complaints.

(Of course, Wilson's Syndrome is not the only possible explanation for each symptom but because it can be so debilitating, and yet is so common, easily recognized, and easily treated, it should be considered first, not last).

Doctors have long been concerned about patients having very high fevers, because it is well known that high fevers (i.e. 106 degrees) can cause denaturing (malforming) of the enzymes, brain damage, and even death. Likewise, if a person is pulled out of an icy lake and has a temperature of less than 85 degrees, doctors consider it a medical emergency because warming will be necessary for survival.

It is also clear that body temperatures 1 to 1-1/2 degrees above normal [of 98. 6] can produce familiar symptoms of fever. Similarly, body temperatures that run 1 to 1-1/2 degrees below normal can also produce a very characteristic set of symptoms. So, it is obvious that the proper functioning of the body vitally depends on it being at the right body temperature.

POP QUIZ (Fill in the blank): If a <u>very high</u> temperature can be <u>very bad</u>, and a **very low** temperature can be **very bad**, and a *pretty high* temperature can be *pretty bad*, then a ***pretty low*** temperature can be?_____. If you answered: ***pretty bad***, you get an A+.

Unfortunately, medical schools have taught doctors not to pay any attention to a relatively low body temperature; perhaps because it is not immediately life-threatening, or because the associated symptoms have been mistakenly considered psychological or attributed to other causes. In this book, Dr. Wilson shows how many different medicines are frequently used in an attempt to address patients' symptoms one-at-a-time, when they would be far more responsive to treating the underlying problem. Immediately life-threatening? No, only enough to make some feel "half-dead."

It's Easy To Check Your Temperature...

Take your temperature, by mouth, with a thermometer (preferably mercury/glass) every three hours, three times a day, starting three hours after waking, for several days (not the three days prior to the period in women since it's higher then). For each day, add the temperatures together and divide by 3 to get the average.

Almost everyone's temperatures are low in the morning, but the temperatures go higher in the afternoon and lower in the evening. So, it's a better comparison to see if the temperatures are running low in the middle of the day when the temperatures are supposed to be at their highest. This is because the symptoms of patients with Wilson's Syndrome are, by far, most likely to resolve when their temperatures are brought up to average around 98.6 degrees during the day. NOTE: People can run consistently low temperatures even if they feel hot all the time or sweat easily— be sure to check it with a thermometer!

Wilson's Syndrome: How Such a Simple, Easily Recognized, and easily treated problem has gone overlooked.

"Because I can't get these symptoms to improve with thyroid medicine, they can't be improved with thyroid medicine."—That's not necessarily so. This condition hasn't been so easily recognized in the past because doctors didn't have a way to get it better.

Because some patients' symptoms did not respond in the past to a certain thyroid medicine given in a certain way does not necessarily mean that their symptoms have been "found" to not respond to <u>any</u> kind of thyroid approach . To think so, is a little like concluding that since certain infection-type symptoms don't reliably clear with a penicillin shot, they can't be from an infection. Commonly, infections that wouldn't respond to a penicillin shot will respond to some other antibiotic, or even to penicillin given in another way (for example, intravenously).

"The people that are more likely to benefit from the thyroid method I'm using have low thyroid blood tests, therefore people with normal blood tests can't have a thyroid responsive problem."—That's not necessarily so either.

This is like concluding that "The pay-phones that are more likely to benefit from a repair-man using his tools to replace their receiver cords are those having cords that have been completely severed, therefore pay-phones that don't have severed receiver cords can't have a problem that might benefit from repair [with tools] ." As it turns out pay-phones <u>with</u> intact receiver cords may <u>still</u> not work properly, because something else might be broken, like the <u>coin mechanism</u>. In fact, the coin mechanism is <u>far more commonly</u> the problem, in pay-phones that are out-of-order, and it's certainly possible for them to be repaired [with tools] . So, just because a problem is more obvious doesn't make it more common or more important. In a similar way, doctors have overlooked a few more common thyroid-responsive problem by preoccupying themselves with the ones that show up on thyroid blood tests.

What makes Wilson's Syndrome so simple and so obvious is how typical the patients' stories are before treatment, and how reproducibly and predictably the symptoms respond to proper T3 therapy.

Why Our Medical System Hasn't Understood The Thyroid System Or Your Symptoms Well Enough To Help You—It's like not understanding that there's more to making ice than just water.

The glandular portion of the thyroid system provides the raw material (what is measured by thyroid blood tests) needed by the peripheral portion (downstream to the glands) to deliver the right mix of the thyroid hormones T3, T4, and perhaps RT3, to provide proper thyroid stimulation of the cells in order to generate an adequate body temperature to prevent symptoms of unbalanced thyroid system function. If the glandular portion, or coarse tuning, wasn't working well enough, then insufficient raw material would be produced, which would show up on the blood tests, and the shortage would be felt all the way down the line, eventually resulting in symptoms. Just as it's hard to make enough ice when there's not enough water. But if the glandular portion were perfectly fine, and there was a problem in the peripheral portion, you could still get symptoms as seen in Wilson's Syndrome. That's because it's also hard to make enough ice when there's plenty of water, but not enough cold . When trying to make enough ice, it's easy to see if there's enough water, but how do you know if it's been cold enough long enough ? That's a little tougher— but the best way is to see how much of it is ice. That's why the fine tuning of the thyroid system is best assessed by the temperature and the symptoms; because it's easy to see if you have enough raw material (normal blood tests), but the best indicator that things are regulated well is when your temperature is normal and you're feeling well.

Our medical system has been distracted by an observation that was made over 50 years ago - that the low-thyroid-type symptoms that were responsive to the thyroid treatment approach they were using at the time, seemed to correlate fairly well with findings on thyroid blood tests. They found that when you're having trouble making enough ice, and it gets easier when you add more water, then you probably weren't getting enough water; which they also found was an easy enough problem to recognize in the first place (with tests). So they decided: "To make enough ice, let's busy ourselves making sure we have plenty of water and the rest will take care of itself;" and that's essentially where our medical system has been ever since. They have been hoping, frequently assuming, and in some cases even pretending that by ensuring there are thyroid hormones such that there are normal blood tests, there would also be sufficient thyroid stimulation of the cells, good temperatures, and good health and well-being.— But that's not necessarily so. As we've discussed, there's more to making ice than just water. **That's where it starts, not ends**. This is how the treatment method for Wilson's Syndrome was developed. By being conscious of the entire thyroid system, including the **peripheral** portion, as well as the **glandular** portion while keeping an eye toward the resulting temperature and symptoms, plenty of ice was made far more reproducibly and predictably. A chapter of this book, is devoted to explaining how Wilson's Syndrome was uncovered. In fact, it has been seen that of the people whose low-thyroid symptoms resolve with the right kind of thyroid treatment given in the right way, probably >95% don't have a problem with the glandular portion of their thyroid systems. In other words, for most people that are having trouble making enough ice, it's not because of a shortage of water; they have plenty of water, they're just having trouble making it ice.

Why Thyroid Blood Tests Aren't Always Conclusive

Thyroid hormones do not have their action in the bloodstream, but in each cell of the body—which can't be measured directly.

The glands of the thyroid system (hypothalamus, pituitary, thyroid) function to provide proper levels of the thyroid system hormones in the blood stream. Blood tests are very good at assessing the function of the **glands** of the thyroid system, because they are very good at measuring these levels. They aren't always conclusive, and frequently don't correlate well with a patient's low-thyroid-type symptoms because the hormones don't have their action in the blood stream but in the cells of the body, and currently there is no way to measure that action directly. **Body temperature patterns correlate better with a person's low thyroid-type symptoms because rather than trying to estimate what will happen at the cell, they better reflect what has happened in the cells of the body.** You know there's got to be something wrong with this picture: Upon hearing your complaints and history, your doctor's first thought is "low thyroid." In fact, your story is so classic for low thyroid function that he's positive your tests will be low, and he's getting excited about the benefit he's confident you'll get. He's just about to explain how you're likely to get a big improvement and how important it will be to take the thyroid medicine properly, as he flips to the results of your blood tests (which are in the "normal range"). And in the next instant he says: "Your TSH and T4 blood tests are fine, therefore you're normal—so, your symptoms are definitely not thyroid system related and can't possibly respond to thyroid treatment" (while perhaps adding in something about whether or not your symptoms are real [when they were real enough moments earlier] and he or she may even suggest psychological counseling). 100% total about face? Discouraged only by a less-than-conclusive blood test? So now you wonder, "Doctor, are you concerned at all about trying to help me with my problems, or are you satisfied with lining up numbers on that piece of paper? Is it possible that there could be a thyroid approach that might work beautifully under these circumstances, that you're just not aware of yet?" These tests, like all tests, provide only limited information so why act like they provide more than they do? Besides, we all know that every test of any kind has false positives and false negatives. So, why jump past the mark, to make wide-sweeping conclusions (based on insufficient information) that aren't necessarily so, and to be inappropriately authoritative?

This book contains a common-sense discussion about how there is far greater variation in thyroid blood tests than in body temperature patterns, and why that's important.

What You Can Do On Your Own That May Correct Your Symptoms And Protect Your System?

Your body is designed to do two things:
1. Not starve.
2. Get things done.

When working properly, it will function appropriately somewhere between these two extremes:
1. Conserve as much energy as possible to protect against starvation and physical threat, even if some things don't get done.
2. Get as much accomplished as possible, no matter how much energy is consumed.

The first extreme would be more appropriate if there was a shortage of food, or if times were tough, but would be very inappropriate if not. The second would be more appropriate if there was an abundance of food and resources, but would be very inappropriate if there wasn't. Wilson's Syndrome is basically when a person's body gets stuck functioning inappropriately close to the second extreme.

So, it would be good to give your body reason to think that times aren't tough, that there is a sufficient supply of food with no threat of impending shortage, and that productivity is preferable. Such measures might be able to coax your body out of "conservation mode" and protect it from getting stuck there again. Inside this book such measures are described in good detail.

Why, When Treatment Is Needed, It Almost Always Is Not Needed For Life, But On The Order Of Months.

This book describes how one's symptoms could respond quickly and completely to the right thyroid treatment given in the right way. **The hallmark of low thyroid problems is that while few things can make folks sicker, few things respond as dramatically to proper treatment. This is what**

makes the area of thyroid so exciting. But, the trick has been determining, in any given patient, which is the right medicine, and how it should be given. And this challenging problem has turned a lot of excitement over the years into a lot of frustration, disappointment, failed assumptions, and faulty conclusions all based on insufficient information.

As it turns out, many people's low thyroid symptoms respond predictably and reproducibly well to their body temperature patterns being raised close to 98.6 degrees (on average) using the right thyroid medicine given in the right way. T3 (liothyronine or triiodothyronine) is frequently more useful in accomplishing this in more people. However, T3 has not been very well tolerated in the past because of it being strong but short-acting. But a sustained-release agent that is used in many sustained-release medicines on the market can be used with T3 medicine to make it far better tolerated. The method developed by Dr. Wilson involves using T3 incorporated with such an agent, to be taken every twelve hours by mouth.

Frequently, the patients' symptoms resolve and remain resolved even after the treatment (which sometimes consists of one or more "cycles") has been discontinued. In this book there is a detailed discussion (about 80 pages worth) about the principles of management, with some special notes. Because of space constraints it is not exhaustive, but it is extremely informative and will give you a very good idea of what's involved in the treatment of Wilson's Syndrome. It's always preferable to be able to get off medicine rather than to stay on, and this result is more often possible when the RT3 levels have been depleted. This also is accomplished with T3 more readily than it is with T4-containing medicines. It is felt that bringing down the level of RT3, by supporting the metabolism in the meantime with T3 for a time, interrupts the vicious cycle of impaired T4 to T3 conversion so that you can make T3 well on your own again. T3 therapy should not be undertaken casually, it must be done precisely and carefully, and is not completely without risk (before a therapeutic trial is prescribed, the potential risks and potential benefits should be considered and discussed on an individual case basis with your doctor). In many, many cases the right thyroid medicine given in the right way can make all the difference in the world in the lives of those who need it.

As discussed previously, our medical system has not been paying enough attention to what is happening in the critical portion of the thyroid system that is downstream from the glands of the thyroid system. Also, they're not concentrating on your temperature and symptoms. They're hoping that by controlling things upstream via your blood tests, that things will automatically work out well at the cell.

It often works out better to concern oneself more with what is happening closer to **where the action is**, in the portion of the system downstream from the glands (peripheral portion). By paying attention to things closer to **"where the rubber meets the road"**...near the cell, your resulting temperature, and your symptoms, one may often improve the symptoms more reproducibly. For example, imagine you were trying to write your name with a rubber pencil that was 3 feet long, while holding the end away from the point. You could press down, but it might wiggle this way, or that, and would be hard to manage. But if you held it down by the point, you'd have a lot better chance of being able to read your name when you were done. Likewise, when a doctor makes sure your T4 levels look about right on your blood tests, that T4 may get converted to T3 (which is 4 times more active than T4), or it might get converted to RT3 which is totally inactive. How much goes one way and how much the other can change readily (on the order of days or perhaps even hours) depending on the circumstances. In fact, in this book Dr. Wilson explains how and why patients with Wilson's Syndrome who are treated with T4 (levothyroxine) can actually get worse; or if they do get better, their symptoms frequently worsen again after 2-3 months. And if the dosage is then increased, and if the symptoms do improve again, they usually worsen again after another 2-3 months, or may worsen "right off the bat" with that increase or a subsequent one. To try to eliminate your symptoms by looking only at blood tests is like trying to write your name from three feet away with a floppy pencil. **Although it is common practice, it is not proper to give thyroid medicine without regard to body temperature patterns.**

Four Myths About The Thyroid System

Myth #1. Once a person needs thyroid medicine to improve low thyroid-type symptoms, or low thyroid blood tests for that matter, he/she will always need thyroid medicine for the rest of his/her life.

Even glandular insufficiencies of the thyroid system can be temporary. This makes it possible for people to be weaned off thyroid medicine sometimes, with their glandular function coming back up to normal. And very frequently, people without glandular insufficiencies can be weaned off treatment successfully after their symptoms have resolved with treatment.

Myth #2. If a person is given thyroid medicine when the thyroid blood tests are normal, or when the thyroid gland is normal, it will damage the thyroid gland.

Whereas, thyroid medicine can rest a person's thyroid system for a time (which can often "reset " things), much like birth control pills suppress a woman's own female hormone cycles (frequently useful when used for a time to correct irregular periods), no studies have ever shown that it can damage a previously healthy gland to prevent it from functioning normally again after the medicine is discontinued. The function of many patients' glands can come back up again after being suppressed for more than 20 years with thyroxin (T4).

Myth #3. Thyroxin or T4 is the most important thyroid hormone, and everything depends on its blood test levels being within a certain range.

Actually, there was once a boy who was born without thyroid function, and he was started on T3 instead of T4. He grew and developed normally and passed, without problems, on into adulthood without ever having a molecule of T4 in his body.

Myth #4. Thyroid medicine, T4 or T3 is absolutely necessary and something "you'll probably need for life" one minute if your blood tests are low, and then automatically become very bad for you if your tests are normal, the next.

Wait a minute. Thyroid hormone (T4, T3) has been floating around in our bodies since birth, and is absolutely necessary for good health. There is nothing inherently bad about the molecules; they can't and haven't directly damaged the tissue of your heart, brain, or other tissues. There is not a shred of evidence that suggests that thyroid hormones, when used properly, can damage the body in any way. But of course, thyroid hormones are medicine, and as with all medicines, should be used only under the thoughtful supervision of a doctor. Taking thyroid medicine is not completely without risk as nothing is.

Yes, it's not advisable to walk through an unfamiliar roomful of furniture at night with the light off. But that doesn't make it dangerous to walk through rooms full of furniture, especially when they can very often be negotiated quite comfortably when the lights are on. The problem has been that our medical system has been concentrating only on the problems affecting the glandular portion of the thyroid system which they were able to correct well using blood tests as a guide, but when the tests were normal they (not surprisingly) were not able to improve low thyroid system symptoms reproducibly with the treatment they were using. And since they did not have the principles of management recently developed (for Wilson's Syndrome), nor body temperature as a guide, they had virtually no way of monitoring treatment and consequently, more commonly encountered problems. Thus, generating very little benefit on one hand and some problems on the other, they gave upon that roomful of furniture, closed the door and decided/pretended it didn't exist.

Does Your Doctor Know What He's Talking About? 7 Polite Questions You Can Ask To See If You Have Reason To Think So.

I . What's the purpose of the thyroid system? **Answer: (See Chapter 2)**

2. a. Where do the thyroid hormones have their action? **Answer: In the cells of the body (at the nuclear membrane receptors).**

b. How many thyroid hormones have any activity? **Two, T3 and T4.**

c. Which has the most activity, or is the active thyroid hormone? **The active thyroid hormone is T3 and it has 4 times more activity than the raw material T4.**

3. a. Where is most of the active thyroid hormone produced? **Outside the thyroid gland.**

b. What, if anything, affects its production? **Stress, fasting, illness, cortisol, certain meds.**

c. If it can slow down is it possible that something can cause it to stay down? **Yes.** If no, why not?

4. a. What do thyroid blood tests measure? **Glandular function, levels of thyroid hormones in the bloodstream.**

b. If the tests measure the levels in the blood, does that necessarily reflect what's happening at the site of action in the cells? **No, blood tests don't measure whether or not there is adequate thyroid stimulation of the cells.**

5. If you give me T4, or if I already have enough in my system to provide for normal tests, how do you know for sure it will be converted well enough to provide sufficient T3 to the active site? **He/she doesn't, because that can't be measured directly at this time.**

6. If very high temperatures are very bad, and very low temperatures are very bad, and pretty high temperatures can cause pretty significant symptoms, can pretty low temperatures cause pretty significant symptoms? **Yes.** If no, why not?

7. Would you please tell me if and how you know for sure? *(Can be used sparingly with all of the above). Also, don't be afraid of, or afraid of asking for medical articles or medical literature on the subject. You can read. Make your own evaluation. If you feel what you're reading isn't logical, that very well might be because it isn't.*

As you ask these questions, realize that this is one area of medicine in which doctors have had really no good reason for much of what they've thought, said, or insisted. This area has been neglected. There has been too little research done, and much of what has been done is poorly designed, with faulty conclusions being drawn from insufficient information. This kind of ignorance breeds confusion, which breeds insecurity. Many doctors feel uneasy about thyroid to begin with because they know it's important, powerful, and vital, but they know they haven't gotten a very good handle on it from what they're being taught by our medical system. So, understandably, they, and the experts who are teaching them, can be a little sensitive, and/or defensive. While in some cases, they can even be surprisingly easily provoked/ offended. Be on the lookout for "studies that have 'conclusively shown this' and 'definitely shown that,'" which have not necessarily shown anything of the kind—this is a favorite of those who love to draw faulty conclusions based on too little information in an effort to justify their point of view. But, doctors are people too, and they have feelings, so be kind.

Also Discussed In This Book

Hypochondriac? Doctors not being able to find a physical problem necessarily means you don't have one? They should be quicker to consider their limitations than to jump to unfounded conclusions. (See Chapter 4).

Emotional and Social Implications. There are very typical emotional and interpersonal manifestations of Wilson's Syndrome (short-suffering, end of the rope, out of resources, and even "not caring," etc.) This may give you and those close to you an explanation as to why (and how) you're just not feeling, or acting yourself. (See Chapter 7).

More and more doctors are recognizing and treating Wilson's Syndrome. The theory behind Wilson's Syndrome is well supported by information already available in the medical literature.

There is also available a Wilson's Syndrome Doctor's Manual that is written for physicians but recommended to patients as well, that makes the treatment protocol easily and quickly understandable. It also includes forms, case studies, and management flowcharts.

Chapter One

1. VERY SIMPLE, BUT VERY SIGNIFICANT

What if there was a condition that was so common that its manifestations, signs, and symptoms were sometimes considered to be a "normal" part of life? Let's suppose that it could make people miserable, but could not be easily proven or demonstrated with blood tests currently available? What if the condition caused signs that might not be obvious to those who came into contact with the suffering person? Or, what if its manifestations were usually attributed to other causes so that the underlying condition would continue to be overlooked? What if the person suffering from the condition was sometimes the only one who could really tell that there was something wrong?   What if the condition was so insidious that it sometimes wasn't even obvious to the suffering person that there was something physically wrong, leading them to doubt their own mental and psychological health? What if the root problem was a physiological deficiency so fundamental that it could virtually affect every function in the human body, and thus cause all manner of symptoms? And finally, what if this condition continued to be overlooked for years in spite of being very recognizable and easily treated?

If one considers the possibilities, it's easy to see the effect such a condition could have upon our lives. It could account for a great deal of lost productivity and decreased quality of life in our families, jobs, and social lives. It could lead to personal discouragement and unfounded conclusions and criticism from others.

If this one problem could be easily treated, then a large number of awful complaints could be relieved with one simple and effective treatment. And so it is with Wilson's Syndrome.

The Story Of Anna

Anna's problems began after she had undergone several surgeries. She never felt well, and on occasion could not even

1

get out of bed. She suffered from severe premenstrual syndrome, migraines, depression, easy weight gain, itchiness, fatigue, and panic attacks that kept her from driving in heavy traffic.

Over a period of time, she went to more than 10 doctors in search of an explanation for her condition, which worsened after each operation (the last being a hysterectomy). She was referred to a teaching hospital for comprehensive evaluation (by internist, infectious disease, OB/GYN, gastroenterologist, dermatologist, and ENT).

In Anna's words, "It was so frustrating since I've always been health conscious and was even a weight-training **instructor**. I ate all the right foods, and did all the right exercise (working out at least three times a week), and I still wasn't feeling any better, so I knew something was wrong."

Fortunately, after being diagnosed as a typical Wilson's Syndrome sufferer, she was able to experience relief almost immediately with treatment.

Anna's reaction was typical. She says, "I was astounded to see that the answer could be so simple. With treatment, it felt like someone had flipped a switch. I was so happy to feel good again."

Anna's experience could be multiplied by thousands who have seen their lives transformed.

Observations That Point To Wilson's Syndrome

There are a few unusual observations that form the basis for this book

First, there are many symptoms that can be associated with decreased thyroid system function. If one carefully questions patients who are seeking treatment for any **one** of these symptoms, it soon becomes apparent that they are often suffering from **many** of the characteristic symptoms.

Second, in such patients, their symptoms often come on together after an identifiable stress, and persist even after the stress has passed.

Third, in these patients, there is almost always (more than 99.5% of the time) found body temperature patterns that average consistently below normal, that is, less than 98.6 degrees Fahrenheit taken orally (usually about 97.8 degrees).

Fourth, when such patients are treated correctly with the **right** thyroid medicine to bring their body temperature patterns closer to normal, the symptoms often predictably and reproducibly resolve.

Fifth, (and what sets the treatment protocol for Wilson's Syndrome apart from any other approach) the symptoms often <u>remain</u> resolved, with body temperatures remaining normal even <u>after</u> the thyroid hormone treatment has been discontinued.

These simple and unusual observations turn out to have profound significance and far-reaching ramifications.

Different people have their own definitions of simplicity. Some consider something simple if people are already aware of it. Some base simplicity on how many people can understand. Simplicity can also be measured by how predictable a certain situation is and how many variables are involved. For example, if one could easily predict the outcome of a certain process with a high degree of success, then one might gain experience with such a process, become more and more comfortable, and thereby consider the process simple.

The smaller the number of variables that one needs to consider to predict successfully the outcome of the process, the simpler the process. One might compare the cockpit of a 747 jetliner with all its switches, gauges, dials, handles, and levers, with a light switch. Flying a 747 involves a great number of variables (a lot of buttons to press, and gauges to read). It would certainly be simpler to switch on a light than to fly a 747. In the same way, the underlying problem in Wilson's Syndrome is extremely simple, because at its root lies **one** important variable, that is, insufficient active thyroid hormone interaction with the nuclear membrane receptors of the cells to produce desirable body temperature patterns. It is difficult for me to conceive of a medical problem that is more simple than the problem of Wilson's Syndrome. There is nothing complicated about it. There is nothing difficult, hard to understand or unpredictable about it.

There are many other things in medicine that are simple in theory also. For example, if a person is cut with a knife, he will bleed. If the bleeding is severe, it's obvious that it is preferable that the bleeding be stopped and the wound treated appropriately with bandages, stitches, or otherwise.

What sets Wilson's Syndrome apart from many other uncomplicated problems is that it just so happens to affect one of the most fundamental regulating processes of the body. And because of this fact, it can affect essentially every other process in the body by affecting the body temperature. This significant point is what gives Wilson's Syndrome its extreme importance. It's like the one card on the bottom of a house of cards that can't be removed without the whole house collapsing.

So we can see that Wilson's Syndrome is not at all complicated. In fact, it is very simple, but its significance cannot be understated.

One Cure For Many Symptoms?

The debilitating symptoms include fatigue, depression, headaches, migraines, PMS, anxiety panic attacks, irritability, hair loss, decreased motivation and ambition, inappropriate weight gain, decreased memory and concentration, insomnia, constipation, irritable bowel syndrome, decreased healing after surgery, dry skin, dry hair, fluid retention, itching, acne, bruising, heat and cold intolerance, asthma, and others. Wilson's Syndrome can cause all these things, and be easily recognized and treated.

4

What if Wilson's Syndrome (WS) is so common that each of us know someone who is greatly affected by it personally, or impacted by it through others (spouses, bosses, coworkers, employees, friends, parents, children, etc.). Let's suppose that WS is not the **only** cause of migraine headaches, but let's suppose for a minute that it is the most **common** cause (which it is). This also holds true for persistent fatigue, inappropriate depression, PreMenstrual Syndrome, decreased memory and concentration, decreased motivation and ambition, mood swings, insomnia, and many of the symptoms that have been listed.

It would be confounding if an underlying factor leading to most cases of migraines, fatigue, premenstrual syndrome and depression were identified and turned out to be easily treated. But what if the underlying factor and the easy treatments uncovered turned out to be the same for all these symptoms? How do you think most people would react to being told such a story? What do you think would be most people's first impulse upon hearing of even the speculation or suggestion of such a condition?

New Things Are Happening Every Day

There seems to be a sort of unspoken sentiment, with some, that we pretty much already know all there is to know in the field of medicine and about the human body. Since there has been such an explosion of medical knowledge and technology, and because we know so much more now than was known 30 or 40 years ago, it's easy for it to seem that we have almost everything figured out. But, as it turns out, we have barely scratched the surface and we are not even close to understanding everything there is to know about the wonderful and complex creation that we call the human body. In this information and technology age, new things are popping up around us all the time.

Another reason for difficulty in grasping this possibility is that we have learned about **big** things in **history** class. And, of course, history happened in the **past**. So it's natural for us to tend to think that, therefore, big things happen **only** in the past.

Even though we know that breakthroughs are happening every day, by the time we know about them they are established in history.

It also would seem that if there was such a simple problem with such profound physiological consequences, that it would have been discovered a long time ago.

But we realize, for instance, that all the working parts of gas string trimmers, like Weedeaters, have been around since World War 11, namely the internal combustion engine, drive mechanisms, grease, oil, gas, and nylon. However, it took until the early 70's for these materials to be combined in such a way as to create a gas string trimmer, a tool that has proven to be extremely useful in the lawn maintenance industry. There is nothing complicated about spinning nylon or the string trimmer, but that didn't keep it from going undeveloped for 25 years.

So, new and different things do happen today just like they happened in the past. They happen every day, and it is often said that "fact is stranger than fiction." But seeing that it is true, the greatest tragedy would be for people to be unaware of the treatment for Wilson's Syndrome.

The sooner WS is recognized for what it is, the sooner we will change the way we address almost every medical problem, and reduce the devastating toll it takes on our productivity and quality of life.

2. BODY FUNCTION DEPENDENT ON BODY TEMPERATURE

The body's function depends on its metabolism.

Metabolism Dependent On Enzymes

The metabolism is basically the sum of all the chemical reactions that take place in the body. People use the term metabolic rate to indicate the rate at which these chemical reactions take place. The metabolism is important because we are nothing if we are not a large combination of complex chemical reactions. All the physical processes and even the mental processes that take place in our bodies are influenced or made possible by chemical reactions. So needless to say, the metabolism is extraordinarily important.

The proper function of the metabolism vitally depends on the proper functioning of the body's enzymes. Enzymes are proteins that catalyze (they're catalysts) virtually all the chemical reactions of the body. Catalysts make it possible for certain chemical reactions to take place in a way they otherwise wouldn't. For example, when one uses epoxy glue to make a repair, it is necessary to mix the two parts together before it can be used. One part is the resin and the other is the hardener. Separately, they are useless as glue because they will not harden. But when the hardener is added to the resin, a chemical reaction takes place enabling the glue to do what it is designed to do. Here the hardener is acting as the vital catalyst. In the same way, if it were not for the important catalysts of the body known as enzymes, the body could not survive.

So, at the very heart of the metabolism are the enzymes. As it turns out, how well an enzyme functions depends on its shape, and its shape depends on its structure. Enzymes are long chains of amino acids that are assembled according to the genetic code of the DNA. Depending on how the amino acids of the enzymes are arranged, the enzymes will take on a particular shape. This shape can change at different times and under different conditions. In fact, this ability to change shape in a characteristic way is precisely what gives them their function. They're like a twisted telephone receiver cord that will untwist when you answer the phone and pull the cord tight, and then twist back into its previous shape when you put it back on the hook.

Enzyme function Dependent On Temperature

The shape of an enzyme also depends on its temperature. When enzymes get too warm, they get too loose. And when they get too cold, then they get too tight. When they are just the right temperature, then they are just the right shape and the chemical reactions that they catalyze take place at the optimal rate and with the most ease. When the temperature is too hot, too cold, or unsteady, the enzymes will spend less time in their optimal shape which simply translates into having a less than optimal metabolism.

An interesting example of how this works can be seen in the Siamese Cat. Its coloring depends upon the production of a certain pigment which is the result of a chemical reaction that depends upon a particular enzyme. Since the function of this enzyme depends on its temperature, the chemical reaction will only take place when the temperature is just right. Interestingly, the only places where the temperature is cool enough for the chemical reaction to take place are found in the cat's extremities. These are the coldest parts of the cat and include the cat's paws, tip of the tail, tips of the ears, and the nose and mouth area of the face. That's why these parts are dark with the rest of the cat being light colored, and thus the characteristic markings of a Siamese Cat. It is said that one might adversely affect his investment in a show quality Siamese Cat by letting the cat be exposed to unusual temperatures. For example, if the cat is exposed to weather that is too cold, too much of the coat may turn dark.

So we can see that temperature plays a major role in the function of enzymes. For this reason, doctors have long been concerned about patients having very high fevers. If the temperature goes too high, the patient's brain enzymes can

8

denature (get malformed) which can cause delirium and can even be life-threatening. Doctors have also long been concerned with the opposite extreme when the body temperature is too low (hypothermia). This is equally dangerous and also can be life-threatening. It is difficult to understand why we have been very concerned about extremely high or extremely low temperatures, but frequently appear to not even consider the effects of milder aberrations in body temperature. If fever and hypothermia are two life-threatening extremes of a continuum, then it is only logical and reasonable that less severe alterations can cause less severe, but never-the-less significant problems.

Studies have shown that when an enzyme-dependent chemical reaction is monitored for how well it takes place at various temperatures, the lower the temperature, the slower the chemical reaction. As the temperature is increased, the reaction rate will go faster with each increase until it reaches its optimum reaction rate. If the temperature is increased too much, the rate of reaction will diminish due to denaturing or change in shape of the enzyme. (See Diagram 2-1).

DIAGRAM 2-1

SAMPLE ENZYME THERMAL STABILITY CURVE

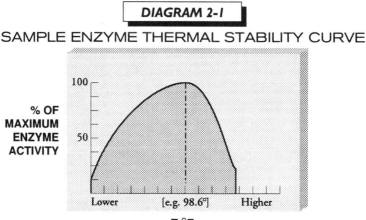

1. Biochemistry, Second Edition, Worth Publishers: 1970,75: Albert Lehninger

98.6 Is About Right

Why is it that 98.6 degrees Fahrenheit is usually the best temperature for people? The best temperature is the temperature at which the body's enzymes function at peak efficiency. Different enzymes work best at different temperatures and the functions of some are more greatly affected by changes in body temperature than others. As it turns out, the enzymes that are most affected by changes in body temperature are also often the enzymes that catalyze some of the more expendable bodily functions. Therefore, when the metabolism slows down, people often develop dry skin, unhealthy nails, dry hair, hair loss, irritability, poor recall, fluid retention, decreased sex drive, and up to 60 other puzzling and, until now, baffling symptoms. This is the body's way of insuring that depleted energy reserves are used to maintain the most important functions, such as vision, hearing, heart function, breathing, and all the other bodily functions necessary for survival. The enzymes responsible for these more vital functions aren't as affected by changes in body temperature.

The temperature at which a particular enzyme functions the best depends on its structure. And its structure depends on its coding as dictated by the genetic code found in the DNA of the chromosomes. The genetic code is what permits the great variation in hair color, height, appearance, weight, hand size, etc.

On the other hand, some factors differ very little from one person to another, such as the important enzymes for life. This is evidenced by the fact that some of the routine blood tests doctors do in an annual physical include tests for liver enzymes. These tests are specifically for enzymes that are normally found in every person's body. The enzymes are extremely similar in structure and therefore, are similar with regard to optimal operating temperature. **So, in a sense, an enzyme's ideal temperature is dictated by the coding of that enzyme, which does not vary a great deal from person to person. And it just so happens that most of the**

important bodily enzymes function best at or near 98.6 degrees Fahrenheit.

It is hard for some people to imagine that most people operate optimally at a *particular* body temperature, often thinking to themselves, "everybody is different." It is a little hard to grasp the wondrous design of it all. It's helpful to remember that it is the nature of all things to move toward disorder. This tendency is called **Entropy**. That's why objects tend to equalize in temperature.

An example of this would be, if you take a gallon of milk out of the refrigerator and put it on the counter top, you would not expect that three or four hours later it would be the same temperature as when it was removed from the refrigerator. It would be much closer to room temperature. Likewise, if a pot of boiling water is taken off the stove and placed on the counter top, it would cease to boil and in a short time would be close to room temperature.

Ambient temperature is the term used to identify the surrounding or environmental temperature. It is the nature and tendency of all things to approach ambient temperature. If you are in a room, then the ambient temperature is the room temperature. If it weren't for your metabolism, then your body temperature would tend to move toward the room temperature.

Let's suppose that the room temperature is 75 degrees. Given the **Law of Entropy**, one might expect that eventually your body temperature would also be 75 degrees. We know, of course, that this does not happen. Instead, you will most likely be very close to 98.6 degrees. That would be 23.6 degrees above room temperature! In fact, this characteristic is one of the things that distinguishes the living from the dead, hence the term "warm bodies" that is sometimes used to refer to living people. When we die, our bodies stop fighting Entropy and cool to room temperature. If there were no specific reason that people should be close to 98.6 degrees, you would expect to find some people running around 78 degrees, others 85 degrees and some perhaps 98 or 105 degrees. But we know that this is not the case, and so we have what is considered to be normal body temperature.

It is far from coincidental that people run about 23.6 degrees above room temperature, especially when you consider that all humans normally maintain a body temperature that is extremely close to 98.6 degrees within a plus or minus of 1.5 degrees. A variation as small as 1.4 degrees above normal (or 100 degrees), is considered adequate reason to be excused from work. Such a situation is about as coincidental as throwing a deck of cards in the air and having them land forming a card house.

We are all familiar with the symptoms that can be associated with fever, including headaches, achiness, fatigue and flu-like symptoms. These symptoms can be distinct symptoms brought on by an abnormally high body temperature in and of itself, and are not necessarily related to the underlying illness that brought on the high temperature. For example, a patient might have a sore throat generating a fever and fever symptoms. The patient's fever symptoms can even be generated without underlying illness, such as the foggy mindedness that can sometimes be brought on by spending too much time in a steam bath or hot weather.

If very small elevations in temperature can cause symptoms familiar to all of us, then it is easy to understand how slightly lower body temperatures can also cause symptoms that are familiar to almost all of us. The same special reason that causes people to run 23.6 degrees above room temperature is the same reason that there is a temperature at which each person's body functions best. It is the same reason that for most people that temperature is 98.6 degrees. And it is for this reason that abnormal body temperature can cause faulty enzyme function resulting in a multitude of seemingly unrelated symptoms characteristic of Wilson's Syndrome. Therefore, we can see that body temperature is of prime importance in the proper function of enzymes and therefore of the human body. The symptoms of Wilson's Syndrome are preeminently and foremost symptoms of Multiple Enzyme Dysfunction (MED) that are caused by aberrations in body temperature patterns.

One way to understand this is to consider a radio. If you want to listen to a radio station with a frequency of 99.7, you carefully tune the radio to that frequency. If it is set a little too low, or too high, or the dial is loose (so that it drifts about easily), then part of the radio program might be received, but it might not be optimal because of static. If the radio is properly tuned, then the static disappears and the reception is clear. So too, if we are not at the optimal temperature, we may still be able to function at some level, but we won't be at our best and may experience characteristic complaints and problems. Our performance will suffer when our temperatures are not tuned for optimal enzyme function.

Temperature Regulated By The Thyroid System

Let's talk about how the thyroid system affects the body temperature and the metabolism. My patients and I are continually amazed at the effects proper T3 therapy can have in the treatment of Wilson's Syndrome. I'm often asked, "How can this **one** medicine make such a big difference and how can it affect **so** many things?" It is not hard to understand the far-reaching and pervasive effects of liothyronine (T3) when we remember its critical role in controlling the metabolism - the sum of all chemical reactions in the body. To understand this critical role, let us look more closely at the thyroid system. The following diagram (diagram 2-2) will be referred to as we discuss more fully the thyroid system.

Briefly, the thyroid system begins in the brain. At the bottom of the brain is the hypothalamus, which is the part of the brain that secretes TRH (Thyrotropin Releasing Hormone). TRH travels to the pituitary gland at the base of the brain and stimulates the pituitary gland to produce TSH (thyroid stimulating hormone). TSH enters the bloodstream, travels to the thyroid gland at the base of the neck and stimulates it to produce T4 (thyroxin). The T4 produced in the thyroid gland is

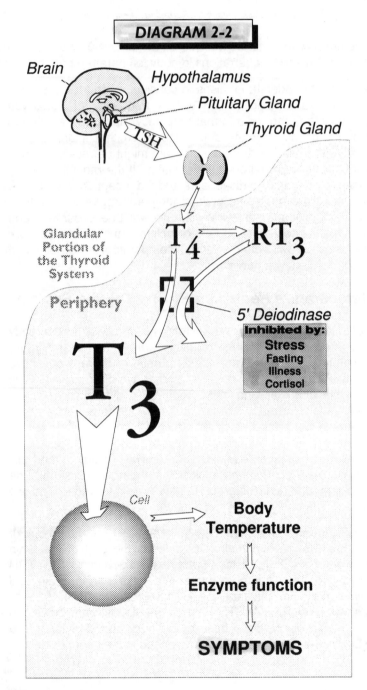

then converted to the physiologically active thyroid hormone T3 (liothyronine). T4 is converted to T3 by an enzyme called 5'-deiodinase, which is found in many of, if not all, the tissues of the body. **By far, most of the T3 of the body is produced from the conversion of T4 to T3 that takes place outside the thyroid gland in the body's tissues.** T3 has its action at the nuclear membrane receptors in the cells of the body. There, the T3 initiates a cascade of chemical reactions within each cell and thereby affects each cell's metabolic rate. The metabolic rate of the cells determines the metabolic rate of the body. The metabolic rate of the body, together with the surface area, activity level, sweating, environmental conditions, and other factors, determines the body's temperature. The body's temperature affects the function of the enzymes which are largely responsible for the most important chemical reactions in the body. These chemical reactions, in turn, are the key to the body's functions. This is the reason that the thyroid system is so vitally important. It affects every bodily function. Indeed, a complete absence of the thyroid system's function is not compatible with life.

DIAGRAM 2-3

THE STRUCTURES OF T4, RT3, AND T3

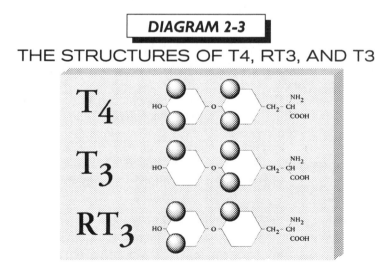

It should be pointed out here that not only can T4 be converted to T3, but also it can be converted to Reverse T3 (RT3). T4, RT3, and T3 look very similar as is demonstrated in diagram 2-3.

They are like three keys that look the same with each key having one notch that's different. All three keys may fit into the lock, but they might not work the same. In the same way, T4, RT3, and T3 each have greatly different capacities to stimulate the thyroid hormone receptor. T4 has a small amount of activity at the site; T3 is four times more active than T4; and RT3 has no activity at all. Since T4 and RT3 look so similar, they both can occupy the active site of the 5'-deiodinase enzyme, thereby competing for the enzyme's attention. It should be noted that stress, fasting, illness, cortisol, and some medicines can also inhibit the action of 5'-deiodinase.

The Inertia Of The Thyroid System

Inertia is the tendency of a body to resist change in its motion. It is the tendency of a body in motion to stay in motion unless acted on by an outside force.

I have paid close attention to the thyroid system (especially the relative levels of T4, T3, and RT3) while treating thousands of patients. Through these observations I have come to believe that the relative conversion of T4 to T3 and RT3, the competition of RT3 and T4 for the deiodinating enzyme, and the relative effect of RT3, T4, and T3 on the nuclear membrane receptors, provide the thyroid system with a great deal of inertia. This means that once the thyroid system is set in a certain pattern, there is a great tendency for it to remain in that pattern. I believe that it is designed this way for a very special purpose.

It would be difficult, within the limits of this book, to convey all the experiences that have led me to this conclusion. But maybe it will help to point out a few observations. Let's remember that T3 is four times more potent than T4, that it is the most active thyroid hormone, and that it has a half-life of 2

1/2 days. (The half-life of a hormone is the amount of time required for 50% of the hormone present at any given time to be eliminated by the body). Let's remember that T4 is less potent than T3, and has a much longer half-life (7 1/2 days), and therefore is more "stable" than T3. And RT3 (Reverse T3) has no activity at all and is rapidly broken down by the body soon after it is produced.

Let's refer to diagram 2-2. Since stress can decrease the amount of T4 converted to T3 by inhibiting the deiodinating enzyme, which causes more T4 to be shunted towards RT3, and since T3 is extremely active and RT3 is completely inactive, it is easy to see how stress can decrease the amount of active thyroid hormone available to the cells.

When the stress passes, there is less direct inhibition of the deiodinating enzyme, which encourages greater T4 to T3 conversion. And there should be less shunting of T4 to RT3, which should result in more T3 being produced. With RT3 being quickly broken down, there should also be less **indirect** inhibition of the enzyme from competition between T4 and RT3 for the activity of the deiodinating enzyme. These changes should allow the T4 to T3 conversion to return back to normal. Our systems are designed this way to allow the body to slow down under conditions of stress, and then return back to normal when the stress has passed.

Remembering that T4 is a longer-acting and less-potent stimulator, you can see how it can have a stabilizing influence. If T4 had no effect, then the unmitigated influence of T3 at the nuclear membrane receptor might cause a system that lacks sufficient stability. However, since T3 is the physiologically active thyroid hormone, if it did not have its effect, then the much weaker influence of the T4 would almost certainly be insufficient to provide for an adequate level of metabolism. So, we see the beautiful balance of how T3 can provide sufficient levels of metabolism, and T4 can help provide the desired stability. Another factor to remember is that when T4 is broken down, a portion of it is converted to T3. So **T4 also serves as a steady, constant supply of the more active T3.**

Even RT3, although it is short-lived, seems to play a role as a recent article in a Japanese medical journal suggests. It states that RT3 may play a biologically causative role in decreased thyroid system function. (Nippon Geka Gakkai Zasshi; Shigematsu, H.; October, 1988, 1989; pp. 1587-93). Reverse T3 may play this role by interfering with the T3 / thyroid hormone receptor interaction and/or by competitively inhibiting the deiodinating enzyme. When T4 to T3 conversion is impaired, there is less T3 to stimulate the receptors powerfully, and relatively more T4 to stimulate them weakly. With less T4 to T3 conversion, more T4 may be shunted to RT3, which results in more competitive inhibition of the deiodinating enzyme. This may result in even less T4 to T3 conversion, more shunting towards RT3, and so on. And so a vicious cycle can be started that can contribute to a persistent T4 to T3 conversion impairment that can remain even after the original cause of the impairment has passed. Such a cycle could last for years, and could get worse in stages with subsequent stresses.

An analogy comes to mind that may help one to visualize the inertia of the thyroid system. Let's imagine a small sailboat placed in a flowing stream. The stream is flowing at a constant speed, but there is a fan placed downstream in front of the sailboat that is blowing upstream. As the sailboat floats downstream and comes closer to the fan, the blowing of the fan keeps the boat at a certain distance, and the flowing water keeps the boat from moving further away from the fan.

Now, if the stream flows more slowly, there is less pressure on the boat to remain close, and it moves upstream, further away from the fan until it settles into a new stationary position. This is because the further the boat moves away from the fan, the weaker the fan's influence, until the influence of the fan and the influence of the stream equalize again.

But when the flow of the stream increases, the sailboat settles into a new stationary position that is closer to the fan as the two forces again reach equilibrium. So, even though the fan is always flowing, and the stream is always flowing, the sailboat has a tendency to settle into a certain position and stay there as long as the influences remain balanced.

The thyroid system behaves similarly, but is more complex. T4 is converted to T3 and also to RT3. RT3 affects the conversion of T4 to T3. Stress can also affect T4 to T3 conversion. In addition, T4 can interact with the nuclear membrane receptor, as can T3 and possibly RT3. So there are at least six or seven influences at work which are constantly moving, but tend to add up in such a way that the thyroid system settles into a certain position and stays there in much the same way that the sailboat finds equilibrium.

The design of the peripheral (outside the thyroid gland) conversion of the thyroid hormones is set up to provide a great deal of inertia. This is no accident. The peripheral conversion design is probably of **far greater importance** in the regulation of the thyroid system's <u>ultimate</u> influence on the metabolism, than the glandular feedback mechanisms (involving the thyroid gland, pituitary gland and hypothalamus) that are currently thought to be most important in this regard.

When You Hear "Thyroid," Think <u>System</u> Not Gland

How people use the word "thyroid" has led to confusion that has contributed to WS being overlooked.

For some reason, decreased thyroid system function is not commonly suspected when one is considering possible sources of physical ailments in people who are ill. Since it is not often considered as a problem, it is not commonly talked about or discussed. When the topic is brought up, people will often be heard saying that "so-and-so" has/had a "low thyroid problem." Most often, people (even doctors) will automatically tend to think of the word "thyroid" as being used as a noun in this context to refer to the thyroid **gland**. This tendency is reinforced if the first statement generates the question "What's thyroid?" One would often tend to answer, "The thyroid is a very important small butterfly shaped **gland** at the base of the neck that ..." and so on. This tendency draws attention away from the fact that the thyroid gland is only one **part** of the

19

whole thyroid system and not even the part with which there's most commonly a problem. As odd as it may seem, I feel that it may be this simple tendency that has caused Wilson's Syndrome to be overlooked by some of the best doctors in the world for decades (by so many for so long). For this reason I recommend that in the phrase "low thyroid problem" the word "thyroid" would best be thought of as an <u>adjective</u> used to describe the entire thyroid **system**. This would help us all to remember that the thyroid gland is again merely a part.

Which link in bicycle chain is the most important? Without any **one** of the links, the chain could not perform its function. Would the link that most often breaks deserve the most attention? I recommend in order to keep the proper perspective that we use instead of the phrase "low thyroid problem," the phrase "decreased thyroid system function" or DTSF. Using this phrase may help us (lay people and doctors alike) from getting too fixated on the gland only. Because when we do this, then we are often led down the wrong path while overlooking some very obvious problems. All the causes of decreased thyroid system function (DTSF) all generate the same symptoms of Multiple Enzyme Dysfunction (MED) that result from body temperature patterns that are too low, but not all causes of DTSF involve the thyroid **gland** itself.

Let's discuss the impairments that have been described to date. Rarely mentioned is the possibility of the hypothalamus not producing TRH as it should. This may be referred to as secondary hypopituitarism since it results in low (hypo) function of the pituitary gland secondary to inadequate TRH stimulation. Hypopituitarism can be primary (as in primary hypopituitarism) meaning that the problem is primarily in the pituitary **gland** itself which results in inadequate TSH secretion. Inadequate TSH secretion leads to hypothyroidism secondary to a pituitary problem (and so primary hypopituitarism is also sometimes referred to as secondary hypothyroidism).

Are we confused yet? The problem may be primarily in the thyroid **gland** itself which results in inadequate T4 production in spite of normal TSH production (this is known as primary hypothyroidism). The impairments of the thyroid system listed above have been fairly well described to date. However, one may see from the diagram (diagram 2-2) that there is still a long way from the thyroid gland to generation of an adequate body temperature. Impairments of this important portion of the thyroid system have thus far not been well described. One may see from the diagram that there could be a problem with the conversion of T4 to T3. It is known that the conversion of T4 to T3 decreases under periods of fasting and severe illness. It has been shown under these conditions that the level of T4 to T3 conversion can drop by 50%. This change has also been shown to return to normal once the fasting or severe illness is over. When the conversion of T4 to T3 decreases, more T4 is shunted to RT3 causing an elevation in RT3.

These adaptive changes in laboratory findings are not considered to be very serious and are sometimes referred to as "Euthyroid Sick Syndrome." Although this syndrome has not been very well defined, it is usually thought of as an adaptive temporary change in laboratory tests [increased RT3, decreased T3, usually with normal T4 (normal thyroid gland function) lab findings] brought on by severe illness that returns to normal when the illness has passed. There is not considered to be a need for treatment for Euthyroid Sick Syndrome except for treating the underlying illness. For years there has been some speculation in the medical literature about the possibility of a **persistent** impairment in the conversion of T4 to T3 contributed to inhibition of T4 to T3 conversion by an elevation of Reverse T3 ("Thyroidal and Peripheral Production of Thyroid Hormones;" *Annals of Internal Medicine*, Schimmel; Dec. 1977). Not only **can** this happen, but it **does** happen.

This condition has, up until now, not been named or well described. I have taken the liberty to name it Wilson's Syndrome and to describe it in great detail in this book. As it turns out, WS can have a tremendous impact on a person's life causing characteristic and often debilitating symptoms and being **quite maladaptive**. It can be brought on by fasting, illness, and stress but rather than going away after the conditions have passed, it can persist; thyroid blood tests are often within "normal range," but it is characterized by a low

21

body temperature; it can be treated with proper therapy (with T3 therapy being very important). With proper T3 therapy the syndrome can be reversed usually with the correction persisting after treatment has been discontinued (although subsequent stress can cause the syndrome to return again).

The symptoms of Wilson's Syndrome are essentially the same as the symptoms of other causes of decreased thyroid system function; yet proper treatment of Wilson's Syndrome has revealed other related symptoms that up until now have not been very much considered to be thyroid (adjective) related (e.g. migraines, PMS, panic attacks, night sweats, ringing of the ears, mood swings, itchiness, allergies, asthma, etc.).

Of all of the causes of DTSF mentioned above, Wilson's Syndrome is by far the most common. As previously discussed, the symptoms of MED can result from low body temperature patterns of various causes. However, DTSF is by far the most common cause of the low body temperature patterns that cause persistent symptoms of MED. And although there are various causes of DTSF, Wilson's Syndrome derives its importance from the fact that it is by far the most common of those. It is at least 50 times more common than any other cause of DTSF and therefore is also the most important.

Other Factors That Can Influence Temperature

There are several factors that can affect body temperature. But whatever does affect it (making it too low, too high, or unsteady) can cause all the symptoms of Multiple Enzyme Dysfunction that are characteristic of Wilson's Syndrome. For example, people who are exposed to cold weather and become hypothermic will often become sleepy and fatigued. Also, when people eat ice cream too fast, their throats get cold causing the blood going to the brain to be more cold, and they can develop a headache.

Surface Area / Volume Ratio

We've discussed how the body temperature depends upon how much heat is generated within the body itself (which is regulated by the thyroid system). But it also depends upon how much heat goes in and out of the body from or to the environment.

The amount of heat going in and out of the body is determined by a couple of factors, one being what environmental conditions the body is exposed to. For example, the body will retain more heat when exposed to the heat from a shower, a sauna, or hot weather, than it will if it is exposed to cold weather or a cooling thermal blanket such as the ones sometimes used in hospitals to lower a patient's fever. Another factor is the body surface that is exposed to the environment.

An analogy that I frequently use to illustrate this point is that if you had a lump of mashed potatoes on your plate that was too hot to eat and you wanted it to cool faster, you could spread the potatoes out on the plate. The more it is spread out, the faster it cools. The reason for this is that for the same volume of food one may increase the surface area by spreading the food out, thus exposing more of the food or mass to the surface so that the heat more easily dissipates.

The laws of physics tell us that the shape in the universe that holds its heat the best is the sphere or ball because it is the shape that has the smallest amount of surface area per unit of volume. The more a person looks like a ball and less like a stick, the harder it is to dissipate calories. This might partly explain why taller people tend to be thinner than shorter people.

Let's consider how this ratio can be extremely important. Suppose that there are two different animals that live in very different climates. Of course, they would face different challenges. On one hand, animals that live in extremely cold climates need to retain enough body heat to maintain their body temperatures to ensure the proper functioning of their enzymes and bodily functions. However, animals that live in extremely hot climates have the challenge of dissipating enough heat to maintain a body temperature that would be adequate for their enzyme and bodily functions. For instance, the desert mouse and certain desert rodents are in some danger of becoming overheated. The shapes of their bodies are formed in such a way that encourages rapid dissipation of heat. That's why their ears are large, their legs and tails are long, and even their bodies are more slender. Incidentally, their urine is also more concentrated so that they can better conserve water.

The desert mouse can be compared to the seal that lives in a much colder climate. To help them preserve their body heat, they have shapes that provide less surface area per unit of volume. They are plumper or more bulky in shape with smaller ears. Only their relatively short flippers are exposed to the environment.

Another simple way to see the importance of surface area/volume ratio is to observe people who are sitting outside in very cold weather. Notice that they tend to sit huddled up in a ball to conserve body heat. If it didn't make any difference, people wouldn't hold their arms and legs in close in cold weather. So our surface/area volume ratio can be affected by our height in relation to our weight, how we stand or sit, how we dress to an extent, and how much of our body is exposed to the environment.

The body's temperature depends also on how much heat is generated within the body. The heat is generated by the chemical reactions of the body that change raw materials, fuel, or food into the products and functions necessary for maintenance of life. The chemical reactions take place, for the most part, within the cells of the body, and of course, the volume of the body is made up of cells. The greater the volume of cells, the greater the volume of chemical reactions, and the greater the capacity for producing heat. **So the amount of heat produced in the body is roughly proportional to the volume of the body.** And of course, the heat generated by the body is directly related to the metabolism (the rate or extent to which the reactions take place).

PMS and Temperature

The symptoms of Wilson's Syndrome are principally the result of aberrant temperature patterns due to impaired conversion of T4 to T3 (thyroid hormones). It should be pointed out, however, that there are <u>other</u> causes of aberrant body temperature which can also cause symptoms.

For example, it is well known that the body temperature will vary up and down during a woman's menstrual cycle, tending to peak at the time of ovulation (useful information for couples who are trying to conceive). The temperature tends to rise just prior to a woman's period and gradually decreases as the period begins and progresses. This explains why symptoms of Multiple Enzyme Dysfunction can change in severity in relation to a woman's menstrual cycle, a problem commonly referred to as PMS or premenstrual syndrome. If one looks at the symptoms of PMS, one sees depression, fatigue, fluid retention, headaches, bloating, irritability, craving for sweets (especially high energy sweets such as chocolate), problems with memory, and essentially the whole list of symptoms associated with Multiple Enzyme Dysfunction. They are termed premenstrual because they are most severe prior to the period. The symptoms of MED can be related to temperature patterns that are too high, too low, or unsteady. Premenstrual worsening of the symptoms of MED are most commonly related to rapid change (usually increase) in the body temperature pattern prior to the period. Interestingly, I have often seen complete relief of the PMS symptoms when the body temperature patterns have been normalized. This observation has made it obvious that the symptoms of PMS are related to body temperature patterns.

Another interesting point is that I have had a few patients whose classic signs and symptoms of "premenstrual" syndrome occurred on a predictable monthly basis just **after** their period (or only during the period rather than just prior to their period). One might call this "postmenstrual syndrome."

25

And again, in these cases, their postmenstrual symptoms of MED have often resolved with normalization of their body temperature patterns. This makes it more evident that these menstrual related symptoms of Multiple Enzyme Dysfunction are related to aberrant body temperature patterns. These symptoms seem to be related to female hormones only to the extent that female hormones can affect body temperature patterns.

Adrenal Hormone Levels Affect Daily Temperature Cycle

Addison's Disease and Cushing's Disease are diseases that can affect the levels of adrenal hormones. Addison's Disease is caused by insufficient levels of cortisol in the body, and Cushing's Disease is due to excessive levels of cortisol. It is interesting to note that these two diseases can cause symptoms that are similar to those of Wilson's Syndrome and/or Multiple Enzyme Dysfunction. These include fatigue, fluid retention, weight gain, depression and headaches. It has long been documented that cortisol, which is the hormone that is produced excessively in Cushing's Disease, can directly inhibit 5'-deiodinase (the enzyme that converts T4 to T3). I have seen cases where patients have developed classic cases of Wilson's Syndrome immediately after having been given injections of cortisone or steroids. Presumably, cortisone can inhibit 5'-deiodinase and set in motion the vicious cycle that results in Wilson's Syndrome. In such cases the symptoms can be treated with proper thyroid hormone treatment. So it's not really hard to understand why someone, when given an injection of cortisone, can gain weight, retain fluid, get tired and depressed, and develop many of the symptoms of Wilson's Syndrome. It's interesting that cortisone is produced by the body's adrenal glands under stress. It is also interesting that cortisol levels go up and down in a daily pattern.

It is well known that the body temperature tends to run lowest in the morning, gradually increasing during the day, usually being the highest in the afternoon, and tending to decrease in the evening. So the body

temperature can follow both a monthly cycle and a daily cycle. This can explain why the symptoms of MED sometimes follow monthly and daily patterns.

Many of the patients that I see find that their symptoms of Multiple Enzyme Dysfunction are worse at certain times of the day. For example, they might do fairly well an hour or two after awakening and getting started in the morning, and become extremely fatigued between 2:00 p.m. and 4:00 p.m.

In the section dealing with depression we will discuss how symptoms of Multiple Enzyme Dysfunction can also follow a seasonal pattern. This might help explain what is known as Seasonal Affective Disorder or SAD. It might be a type of biological clock phenomenon similar to hibernation in animals.

Pregnancy

It should be pointed out that a fetal hormone known as human chorionic gonadotropin also can affect body temperature patterns. When a woman becomes pregnant, the baby begins to produce human chorionic gonadotropin or HCG. HCG can increase the body's metabolism and body temperature patterns. This can explain why women suffering from Wilson's Syndrome frequently do their best while they are pregnant. Unlike other women who often feel tired, feel depressed, and gain weight easily during their pregnancy, some women who are suffering from Wilson's Syndrome actually fare much **better** during pregnancy, enjoying much more energy, less depression than usual, and often having unusual success at being able to control their weight. Some women actually report that during their pregnancies were the **only** times that they were capable of losing weight with proper dieting and exercise. Interestingly, HCG has been used in the past as a treatment to help people lose weight.

Blood Sugar

Blood sugar levels can also affect body temperature patterns, and body temperature patterns can affect blood sugar levels.

It isn't too hard to understand, then, why the symptoms of hypoglycemia are so similar to the symptoms of MED. It is also easy to understand how nutrition can be an important influence on overall function of the metabolism.

Thyroid Not The Only System Of The Body

It is interesting that adrenal, female and thyroid hormones can all affect body temperature patterns. It is also interesting to note that the most common cause of Wilson's Syndrome (a thyroid system problem) is childbirth, which involves the female hormone system; and that proper thyroid hormone treatment can frequently correct the symptoms of premenstrual syndrome which is also female hormone related. We have also seen that cortisol in the adrenal hormone system is known to directly inhibit T4 to T3 conversion which is the most critical step in the thyroid system because it is the step in which there is most often a problem.

I have treated more than 5,000 patients with Wilson's Syndrome to date. The more I work with these patients, the more apparent it becomes to me that the human body is a highly integrated system. One part of the system may affect another, which may affect others, and so on. So a change in one part of the system may start a chain reaction of events that can affect the whole system. For example, it is well know that proper exercise can help one's whole system to function better. Likewise, lack of sleep can adversely affect a person's muscle strength, digestion, resistance to infections, mental function, and many other functions. In that way, sleep deprivation can help tear down one's whole system. The same can be said for one's nutrition and stress levels.

The system is influenced by sex hormones, adrenal hormones, stress, thyroid hormones, medicines, blood pressure, sleep, nutrition, exercise, infections, digestion, respiration, blood circulation, and many other influences.

One way to visualize this is by picturing many ropes tied to a single ring. The ropes represent the influences and the ring represents the system. Picture the ropes all pulling in different directions. The position of the ring depends on the amount of tension in each of the different ropes. If one is able to increase the tension in one rope enough, one can affect the position of the ring and therefore the position of the other ropes as well. I often see evidence that when more pressure is exerted on any one of the adrenal, female, or thyroid systems the position of the metabolism, in general, and the remaining two hormone systems can be affected. The same can be observed with positive changes in diet, exercise, sleep habits, stress management, etc. When one effects a correction or normalization in one part of the system, the remaining parts tend to follow suit and settle in behind the changes made in the first. So if one's whole system is out of position, then one's whole system may have to change, to an extent, to make things right.

The ideal whole body system position depends on a proper balance of tension in all the various "ropes" or influences affecting the system. Interestingly, different combinations of tensions may result in the same overall effect. Thus, when trying to improve the body's "position", one should strive to affect favorably as many influences as possible.

For example, if the thyroid system malfunctions, it pulls the entire body system into a new position of functioning which is determined by the new balance of influences involved. If the changes in "rope tension" are mild or short-lived, they may be insufficient to cause a persistent change in the system. However, if the changes are severe or long-lasting, the entire system may settle into a new balance that persists long after the precipitating changes in "rope tensions" resolve.

This analogy shows how the whole body system or metabolism can settle into positions of functioning that have a great deal of inertia. It also can explain how the body's functioning can change for a time (because of external factors like staying up for 72 hours, or by drinking too much caffeine for two weeks) and return to normal once conditions return to normal (plenty of rest, stopping caffeine). It also explains how the body's functioning can go down and stay down even after the change (divorce, job stress, death of a loved one) has passed. It can explain how the body's functioning can get progressively worse in stages, and also how it can improve in stages. It can explain how the body's system can be returned to "normal" and how it can stay normal even after the correcting influences (treatment) have been discontinued. Most of these situations are common in, and even characterize, Wilson's Syndrome.

This illustration also makes it easy to understand how symptoms similar to the symptoms of MED can accompany many different influences; depression, female hormones (PMS), adrenal hormone conditions, dietary habits (hypoglycemia), and others. It can explain how some physicians do have some success in treating the symptoms of Multiple Enzyme Dysfunction with female and/or adrenal hormones. For example, progesterone for PMS is sometimes useful if one can find a dosage regimen that works for the patient.

Many things (diet, activity, stress, hormones, illness, sleep deprivation) can knock your whole system out of whack. As a result, you can suffer from MED due to aberrant body temperature patterns. Likewise, these same things (diet, activity, sleep), can improve the function of your system. However, these influences are often insufficient to correct the whole problem. In such cases, T3 therapy can often be used to predictably, effectively, reproducibly, and quickly influence the system to return to a normal pattern of function.

With exercising, one may need to pick the right kind of exercise, done at the right times of day, in the right pattern during the week; with diet, one may need to pick the right kinds and number of foods from the thousands available, and eat them at just the right time in just the right way; with psychotherapy, one might need to choose just the right words in just the right combination at just the right time; with female hormones, one may need to pick the right combination of progesterone and estrogens of the right kind (there are many on the market, some not found in nature) given at just the right times. The same can be said for sleep cycles and other medicines and influences. **But with T3 therapy, one need only take the right kind of T3 in the right way to get the**

body temperature to normal. This may explain why there are so many diet, exercise, psychological and medical books describing different detailed approaches to these sorts of problems. No doubt they work well for some people. However, as many people well know, these approaches don't work for everyone.

T3 IS A TEMPERATURE TOOL

Although there are other possible approaches to the symptoms discussed in this book, the appeal of T3 therapy for WS is its simplicity. It's no-nonsense. You get the temperature up and you either feel better or you don't. With many approaches there is no way of knowing if one is headed in the right direction, but with T3 therapy **there is a guide! The body temperature!** It's so nice to have a guide. One can usually get the temperature up and see if one is on the right track in just a couple of weeks. And when patients do respond, they often <u>remain</u> improved even after the treatment has been discontinued. T3 therapy is deliberate and direct.

To illustrate, let us suppose that you bought a certain computer. The owner's manual states that the computer has a special safety feature that causes its function to slow down when under too much strain. This is to avoid costly damage to the machine. It also states that the computer should only be connected to a certain number of terminals, run certain types of programs, be run for only a certain number of hours per day, and be kept in a room at a certain temperature and humidity. During a particularly busy period of time, long after the owner's manual has been stuffed in a closet and you've started paying less attention to the manufacturer's recommended do's and don'ts, you notice that the machine's function is beginning to slow down. The screens are becoming dim, the printer is barely working. You retrieve the owner's manual and correct all of the abuses. Although there is some improvement, the computer's function still does not return to normal. Puzzled, you take the printer apart, clean it, inspect it, and reassemble it with no resulting improvement. You replace the software, dismantle the computer itself, and after several weeks you still cannot find the answer to your problem. Being very concerned about your costly equipment and the work you still need to accomplish, you finally break down and call the manufacturer to send a service man. He recognizes immediately that the system has slowed itself down to protect itself. You are very relieved to hear that your $25,000 computer is not ruined. The service man points out that the system will sometimes stay a little slow after it has saved itself from destruction. He also points out that it was for this reason that the manufacturer installed a little green reset button on the bottom of the machine, described on page 127 of the owner's manual. Within one second of pressing the tiny button, the function of the machine "miraculously" surges back to normal. Stunned, you realize at once how much more effective, quick and simple it can be when one directly addresses the fundamental underlying problem.

I feel that it is for a similar reason that so many people suffering from persistent symptoms of MED respond so well to proper T3 therapy and why the results can seem so miraculous. We are in a sense pushing the "temperature button" on the body and getting all the other functions to respond, or come back.

Chapter Three

3. WHY THE METABOLISM WORKS THE WAY IT DOES

Conservation Mode Versus Productivity Mode

The thyroid system is well known to be important in the regulation of the body's metabolic rate. It can decrease or increase the metabolic rate under certain circumstances. Why is this important? We can think of the metabolism as having two speeds or modes, one that uses less energy and one that uses more. I'll call the slower mode the **conservation mode** and the fast mode I'll call the **productivity mode**.

There are two things that your body is designed to do:
1. Not starve
2. Get things done

It is easier to survive famine if your body is not using as much energy (conservation mode). On the other hand, the more energy you spend (productivity mode) the easier it is to get things done. If you didn't have a conservation mode, then when food was scarce you'd be more likely to starve. And if you didn't have a productivity mode, then when resources were plentiful you'd have a hard time getting as much done. People who are in the conservation mode frequently tell me: "I don't have any interest in anything anymore, and I just don't feel like **doing** anything." What a way to conserve energy!

It is normal for the thyroid system to enter into and out of the conservation and productivity modes at the appropriate times and under the appropriate conditions. This helps the body to cope with the changes and challenges of life. The body enters into the conservation mode under conditions that threaten the survival and/or physical, mental, emotional resources of the body, such as childbirth, divorce, death of a loved one, job or family stress, surgery or accidents, etc., and starvation (not very common in the United States except for severe dieting). It seems that stress is not always measured by the challenge itself, but by the relationship of the presenting challenge to the available resources. When the brain determines that there is a threat, or that there may be insufficient resources available to easily meet a presenting challenge, a signal is sent to the body to begin entering into the conservation mode to conserve energy. When the stressful conditions have passed, the body is supposed to return to the productivity mode; but in Wilson's Syndrome it doesn't, leaving people to suffer with frustrating and often debilitating complaints long after the stress has passed. So essentially, Wilson's Syndrome is a natural and normal starvation/stress coping mechanism gone amuck.

How The Thyroid System Gets Into Conservation Mode

Under stress, the body slows down by decreasing the amount of raw material T4 that is converted to the active thyroid hormone T3, while increasing the amount that is converted to the inactive RT3. It has been shown that during fasting, the T3 level in the bloodstream can drop by 50% with the RT3 going up by 50%. Since T3 is an extremely active thyroid hormone and since RT3 has no thyroid hormone activity, it is obvious that this shunting process can greatly affect the amount of physiologically active thyroid hormone at the level of the active site. Studies have shown that the metabolic rate drops during these same conditions of fasting.

Incidentally, it has been shown that some of the highest levels of RT3 found in man are in newborn babies. Cord samples of blood taken from the umbilical cord at the time of birth often show elevated levels of RT3 and low levels of T3 (which begin to increase soon after birth). This may be a survival mechanism to help the baby to conserve as much energy as possible and get a foothold in this world. I have often wondered if this is why babies spend so much time sleeping. Basically, all they do is eat, sleep, and gain weight and can often be on the irritable side. A little hunger seems to be so much more painful for them, and their hunger-pang screams seem so much more urgent and desperate, as if they're faced with a life-threatening situation. But after they are fed they are extremely content and satisfied. As we will discuss next, it seems that the conservation mode is triggered when the body perceives a threat that there may be insufficient resources to meet apparent challenges. The lower the resources, the more desperate the situation. Probably few of us can think of an animal or organism with fewer resources or that is any more vulnerable than a human baby.

When the body is faced with stress or starvation, and T4 to T3 conversion decreases, the cells of the body slow down, so the body temperature drops. When the temperature drops, many of the body's enzymes do not function as well.

Conservation Is Bought With A Price

As the body conserves energy, it cuts down on some of the more expendable functions that are not absolutely necessary for survival. This can lead to a long list of unfavorable symptoms listed in Chapter 9 (fatigue, depression, PMS, migraines, fluid retention, etc.).

This is accomplished by the fact that some enzymes are more susceptible to a decrease in body temperature than others. It is fascinating that the most susceptible enzymes happen to be related to some of the body's more expendable functions. For example, the largest organ in the human body is the skin, and a huge amount of energy is expended in maintaining the skin. The skin is quite durable and can continue to function for many weeks even when maintenance levels drop significantly. So a person's body can get away with significantly decreasing the energy expended on maintaining the skin for a period of time, thereby conserving a huge amount of energy. In this way, the body's conservation of energy can result in **dry skin, dry hair, hair loss, dry, brittle nails, etc**. It's not surprising that luxury functions, such as the sex drive, are among the first to go. The more important functions (for personal short-term survival) like vision, hearing, heart function, and breathing are not as greatly affected by changes in temperature. Thus, the body has a very effective way of conserving energy under periods of stress by decreasing energy expenditures on some of the more expendable bodily functions, while preserving some of the more vital functions.

Conservation Mode Sometimes Maladaptive

It might sound at first that it would be good for people to constantly be in the conservation mode. For, after all, one can never have too many resources and it is always good to conserve energy and resources, even if you have plenty, for potential problems that may lie ahead. However, resources are only of any value when they are put to use. The physical, mental, social and emotional resources that human beings have are necessary for their survival and productivity. They are put to use in providing for food and clothing, building shelters and homes, and building important interpersonal relationships that are of great value in times of difficulty. These resources are also important for the building of strong communities and societies. They are important in creating new ventures and making machines and tools that make life easier and increase the standard of living. They are necessary for the building up of mankind in general. So conserving resources continually can be a very big problem, especially when it prevents the resources from being used appropriately under the right conditions.

I believe that the body entering into conservation mode is an adaptive response in times and places where there is insufficient food, nutrients, or resources available to maintain life. For example, if a man was in prehistoric times and he broke his leg and was unable to hunt or obtain food efficiently, he would probably survive longer without food if his metabolism would appropriately decrease under the given circumstances. Likewise, his family could better survive the period of time without food if their metabolism slowed down appropriately. When his injured leg healed sufficiently to enable him to hunt again and obtain food for himself and his family, it would be appropriate for their metabolism to return to normal, enabling them to be more healthy and productive. If this response were not present when he broke his leg and was unable to feed his family, the metabolism would continue at the same pre-injury rate and there would be a greater chance that he and his family would starve and die.

This adaptive response can become maladaptive in the 20th century when an injured person can be taken to the hospital and given meals or I.V. nutrients to prevent starvation. His family may be able to go to the supermarket to purchase food, thereby eliminating the possibility of starving to death as the man is healing. In this situation, the response can be maladaptive because his metabolism may automatically drop in response to his injury. The function of his enzymes and his utilization of energy in order to heal may be impaired because of a less than optimal body temperature. The body enzymes, including those responsible for healing, may not function as effectively as they could.

Poor healing is a common finding in the patients that I see suffering from classic cases of Wilson's Syndrome. They frequently do not heal as quickly, and often will have sores that will persist much longer than would be otherwise expected. Many patients have undergone surgery and have, during convalescence, developed many other symptoms of Wilson's Syndrome. They can even suffer complications from the surgery in terms of wound infection, poor healing, and may even have to be opened again for revision of the wound because of infection and/or poor healing. Many of these patients notice that they do not heal as well with the onset of the symptoms of Wilson's Syndrome. Thus, Wilson's Syndrome is a great condition to have in response to periods of fasting or famine, but it is not the most productive condition to have when there are good hospitals and food supplies available.

Thus, the conservation mode is maladaptive when it keeps the body from being happy, healthy, strong, and productive when there is no real threat of starvation. And the productivity mode is maladaptive when the body does not slow down under appropriate conditions and when it puts the body in danger of starving.

I frequently tell people with Wilson's Syndrome that it is not all together bad that they have the ability or tendency to develop the condition, because they have the capacity to slow down under adverse conditions and are probably less likely to starve if the supermarkets close down. But it is not the best condition to have if they want to enjoy healthy, happy and productive lives.

As I discuss later, there are a large number of disturbing symptoms that can result and maladaptively persist from Wilson's Syndrome. Many of these symptoms are familiar to all of us and are therefore often considered "normal." But there is a difference between common and ideal. It should not be assumed that these symptoms are mild, because they are often extremely debilitating. They can be so incapacitating that they can render a person almost a "metabolic cripple." It is maladaptive when these disturbing and burdensome complaints and symptoms persist inappropriately, when there is no need for the body's metabolism to be slow.

Since Wilson's Syndrome is essentially a stress and starvation coping mechanism gone amuck, one may be able to see how certain maladaptive situations can present themselves. For example, a person may be faced with being laid off from work because of the closing out of their department, and begin to have feelings of being overwhelmed and may enter into some depression and may develop headaches and other symptoms of the conservation mode. These symptoms are often brought on by a drop in body temperature patterns. The person may also have a tendency for increased fatigue and decreased motivation, and all these complaints may make it more difficult for the person to find alternative work If the person does have difficulty finding another job, then the temperature might drop further in response. This may result in worsening of the symptoms and thereby further decrease the available resources the person may need in order to find a job.

In Summary, the greater the tendency a body has to enter into the conservation mode, the greater the tendency a body has to remain in the conservation mode. The proper functioning of the body depends, in large part, on how effectively and how appropriately the body enters into and out of the conservation and productivity modes.

4. HOW HAS WILSON'S SYNDROME BEEN OVERLOOKED FOR SO LONG?

Where We've Been

Brief History Of Thyroid Tests And Medicines

It has long been known that thyroid hormone deficiency can lead to severe physical impairment and even death. Recognition of the signs and symptoms of deficient thyroid hormone in subtle cases was first made possible by experience that was gained in the more severe cases. Severe thyroid hormone deficiency is called **myxedema** or myxedematous coma. It was called this because in severe cases of thyroid hormone deficiency patients become edematous or severely swollen, they can have decreased levels of consciousness and can even fall into a coma.

It wasn't many decades ago that doctors first began to understand the significance of the thyroid system. Patients would sometimes develop dry, coarse skin, slowed reflexes, hair loss, brittle nails, thinning of the lateral one-third of the eyebrows, thick swollen tongues and other severe complaints. When these patients were identified early enough and treated properly with thyroid hormone supplementation, their rapid and dramatic response to thyroid hormone supplementation was extremely gratifying. As the patients gradually improved, doctors were able to become familiar with the varying degrees and effects of thyroid hormone deficiency.

In time, a test was devised known as the Basal Metabolic Rate Test or **BMR** Test, which was intended to help identify patients suffering from thyroid hormone deficiency. The test consisted of the patient waking up in the morning, remaining motionless, and breathing into an oxygen mask with the doctor measuring the amount of oxygen consumed by the patient in a given period of time. With the amount of oxygen consumed, the doctor could calculate the patient's Basal Metabolic Rate and compare it to the Basal Metabolic Rate of other people both normal and ill to help determine whether or not the patient might benefit from thyroid hormone supplementation. The test was cumbersome to perform and therefore was often done improperly, which added to its inaccuracy.

The BMR test did not have as much predictive value as was hoped for. Later a protein bound iodine (**PBI**) test was developed. It was felt that the level of protein bound iodine in the blood should somehow be closely proportional to the level of the thyroid system function in the body (which is not always the case).

Then tests were developed for **T4 and T3** specifically. These tests still do not have the predictive value that would be preferable in the treatment of decreased thyroid system function and the consequent symptoms of MED.
Since then, a myriad of other tests have been devised in an attempt to find a more reliable test, one of greater predictive value, in the treatment of patients suffering from symptoms of thyroid system deficiency.

One test known as the **Radioactive Iodine Uptake test** involves radioactive iodine being ingested by the patient and taken up by the thyroid gland which is then scanned with a radioactivity scanner to detect the level and pattern of radioactive iodine in the thyroid gland in an attempt to get an idea about the thyroid gland's function. There is the **Thyroid Stimulating Hormone test, Thyrotropin Releasing Hormone, T3 uptake, T4 index, T3 index, T7, RT3,** and others. These tests have their uses and are directed at assessing various levels of the thyroid system but are not extremely useful in predicting the onset and/or resolution of the **symptoms** of decreased thyroid system function. It should be pointed out that some of the thyroid tests available are actually measurements that have been mathematically manipulated in an attempt to increase their usefulness - without much success.

Medicines Used

In the beginning, patients were given thyroid hormone supplementation in the form of desiccated (dried out) animal thyroid gland tissue and patients are still treated today with thyroid hormones that have been purified and extracted from animal sources. Later, synthetic sources of thyroxin (T4) and liothyronine (T3) were developed. These medicines have been on the market for decades. Currently, synthetic sources of thyroid hormones are often considered better because of the greater consistency from pill to pill.

Inherited Attitudes Of Doctors

Let us explore, briefly, the attitudes that doctors may have had over the years. Early in medicine, a doctor may have been able to be well-versed with all the available medical information, and he might have felt comfortable in having mastered a certain body of information. When teaching the next generations of doctors he might have said confidently that he was teaching the young physicians everything that they needed to know about a particular field. Those young physicians may have believed it, and they may have admired their professor and tried to emulate him by trying diligently to study the expanding medical information and to master it. As they taught the next group of physicians, they too may have passed on the notion that they were being taught everything that there was to know. For what other purpose does a doctor attend medical school? I think this pattern may have repeated itself over the years. Believe it or not, even in my medical training, which was not many years ago, on more than one occasion did a professor or an attending physician imply, if not come right out and say, that we were being taught everything important that there is to know. Unfortunately, those who believe that they are being taught everything, tend to stop looking for anything else. Thankfully, there were some professors and doctors who admitted that it was impossible for any doctor to know everything, and they emphasized more fully in their teaching the importance of being able to evaluate the available medical information and apply that information with proper problem solving techniques in the treatment of patients' problems. It is always amazing when any doctor seems to be able to muster the confidence to think for a moment that his medical knowledge is exhaustive, and therefore that his opinions are necessarily correct.

We all know that many times the things that we assume to be true aren't even close to being true or correct. In fact, it is often surprising how far off base some of our assumptions can be. As we discussed earlier, it was assumed that because the earth **seemed** flat, that it **was** flat.

All these factors have led to surprising assumptions, surprising attitudes, and surprising conclusions regarding decreased thyroid system function, its treatment, and the patients who suffer from it. For example, because DTSF can cause certain symptoms and can sometimes lead to death, doesn't necessarily mean that a treatment that prevents death sufficiently corrects the symptoms. And because severe symptoms could be, in the beginning, correlated to diseased thyroid glands, doesn't mean that they were caused **only** by diseased thyroid glands. Diseased pituitary glands were later discovered to be able to cause severe symptoms, even with normal thyroids, and it was seen that the previous assumption was incorrect. However, because diseased pituitary and thyroid glands can cause severe symptoms, again, does not mean that they are caused **only** by them.

Another assumption is that since patients that have excessive thyroid hormone activity in their bodies sometimes exhibit nervousness, fatigue or headache, that therefore, anyone on supplemental thyroid hormone treatment who exhibits these symptoms is necessarily on excessive amounts of thyroid hormone medication. This is in spite of the fact that decreased thyroid system function can also cause symptoms of nervousness, headaches, and fatigue.

Throughout history, we have seen how wrong and sometimes silly assumptions can be when based on a limited perspective.

This points out the wisdom of a principle that a doctor once taught me. He pointed out the distinction between people who are sick and people who are ill. People who are ill, are uncomfortable or unhappy for some reason, and feel that they have something wrong with them for which they may seek help. He pointed out that people who are ill may also be sick, meaning that they have some physical problem that can be shown to be the source of their complaints or illness. He went on to say that there are some doctors who only treat patients who are sick. When it is determined that the patient does not have an easily identifiable physical problem, then they may feel that the patient does not need help and completely overlook his illness. Better doctors, he said, address themselves to patients' illnesses by trying first to find a sickness that is causing their illness. But when and if they are unable to find any sickness, they, nevertheless, endeavor to address the patient's illness by acknowledging it and by endeavoring to help them deal with it as well as possible.

I believe that the doctor was trying to teach the importance of compassion, empathy and being supportive. But I see additional wisdom in this principle, because it points out that people who are sick are people who have physical conditions that can be diagnosed and detected using available medical technology.

But, what if a patient's illness is being caused by a physical problem that is not yet easily detected by available medical technology, and what if a patient is told that he or she does not have a physical problem, when in fact, he or she does? So, to me, the principle emphasizes and helps one to remember an extremely critical fact that all physicians and patients should always be aware of. That fact is, that current medical science is not exhaustive, and just because someone is suffering from a condition that cannot be easily identified or treated, at this time, doesn't mean that the person does not have a physical problem that may even be severe, and that could be treated if our understanding was more complete.

Where We Are

Unfortunately, in spite of the development of the many and varied **testing** approaches for the thyroid system and the various thyroid hormone **medicines** available on the market, doctors still have been unable to find a very predictable method for relieving the symptoms of decreased thyroid system function, <u>particularly not through the use of thyroid blood tests as a guide</u>. There are many patients who, after developing symptoms of decreased thyroid system function, enjoy improvement of their symptoms through the use of thyroid hormone supplementation to the satisfying of thyroid blood test criteria (returning of the thyroid blood test values back once again within the normal ranges), <u>without</u> enjoying anything close to a complete resolution of their symptoms to pre-illness levels.

What Most Doctors Learn About Thyroid

As I look back on the lectures that we were given on the thyroid hormones and the thyroid hormone system in medical school, I can remember the general consensus among the students being that the lectures on thyroid hormone physiology were among the most confusing lectures in medical school. There was a complete review of all available thyroid hormone testing procedures and how the values of these tests would change under various conditions. Some of this information was comprehensible, especially the part relating to the expected thyroid hormone level changes found in the different glandular abnormalities of the thyroid system. For example, learning the changes in the levels of T4, T3, TSH, and TRH, in primary and secondary hypopituitarism, hyperpituitarism, hypothyroidism, and hyperthyroidism. However, much of the other material presented was considered by the students to be quite confusing.

I will present at this time, **very briefly**, some of the information that was incomprehensible. Note to the reader: If you find this information confusing and hard to understand, don't feel badly. Doctors do too. Just quiz a few. Even doctors who do understand it, usually can't use it to best resolve the symptoms of DTSF in the most effective and predictable manner. **"Even when clinicians suspect hypothyroidism [one cause of DTSF], correctly interpreting thyroid function tests is a difficult challenge. For example, a reliable means of directly measuring serum thyroxin (T4) is still not routinely available. And indirect measures of estimating free T4 are prone to misinterpretation...."** (Overcoming Diagnostic and Therapeutic Obstacles in Hypothyroidism, Emergency Medicine Reports; Vol. II, Number 23, November 5, 1990).

We often try to "guesstimate" how much T4 is floating freely in the bloodstream **(as if knowing that amount exactly would necessarily permit an adequate evaluation of thyroid system function!).** We do this by measuring the total T4 in the blood. But we know that the results of this test can be affected by the level of Thyroid Binding Globulin or **TBG** (the globulin to which T4 is often bound in the bloodstream). Increased TBG levels can **display** decreased T4 levels. TBG levels can be increased in pregnancy, the new-born state, birth control use, and other conditions.

TBG concentrations can be decreased when male steroids are used, cortisone is used, there is chronic liver disease, there is other severe illnesses, and under other conditions. One can see how the interpretation of a T4 test would be difficult because of the effect of TBG.

A test was devised, called the T3 resin uptake (**T3RU**) test, in an attempt to help one estimate the effect of TBG on the value of the T4 test to help one better "guesstimate" how much T4 is floating freely in the bloodstream (**even though knowing this amount exactly still would not necessarily correlate with thyroid system function**). These preceding tests are not even considered to very adequately reflect thyroid gland function, much less system function. For this reason, thyroid stimulating hormone is considered to be a more sensitive indicator of thyroid **gland** function (which many mistakenly equate to thyroid **system** function).

Since the purpose of the glands is to secrete hormones into the bloodstream as influenced by the levels of other hormones present, measurements of the levels of these hormones can well reflect the function of the **glands** (thyroid gland, pituitary gland, and hypothalamus). The function of these glands is quite important in maintaining adequate available levels of the raw material, T4, in the bloodstream. **However, T4 is not the physiologically active thyroid hormone. T3 is the physiologically active thyroid hormone.** Most of T3 is produced from the peripheral conversion of T4. It is called **peripheral** because it takes place **outside any gland**.

Knowing What We Don't Know

Many people (even doctors) mistakenly assume that doctors know everything, and that if a doctor doesn't know everything, then he should know everything, because everything is known.

However, medicine is far less of an exact science than some people make it out to be. If it were exact, doctors could fix 100% of the people 100% of the time. It must be remembered that not everything that is written in the medical literature is correct. We have often seen how opinions in medicine can vary tremendously, even in a short number of years. For example, most people are aware of the controversy surrounding female hormones. In the beginning, it was suggested that they should be taken to prevent symptoms, then it was feared that they should not be taken due to an increased risk of cancer. Then it was recommended, again, that they should be taken to prevent osteoporosis, and still the controversy continues. The same can be said about the amount of fiber in a person's diet. We have seen wide shifts in recommendations from the medical community. First, fiber should be taken in the diet, then a person should eat no fiber in the diet, and then again that they should eat fiber, etc.

While I was in medical school, I heard it said that if one doctor were to read everything that was printed in the field of medicine in the year of 1978 alone, that it would take 54 centuries to read. Of course, since the year of 1978, the situation has grown far more formidable. So, of course, it would be impossible for a doctor to absorb, comprehend, and analyze even a fraction of the available information in an entire lifetime, much less within four years, or twelve years, or even twenty years of medical training and practice. Nevertheless, there are some unfortunate doctors who seem to suffer from the misconception that they do know everything that there is to know about the human body in any of its areas.

Considering that the entire mass of information cannot be comprehended at one time by any human mind, it seems that it would be difficult for any person to determine which, of all that information, is the most significant and what parts of that vast amount of information should be taught in medical school. And even if it were possible, doctors don't always agree on what is most significant. That's what second opinions are for. The things that are taught in medical school are extremely small portions of the available medical information, almost like needles removed from the haystack. It may lead one to wonder how it is being determined what needles are the most significant and what needles are not.

It is understandable that the information pertaining to some conditions (especially those that are life-threatening) have gotten more attention than others. But that's unfortunate for people who happen to be suffering from other conditions. Because, even though their condition may not be life-threatening, they can feel so miserable that they sometimes say that they "would have to die to feel better." It should be remembered that simply because symptoms are not life-threatening does not necessarily mean that they are mild, or not severe.

Our Technology Only Reaches So Far

It probably should be pointed out at this time why there are some things that are easier to document and test than others. The human body is extremely complex in design. It is a highly organized system and it is organized in various levels. The organism is made up of systems. The systems are made up of organs. The organs are made up of tissues and the tissues are made up of cells. The cells are made up of subcellular

47

organelles which are made up of molecules. Molecules are also involved in the chemical reactions.

In general, the higher the level or organization wherein lies the problem, the more specific and documentable the complaint. The lower the level of organization wherein lies the problem, the more generalized and the more difficult to document the complaint. For example, the highest level of organization is the organism taken as a whole. It is easy to see whether or not an organism is alive or dead. When one goes down to the next level of organization of the body, the systems, it is also not difficult to recognize the problem. For example, if someone suddenly pushed himself away from a steak dinner clutching his throat, turned blue in the face and fainted, it would not be hard to see his problem as being respiratory. Neither is it difficult to recognize when someone has a digestive system problem when they vomit everything they eat, and when they stop having bowel movements.

Things are a little less obvious when one goes down to the level or organization of the body represented by the organs. Nevertheless, certain groups of signs and symptoms are usually easy to recognize as being related to a particular organ. For example, not being able to move the left side of one's body is consistent with having a stroke in a particular part of the right side of the brain. Severe pain in the right lower quadrant of the abdomen coupled with significantly elevated body temperature often leads one to think of appendicitis or inflammation of the appendix. Shortness of breath and wheezing often leads one to think of asthma

The problems that are related to the next lower level of organization of the body, namely the tissues, are even more difficult to recognize. Problems at this level are somewhat harder to identify and frequently require the technology that is available through various tests to help identify them. For example, different problems at the level of organization of the tissues can cause fatigue. It is known that patients with liver problems, kidney problems, anemia, and even thyroid gland problems can develop fatigue. Blood tests, urine tests, x-rays, and scans can often help us to determine the source.

The even lower levels or organization, such as the function of cells and the chemical reactions among the molecules, are among the most fundamental processes of life. Symptoms that result from problems lying at these levels are that much more difficult to document. Yet that does not mean that they don't exist. It only means that we have not yet been able to devise tests that can reproducibly and predictively evaluate certain problems and their symptoms. For example, the symptom of depression can be caused by a number of things such as chemical imbalances in the brain that can result from various chemical processes resulting from various causes such as abnormal production or breakdown of neurotransmitters, imbalances brought on by stress, and imbalances that result from substance abuse. It is extremely difficult to measure the levels of neurotransmitters, and the functioning of the cells and chemical reactions within the brain to determine the exact cause of a patient's depression. Nevertheless, that does not prevent depression from being recognized as a debilitating symptom that often responds well to treatment. And it does not prevent antidepressants from being some of the most widely prescribed medicines in the world.

It is understandable that more easily documented and observed processes should be given a lot of attention by medical science. But some of the more fundamental processes of the body are extremely important also, even if they cannot be easily monitored or measured. Is it any wonder that some of the more fundamental processes of the body have not gained as much attention from the medical profession as other more easily documentable problems? (It is commonly joked, for example, that doctors don't know much about nutrition.) It should be remembered though, that just because things are not easily documentable or measurable doesn't necessarily mean that they are not important or that they do not exist.

The assumptions that are made and the theories that are formulated to describe things that aren't easily documented are worth looking at. However, just because people were not able to see that the earth was round, didn't necessarily mean that it was flat. In fact, there are still many things in medicine that have been difficult to document and measure, but we don't have to jump to conclusions.

Limitations Of Tests In General

It is interesting how much stock people are willing to place in blood tests and any other kind of test for that matter. It must be remembered that computers only do that which humans program them to do. Likewise, the significance of certain statistics depends on who's interpreting them and the usefulness of tests also depends upon how they are being interpreted. It is interesting that we (possibly because of our perception of our medical technology) are easily convinced by the results of almost any scientific tests. Let me take a moment now to put tests into a little perspective. Contrary to popular thinking that tells us that blood tests, x-rays, or other kinds of tests are always conclusive, they are more frequently than not equivocal and non-conclusive.

Nevertheless, with our increased reliance on technology, frequently people are led to believe that these tests are extremely conclusive. Somehow this might be brought about by the notion that if a machine costs $600,000 or $700,000 and it can measure intricately the vacillations of the electron clouds of the tissues of the body or something equally amazing and mind boggling, then the results must necessarily be conclusive and useful in all situations, which is, of course, not always the case.

One must realize that tests are not 100% accurate. When one uses a test to determine whether or not someone has a disease, the test sometimes will be positive and sometimes negative. When a test is positive and the test is correct, then that is called a true positive. When the test is positive and the test is incorrect, it is a false positive. When the test is negative and it is correct, then it is a true negative. When the test is negative and the test is incorrect, then it is a false negative. One must remember when choosing a test one is attempting to find a test that has few false positives and few false negatives. In medicine there isn't anything that is exact or 100%. The
50

fewer false negatives and the fewer false positives a test has, the more reliable and the more useful it is.

Normal Range

A few comments should be addressed to the "normal range," since so many people are often dismissed as having no physical abnormality on the basis of their blood tests being within the "normal range." When they do have a physical abnormality that doesn't show up on a particular test looking for a particular problem then this is what is known as a false negative. It must be remembered that the "normal range" is an arbitrary setting of upper and lower limits in order to establish who does and who does not have a problem. As everyone well knows, what is normal for one person is not necessarily normal for another. Everyone is different. Some people are low, some people are a little higher, and some are higher still. If one plots the number of people having a certain value against the possible values that the tests can give, one finds that in almost any type of medical test, the distribution will follow what is known as a "Bell Curve". It is called this because it is shaped like a bell (see diagram 4-1). Most people will tend to have similar values (representing the middle of the

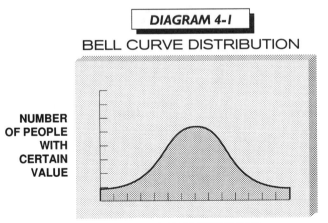

DIAGRAM 4-1

BELL CURVE DISTRIBUTION

NUMBER
OF PEOPLE
WITH
CERTAIN
VALUE

VALUE OF TEST RESULT

distribution). With fewer people having extremely low or extremely high values, the curve takes on a bell shape.

Let us consider the next diagram (diagram 4-2). Let's suppose there are three groups of people. Group A are people who have a physical abnormality that causes their values to run below normal, on average. Let's suppose that Group B is a group of persons who are not sick with an illness with which this particular test correlates. Group C are people who are sick with an illness that causes the values of this particular test to be above normal, on average. By looking at the first shaded area, we can see that some people who are normal have values that are actually more typical of those who have an illness that causes low values. In the second shaded area, we can see that there are some people who are sick that have values that are very much at a level that would be consistent with a normal person. In section three we can see that some of the people who are sick with a sickness that can cause high values also have levels that are more consistent with people who are without illness. In section four we can see that there are some people who are without sickness, who have values that are typical for people who have a sickness that causes

DIAGRAM 4-2

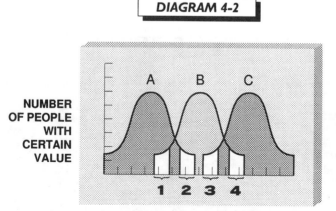

NUMBER OF PEOPLE WITH CERTAIN VALUE

VALUE OF TEST RESULT

elevated levels, on average. So this diagram points out what everyone already knows, and that is: what is normal for one person is not necessarily normal for another.

Without getting too deep into statistics, I would like to point out some common sense reasoning as it relates to "ranges of normal."

The Bell Curve shape has a curved central portion with tails on either side (see diagram 4-3). These bell curves can be of different shapes for different tests. Some may be broad and some may be narrow. Broad central portions indicate that the observations obtained have a greater degree of variation in different people, and narrow ranges of normal indicate that the test value of each person tends to be much more similar to the values of other people.

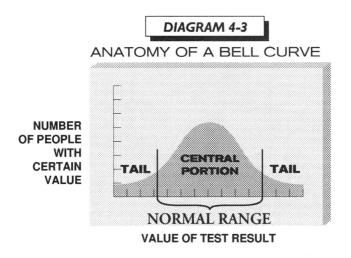

DIAGRAM 4-3

ANATOMY OF A BELL CURVE

NUMBER OF PEOPLE WITH CERTAIN VALUE

TAIL — CENTRAL PORTION — TAIL

NORMAL RANGE

VALUE OF TEST RESULT

As we discussed earlier, entropy is the nature of all things to go toward disorder. If there is no influence causing things to be otherwise, things naturally tend to be random. Tests that have random results form a curve shaped like a rectangle as seen at the top of diagram 4-4. There is no influence that is causing any one particular value to be found any more commonly than

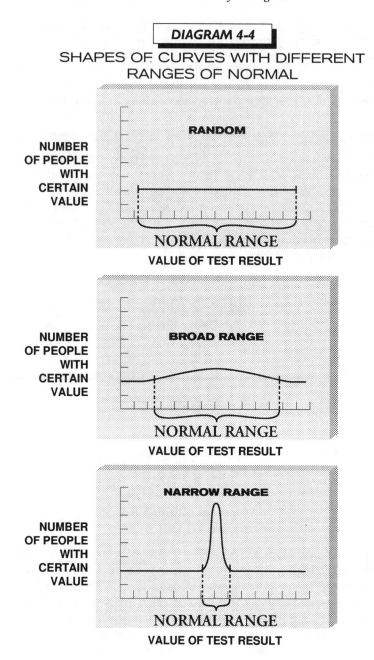

DIAGRAM 4-4

SHAPES OF CURVES WITH DIFFERENT RANGES OF NORMAL

RANDOM

NUMBER OF PEOPLE WITH CERTAIN VALUE

NORMAL RANGE

VALUE OF TEST RESULT

BROAD RANGE

NUMBER OF PEOPLE WITH CERTAIN VALUE

NORMAL RANGE

VALUE OF TEST RESULT

NARROW RANGE

NUMBER OF PEOPLE WITH CERTAIN VALUE

NORMAL RANGE

VALUE OF TEST RESULT

any other possible value. This causes the curve to take on a flat shape. But as influences become stronger in affecting the outcome of a certain test, the shape of the curve becomes less like that of a random test and will take on more of a bell-shaped curve. The stronger the influence, the stronger the shaping effect on the curve. It is the nature of tests to come out with a disordered, random, or flat-shaped curve. If some values occur much more commonly than others, it is not an accident. The stronger the tendency for obtaining a certain result over others, the stronger the likelihood that there must be a very strong influence. So in that sense, the flatter the curve, the more random its nature, and the less specifically the values of a particular test are being influenced. The more peaked the curve, the more likely it is that there is a very specific reason for the peaking, and the more meaningful the test may be (Diagram 4-4).

Limitations Of Thyroid Blood Tests

As it turns out, there is a very good reason that thyroid hormone blood tests are not always of great predictive value in the resolution of the *symptoms* of decreased thyroid system function.

It's because thyroid hormones don't have their action in the **bloodstream**, they have their action at the site of the nuclear membrane **receptors of the cells**. The thyroid hormones, especially T3, interact with the thyroid hormone receptor much the same way a key interacts with a lock so that it may be opened.

At this time, in spite of our vast technology, there is **no way to measure that action**. Not for the past forty years, not now, and probably not for another twenty years, can that be measured **directly**. Historically, doctors have tried to estimate or predict that action based on what floats around in the bloodstream. But common sense tells us that, at best, these blood tests are just an indirect measure of what happens at the cells. And the symptoms of DTSF are caused specifically by low body temperature pattern abnormalities resulting from inadequate thyroid hormone stimulation of the thyroid hormone receptor sites.

So blood tests are very useful in assessing the function of the **glands** of the thyroid system, however, they are frequently hard to correlate with the onset and resolution of the symptoms of DTSF. The symptoms of DTSF ultimately depend on what happens in the **cells** of the body, not the bloodstream. Therefore, the thyroid hormone blood tests are useful in assessing the function of the glands of the thyroid system, but cannot and do not directly measure where **the "rubber meets the road"** in terms of the presence or absence of the symptoms of DTSF.

Most cases of DTSF are caused by Wilson's Syndrome. Since WS is an impairment in the peripheral conversion of T4 to T3 (outside the glands of the thyroid system), it is easy to understand why blood tests are not very predictive in directing treatment of the *symptoms*.

Historically, thyroid blood tests have been used in order to try to estimate what will happen at the active site, but the **body temperature can be used to get a better picture of what actually has happened at the active site.**   Thus, the monitoring of body temperature patterns is a more direct reflection of the adequacy of the thyroid hormone/thyroid hormone receptor interactions of the body.

Since the symptoms are due to abnormal body temperature patterns, it is also easy to understand why body temperature patterns are so useful in the treatment of the symptoms of DTSF. **It is the best indicator that we have.** So treatment of DTSF that does not take body temperature patterns into consideration, isn't being done correctly.   If thyroid hormone/thyroid hormone receptor interactions are ever able to be measured **directly**, such a measurement will add very little to the predictive value already provided by the body temperature patterns (because the temperature already measures the bottom line: the body temperature!).

These facts have led to a great deal of confusion and frustration. I feel that because the limitations of thyroid blood tests are not always borne in mind, false assumptions are made which is one of the biggest reasons that DTSF is so frequently overlooked.

Do Blood Tests Or Temperature Better Reflect Thyroid Stimulation Of The Cells?

It is well known that thyroid hormone levels and body temperature patterns are related. And, it's known that if thyroid hormone levels in the blood drop to very low levels, then a patient's body temperature can drop well below normal and the patient can even become comatose. It is also well known that patients who have thyroid blood tests that are exceedingly high can often have fevers well over 100 degrees in a condition that is sometimes called "thyroid storm."

When thyroid blood levels go too high, the temperature can go too high, and when thyroid blood levels go too low, the temperature can go too low. In either extreme, severe symptoms can result. So both tests, **thyroid blood tests**, and **temperature tests** can both be correlated to conditions and sickness.

Which test, then, is best able to predict when a person is suffering from **inadequate** thyroid hormone stimulation, or when a person has excessive thyroid hormone stimulation at the site of the thyroid hormone receptors? To help us answer this question, let us consider the shapes of the curves of distribution of values of these tests when they are performed in a large number of people. To do this, let's again remember the principle of entropy, the tendency of all things to go toward disorder. Let us remember, also, that the significance of any test values can be measured, to an extent, by considering how that value compares to what value one would expect in a random situation.

Considering The Thyroid Blood Tests

Thyroid hormones do not grow on trees and they don't exist in nature by accident. That can be demonstrated when one considers that without a thyroid gland there is no thyroid hormone production and, therefore, no thyroid hormone levels would be found in the body. So if the thyroid gland was not present or not functioning, then one would expect to find no hormone. So any thyroid hormone levels detected in the body represent a non-random occurrence.

For our purposes, let us consider four of the more than ten thyroid hormone blood tests available. Generally speaking, ranges of normal contain primarily the central portion of a bell curve (see diagram 4-3). Regardless of how narrow or broad a bell curve, the central portion of the curve contains a constant percentage of the measurements taken.

For our purposes, let us say that percentage is 80%. So that means that the central portion of each bell curve contains 80% of the measured values. In medical tests, normal ranges are often obtained by finding the central portion of the bell curve. The lower end of the central portion is represented by the "lower limit" of normal and the upper end of the central portion is represented by the "upper limit" of normal.

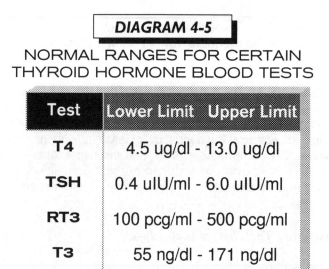

DIAGRAM 4-5

NORMAL RANGES FOR CERTAIN THYROID HORMONE BLOOD TESTS

Test	Lower Limit Upper Limit
T4	4.5 ug/dl - 13.0 ug/dl
TSH	0.4 uIU/ml - 6.0 uIU/ml
RT3	100 pcg/ml - 500 pcg/ml
T3	55 ng/dl - 171 ng/dl

Let us now consider the upper and lower limits of normal for four of the thyroid hormone blood tests available (Refer to diagram 4-5). The first test to be considered is the **T4 test**. The lower limit of normal equals 4.5, and the upper limit of normal equals 13.0 micrograms per deciliter.

The second test is **TSH**. Lower and upper limits of normal are 0.4 and 6.0 microinternational units per milliliter respectively.

The third is Reverse T3 (**RT3**). 100 is the lower limit of normal and 500 picograms per milliliter the upper.

The fourth test is **T3**, lower limit of normal is 55, upper limit, 171 nanogram per deciliter.

Considering that in the random situation one would expect no thyroid hormone levels to be present, since they are not formed out of the blue by themselves, then these upper and lower limits of normal can be considered to represent a certain number of units **above** what one would consider random. Referring back to diagram 4-4 of a random curve, a broad curve, and a very peaked curve, you can see that the random curve is flat which causes the two ends of the "central portion of the curve" to be as far as part as possible. In the broader bell-shaped curve, one can see that the upper and lower ends of the central portion of the curve are closer together yet still wide apart. In the extremely peaked bell-shaped curve, the two ends of the central portion of the curve are extremely close together. So, the closer together the ends of the central portion of the curve, the more peaked the curve is. The more peaked the curve, the more dissimilar the curve is to that of a random situation.

Let us now consider, in percentage form, how far apart the ends of the central portion of the curves are for the four thyroid hormone blood tests previously discussed. With T4, the upper limit of normal is 2.9 times higher than the lower limit of normal. For TSH, the upper limit is 15 times higher than the lower limit of normal. For RT3 the upper limit is 5 times higher than the lower limit, and with T3 the upper limit of normal is 3.1 times the lower limit of normal. Therefore, in a T4 test, there is a 190% difference between the upper and lower limit of normal. For TSH there is a 1400% difference. For RT3 there is a 400% difference. And with T3, there is a 210% difference between the upper and lower limits or normal. One can see by these considerations that the TSH curve is much broader than the T4 and T3 curves. Therefore, the TSH curve more closely approaches the shape of a curve of a random situation.

Considering The Body Temperature's Range Of Normal

When one considers that it would be the natural tendency of a body to be the same temperature as its surroundings, then one may consider the number of degrees a body temperature is above room temperature to be the number of units away from what one would consider a random situation. We shall use 75 degrees as room temperature. Fever is considered to be 100 degrees Fahrenheit and we will consider this to be the upper limits of normal. 97.0 degrees is probably lower than the lower end of the central portion of the curve for body temperature, but for our purposes we will consider this to be the lower limit of normal. 100 degrees minus 75 degrees equals 25 degrees, which we will consider the upper limit of normal as compared to the random situation (room temperature). 97.0 degrees minus 75 degrees is 22.0 degrees which we will consider the lower limit of normal above the random situation. 25 degrees is 1.14 times higher than 22.0 degrees and therefore, the upper limit of normal is 14% greater than the lower limit of normal. We can see by comparing this percentage difference to the percentage differences of the thyroid hormone blood tests that the ends of the central portion of the temperature curve are much closer to each other than the ends of the central portion of any of the thyroid test curves. This indicates a much less random situation, therefore, there must be an extremely strong influence involved. This 14% difference between the upper and lower limits of normal is especially interesting when compared to the hundreds and hundreds of percentage points difference in the upper and lower limits of the thyroid blood tests.

Extremely peaked bell curves do not happen by accident and the greater the peaking, the less accidental the situation.

Again, they are about as likely as tossing a deck of cards in the air and having them land as a card house. The values of the thyroid hormone blood tests and the body temperature are related to the extent that extremely low blood values can be related to extremely low temperatures and extremely high blood values can be related to extremely high temperatures; and both the thyroid hormones and body temperature are intimately related to the thyroid hormone/thyroid hormone receptor interaction at the nuclear membrane of the cells.

The question remains, which test better reflects the influence and purpose of the all important thyroid hormone/thyroid hormone receptor interaction? Since they are related, it would seem that if it were critical that the body maintain a particular set of values for the thyroid blood tests, then the body temperature patterns would vary widely from person to person to accommodate specific thyroid blood test values. Conversely, if it were critical that the body maintain a particular body temperature level, then it would make sense that the thyroid blood tests values would vary widely to maintain a certain body temperature level. When one considers that the percentage difference between the upper and lower limits of normal for TSH are 1400%, and the percentage difference between the upper and lower limits of normal for the body temperature is 14%, it's easy to see which curve more represents a nonrandom situation and which one fluctuates widely to keep the other at a certain level. **It appears that the thyroid hormone blood levels are regulated to fluctuate widely in order to provide for the temperature rather than the other way around.** If it is the purpose of the thyroid hormones to fluctuate widely to ensure a certain temperature, then would the thyroid hormone that fluctuates the widest be any more important than the others in accomplishing that purpose?

It is interesting to see that the TSH (thyroid stimulating hormone) test has the widest range of normal of the thyroid blood tests, suggesting that it may be designed, more than any other thyroid system hormone, to ensure a normal body temperature pattern. It is interesting, because TSH is the blood test currently regarded as the most sensitive reflection of thyroid gland function. But if <u>TSH</u> is regulated to fluctuate widely to help ensure a normal temperature pattern, then it is easy to see how the best indicator of the adequacy of the process is the end result, the <u>body temperature</u>, itself.

> For example, the study habits of students who are trying to score well on a certain test may vary widely. A more confident student may decide not to study very hard, while one with less background might choose to be more diligent. One could try to measure the adequacy of their preparation for the test by how hard they studied, but a more accurate method would be by their actual scores.

Some people consider body temperature patterns to be a more vague and non-conclusive reflection of thyroid system function, because, "everyone's different, and a lot of people have body temperatures that are lower than the average." This is an unusual argument, considering that just as many people have thyroid blood studies that are lower than the average, and their values vary to a much greater degree than do their body temperature patterns. We must remember that the "ranges of normal" are arbitrarily set in an attempt to make the thyroid tests as useful as possible. Thyroid hormone blood tests are invaluable in helping to evaluate and regulate the thyroid system, especially the portion in which the function of the glands are important. However, the fact that there is only a 14% difference between the upper and lower limits of normal for body temperature readings indicates that the body temperature readings far better reflect the status of the thyroid hormone stimulation of the thyroid hormone receptors.

This leads me to believe that the thyroid hormone/ thyroid hormone receptor interactions are regulated in such a way as to provide such specific and consistent body temperature patterns for an extremely important purpose. And I believe that extremely significant purpose is to help provide the optimal conditions for the enzymatically-catalyzed reactions of the body, thereby affecting virtually every bodily function. Thus, the reason for the maintaining of extremely specific and consistent body temperature patterns is that essentially all the bodily functions depend upon it. Since thyroid blood tests fluctuate widely, it is easy to see why temperatures end up having much greater predictive value, in relation to the symptoms of DTSF, than thyroid hormone blood tests. Just because a test is more expensive or difficult to perform does not necessarily mean it is better or more useful.

When Technology Can't Reach It's "All In <u>Your</u> Head?"

There's Even A Word For It: Hypochondria

Somewhere along the line, someone noticed that when patients go to the doctor with <u>specific</u> complaints, many times they can be diagnosed easily and treated effectively. On the other hand, when patients go to the doctor with a long list of <u>generalized</u> complaints, it is often more difficult to ascertain the diagnosis and to find a suitable treatment. So it may have been incorrectly concluded that the patients with the more generalized complaints were healthy, having no physical problems, since the level of medical technology available at the time was unable to provide a reasonable explanation for the patients' complaints.

This may be what has led to the sentiment that when patients go to the doctor with a few well-circumscribed complaints they are sane, good people with a medical problem. When patients go to the doctor with a long list of non-specific, generalized complaints, they are more likely to be thought of as fakers, hypochondriacs or a little bit odd. As a matter of fact, I was taught this rule of thumb in medical school. I remember our class being taught that if a patient came in with a hand-written list of complaints, that red flags should go up in our minds as an alert that these patients might have a large hysterical or psychosomatic component to their complaints. The reasoning offered was, that if they had to write the complaints down, then they must not be very significant (if they couldn't remember them without notes), or that they were probably fishing for attention.

I remember having had a hard time understanding that reasoning then, and I continue to struggle with it now. Especially when I consider that it is possible that patients can have a large multitude of complaints, some of which may come and go at different periods of time. It seems understandable to me that under the pressure of being asked point blank by a doctor what he is complaining of, that the patient might have a hard time remembering all the complaints. And it is understandable how patients would want to write their complaints down to ensure that their money is well spent on the time they have with the doctor and so that they do not leave some of their questions unanswered. This circumstance is so pervasive in the medical profession that there is even a word for it: Hypochondriasis. A hypochondriac is a person affected with hypochondriasis. The definition of a hypochondriac out of Dorland's Medical Dictionary is: "A person who has an unhealthy apprehension about one's health, with numerous and varying symptoms that cannot be attributed to organic disease." But just because a person's complaints cannot be attributed to organic disease with available medical technology does not necessarily mean that they are not due to organic disease, nor does that necessarily make the person's apprehension about his health neurotic. And just because a patient has numerous and varying symptoms does not necessarily mean that they are not due to organic disease.

This sentiment has also helped the word, "hypochondriac," to take on a derogatory nature. Patients I know are aware of this sentiment because many times they will comment to me, as they sheepishly rehearse their physical complaints, that they hope that I don't think they are a hypochondriac. It is clear from their comments that they are aware that people who notice and complain of a large number of symptoms are often thought of as complainers with no real problem. In fact, there is nothing unexpected or unusual about a patient having a larger number of generalized complaints when he has a medical problem that is affecting a more fundamental level of the body's organization. Indeed, it would be more surprising if there weren't a large number of related complaints. It's understandable, then, why patients are often reluctant to recount all of their aches, pains, symptoms, and complaints to their physicians. Many times a patient will only volunteer one symptom or maybe two, usually pointing out those that are the most bothersome. It is interesting that if a doctor asks the patient the right questions, he may find that the patient suffers from quite a few more complaints.

What is strange is that since the first time a patient went to the doctor and died from severely decreased thyroid system function caused by severe hypo-thyroidism, it has been well known that patients with DTSF suffer from a large number of generalized complaints. Since then, doctors don't discount the possibility that a patient with numerous generalized complaints might be suffering from DTSF— until the blood tests come back. Many times a WS sufferer's complaints can be so characteristic of DTSF that a doctor will run thyroid blood testing, being certain that he will find evidence on thyroid blood tests that the patient is suffering from severe hypothyroidism. However, when there is no evidence found on the thyroid hormone blood tests that the patient is suffering from DTSF, the patient may be told that he has no medical problem and he may be thought of in a derogatory light.

What is surprising is how much doctors sometimes seem to think our still fledgling understanding of the human body to be complete and exhaustive. One minute, the doctor can easily recognize the patient's severe and debilitating symptoms of Multiple Enzyme Dysfunction as being a classic presentation of DTSF in need of immediate treatment. The next minute, when the blood tests come back normal, the doctor may think that the patient's large number of generalized complaints can't possibly be related and that they are all in his mind. The doctor may make this "about face" all on the basis of a set of thyroid hormone concentrations measured in the patient's blood (which can't possibly be conclusive).

When the thyroid hormone blood tests come back abnormal, indicating that the patient is suffering from the symptoms of DTSF due to a pituitary or thyroid gland problem, then the symptoms appear to the doctor as being anything but vague and unrelated. When the thyroid hormone tests are low, no one is shocked at all if the patient is fatigued, suffering from fluid retention, depression, dry skin, dry hair, decreased memory/ concentration, abnormal throat/swallowing sensations, numbness or tingling of the hands, inappropriate weight gain, irregular periods, and infertility. No one would be shocked that the huge number of generalized complaints could possibly be all related to one another and could all be caused by the same single problem, because it is well known that one cause of DTSF namely hypothyroidism can cause all of the symptoms discussed.

So it seems strange that a person can present with the exact same symptoms, having an even more classic and severe presentation of DTSF than a patient with blood test-documented hypothyroidism, and the possibility of DTSF is not even entertained, just because no other causes of DTSF have been well described up until now.

It is interesting that the greater our understanding and technology has grown over the years, the fewer and fewer cases of "hypochondria" that are found. More and more illness can be attributed to organic disease, leaving fewer and fewer people in the hypochondria waste basket. I am almost convinced that there is no such thing as hypochondria in the derogatory sense. There is just imperfect medical understanding and technology. I'm not saying that our feelings, thoughts, actions, and physical health are completely out of our hands. I know that the choices that we make in terms of attitudes, diligence, tolerance, etc., do have a tremendous bearing on ourselves, other people, and the things around us. But that might be getting into spiritual questions which are also difficult to measure.

I have gained my perspective on hypochondria from my unusual vantage point of having seen thousands of people, many of which have been told over the years (often not in a nice way) by some of the most highly trained doctors in the world that there is definitely nothing wrong with them. I have often seen their symptoms improve quickly and dramatically, if not completely, with proper thyroid hormone therapy, and with their complaints often staying resolved even after treatment has been discontinued. So needless to say, it can be quite an eye-opener when a patient who has been suffering for years with a characteristic set of complaints ever since the death of their spouse; and has gone through every test and treatment imaginable over the years with little or no success; has their symptoms and complaints corrected sometimes within two weeks with proper thyroid hormone therapy; and has their symptoms stay corrected even after treatment has been discontinued. A very large number of such situations has a way of changing one's point of view.

I don't believe that people go to the doctor for recreation. I think that they can find more use for their entertainment dollar and I don't think they really do enjoy playing the sick role solely for the sake of attention and special considerations from those around them. I really do know that there may be a few people that suffer from such a psychological disturbance only because I know that probably whatever can go wrong does go wrong; and because I know that people are so varied that if a certain psychological disturbance can be imagined, then it probably does exist somewhere someplace. But if I was led to believe in medical school that five to ten percent of people who go to the doctor really do not have a physical ailment and have their problems all "in their head," then I now think that if such a situation does exist, it is extremely rare, being perhaps less than one in ten thousand.

One of the experiences that has helped my perspective change on this matter involved a particular woman. I remember one lecture in medical school when we were briefed regarding what attributes to look for in a patient, that when present, would increase the probability of that patient's symptoms having a mental origin. The patient's initials were S.F. As I have discussed with S.F. herself, if anyone fit the bill for being a "hypochondriac" she did. She was disheveled, and preoccupied with her personal belongings, continually making sure that her comb was in her purse, that her purse was on her lap, and that she knew where her sunglasses and keys were, to the extent that these issues seemed to be the most pressing things on her mind. She had difficulty in maintaining her train of thought, and remembering all of her complaints and all of the points that she wanted to discuss. Overall she behaved rather inappropriately, making the other people in the waiting room and the staff little uncomfortable. So if there was ever a time when I believed a patient's symptoms were all in his or her head, this would be it.

The only nagging problem was that the patient's symptoms were classic for DTSF, and the clinical picture and presentation of those symptoms were classic for Wilson's Syndrome. They came on after a major stress, worsened with a subsequent stress together in a group, etc. Knowing that, at the time, the classic presentation of Wilson's Syndrome wasn't exactly common knowledge, I felt that there was no way that this patient could make up on her own such a classic description of a typical case. So I suspected that the patient may have indeed been suffering from DTSF, and she was started carefully on proper thyroid hormone treatment.

The staff and I will never forget the unbelievable change that came over S.F. within a few short weeks of treatment. She became coherent, appropriate, lucid, and as normal as the day is long. Prior to treatment she had lost several jobs in succession because of the simple mistakes she would make, and she was unable to hold down a job and remain gainfully employed. After treatment, she was able to easily obtain and maintain employment for which she dressed neatly and professionally. She was glad to once again consider herself a contributing member of society, which was especially important for her since she was divorced and needed to provide for herself and be of some support to her adult children. I'll never forget how shocked and amazed I was at the clarity, organization, and eloquence of the appreciation letter she wrote to me. It was just incredible that this letter could have been written by the same person that I had first met. S.F. would agree to this characterization of herself since she was able to see the obvious changes also. She was aware also of her inappropriate functioning and behavior prior to treatment.

In countless other cases, I have seen patients who had previously been labeled "hypochondriacs" enjoy complete resolution of their symptoms with proper thyroid hormone therapy. These experiences have been real eye-openers for me because I have been able to see what our current medical technology labels as being "normal" sometimes isn't even close to being normal at all. I have also been able to see just what can be easily corrected in a predictable way, in a short period of time, with proper treatment. Is it not possible that there may be some common and treatable medical problems that we are not yet even aware exist? (Almost like not seeing the forest for the trees).

To add a little perspective, let me point out that if doctors cannot tell a hundred patients out of a hundred exactly what's wrong with them, exactly the cause, and exactly how to fix it so that it goes away a hundred times out of a hundred, then doctors don't yet know everything there is to know about the human body. For if they did, they would always be correcting the problems rather than sometimes just treating the symptoms.

With the specialization and fragmentation of medicine, there is now more focus on specific **symptoms**, and the diagnosis and treatment of these symptoms. It is interesting how much of medical treatment is symptomatic. For there are many things in medicine for which the underlying cause cannot yet be determined. So, doctors are forced to resort to treating the symptoms while not being able to ascertain fully the underlying cause.

Blood pressure medicine, for example, is used to control high blood pressure. But if it could be easily determined what is causing a patient's high blood pressure, and if the underlying problem could be corrected, then there would not be a need for symptomatic control with blood pressure medicine. Likewise, if a patient had a tendency for developing ulcers because of increased acid secretion in the stomach, and if the underlying cause could be found and corrected, then the patient would not need to take antacid medicine.

One measure of how well a treatment addresses the underlying problem rather than just the symptoms, is how well the symptoms remain corrected after the treatment

has been discontinued. So our medical understanding and technology is not yet complete and there is still a long, long way to go.

Wilson's Syndrome is easily diagnosed and treated (since there are few things in medicine in which it is easier to do so). It is fortunate that the sickness of sufferers will no longer be overlooked and that they will no longer be subjected to the prejudices and criticisms that are often placed on those who are unfortunate enough to suffer from conditions that medical science does not yet understand.

Working with patients that suffer from Wilson's Syndrome has been an extremely humbling experience for me, because I now realize that, just maybe, we **don't** know everything there is to know. It won't be a problem for Wilson's Syndrome sufferers any longer, but for the sake of all those who are unfortunate enough to suffer from physical abnormalities that are not yet fully understood and recognized by the field of medicine, I hope that we, as doctors, can be open-minded and honest enough to say, "I don't know what's wrong with you, but maybe someone else does or maybe someday someone else will."

Patients don't want excuses; they don't want to be patronized; they don't want smooth talk; they want to get better. I don't want Wilson's Syndrome patients and people suffering from as yet undetermined maladies to be given excuses either, I also want them to get better. When the going gets tough its good for the tough to get going, especially if they **can**. But sometimes the blind can't see, the lame can't walk, etc. There are some people who have physical conditions that hinder them from functioning as well as they would like to. It is sometimes a little easier for us to be empathetic towards those whose hindrances are more obvious to us, like, for instance, a man who walks with a seeing eye dog and carries a white cane with red tip. But we must remember that just because we can't easily detect a person's hindrance, such as a chemical imbalance causing depression or premenstrual syndrome, doesn't mean that they don't have one. So if all of medicine, with all of its tests and understanding and knowledge, cannot always detect a person's physical abnormalities, then certainly we cannot, as passers-by, always tell what a person's hindrances are.

I don't want to spend a lot of time on it, but I think there is a point that deserves mentioning. With such a clear description of Wilson's Syndrome (including a predictable and reproducible response to treatment), will there be those who would resist it? Yes. There is opposition in all things and there are very few things that doctors can agree on. Medicine, for some of the reasons that we have discussed, can be a little slow to change. There is a great deal of tradition and a tendency to do things the way they have always been done. But things can't be done any better unless they are done differently. It's gratifying, though, how quickly people are recognizing Wilson's Syndrome for what it is.

Doctors disagree with one another for all kinds of reasons (some of them noble, and others not so noble). It is good that doctors question one another, working through one another's thought processes and conclusions. This helps to provide a more balanced set of thinking. But some doctors may find it easier to say that certain information is wrong, than to say, "I don't know about this yet, even though I am a doctor and I would like to think of myself as being up on the latest developments in medicine." Or the doctor may feel that certain information is wrong because "I have not learned it or been made aware of it through **my** sources." But we have already seen that <u>no</u> source can present to a physician in one lifetime the entire "haystack" of available medical information. Neither can any source necessarily best analyze which "needles in the haystack" are the most important and which it should emphasize to physicians. In addition, "needles" are being added every day.

Psychological

One might say that some of the symptoms related to Multiple Enzyme Dysfunction are psychological, in that the existence of these symptoms and their resolution are all in the patient's head. Some might tend to think so since there is no way of measuring directly the thyroid hormone influence at the level of

71

the cells. But what about when patients' classic low thyroid symptoms get better when thyroid medicine normalizes their temperatures, and their symptoms remain improved even after they wean off the treatment (regardless of what their blood tests show)?

More Reasons WS Overlooked

To compound matters, cases of DTSF that <u>do</u> show up on blood tests are not very common. So doctors aren't always alert to **obvious** cases (out of sight, out of mind). Recently, one of my patients had a classic presentation of thyroid hormone deficiency with many, if not all, of the symptoms of decreased thyroid system function. She had been seen by five different specialists before anyone thought to check her thyroid hormone levels. When they finally were checked they were found to be **abnormal.** She was treated with thyroid hormone replacement and her symptoms improved dramatically. Thus, if **obvious** cases with *abnormal* blood tests are easily overlooked, how much more easily overlooked are cases with **normal blood tests**?

Not Life-Threatening

As was pointed out previously, doctors were first alerted to the existence of DTSF through cases involving deficient **glandular** function. Patients presented to their offices extremely sick, sometimes comatose, and they sometimes died. Physicians at that time were able to work backwards to learn more about the underlying cause. Doctors found that if they normalized the patient's blood tests, they could often prevent the patient from dying. Nevertheless, doctors have still been unable to use blood tests to predictably and reproducibly correct the symptoms of DTSF since many times patients can suffer from the symptoms of DTSF, even when thyroid blood tests are normal. I imagine that if patients continued to die frequently, even when the thyroid blood tests were normal, then more investigation and research would have been done and the importance of body temperature patterns probably would have gained much more attention than it has up until now.

It's ironic that although the glandular causes of DTSF are more life-threatening than Wilson's Syndrome, **Wilson's Syndrome** is by far the **most common** cause of DTSF and the resulting symptoms of MED.

Needed A Treatment

WS has gone overlooked because no one knew how to treat it. There has previously been no good rationale for treatment of the symptoms of Multiple Enzyme Dysfunction, especially when caused by DTSF. For this reason doctors have been unable to get reliable, reproducible, and predictable responses to treatment. Generally speaking, a good rationale for treatment should include an effective therapy and the means to guide that therapy.

When it was discovered that patients suffering from a characteristic pattern of illness would often respond very favorably to thyroid extract given by mouth, many lives were saved. In fact, there are **few** problems in medicine wherein a patient can be so sick and have his symptoms resolve and health restored **so dramatically**, quickly, and easily.

It was also found that some patients, when given too much thyroid supplementation, developed signs and symptoms similar to those of thyroid gland problems that cause excessive thyroid hormone stimulation of the body. So in the beginning, the rationale for treatment of DTSF was limited to giving thyroid medicine to severely ill patients to decrease their symptoms and prevent death. However, there was a need for a better guide than just trial and error to help determine how much thyroid hormone medication was needed.

Later, the thyroid hormones, themselves, were discovered and identified. This led to the development of thyroid hormone blood tests. With this development, it became possible to measure the level of thyroid hormones in patients who were sick and also in normal people. It was found that thyroid system symptoms correlated fairly well with the patient's thyroid hormone blood tests. The symptoms of excessive thyroid hormone treatment corresponded fairly well to elevated thyroid hormone blood levels. And, inadequate resolution of deficient thyroid system symptoms could often be correlated with thyroid hormone blood tests that were below normal. Many times, however, the symptoms of DTSF remained or appeared even when thyroid hormone blood tests were normalized. Many of these symptoms, however, are rather subjective. For example: fatigue, headaches, depression, decreased memory, decreased concentration, and others. Although it was easy for doctors to document whether or not patients died and how their survival or death related to their thyroid hormone blood levels, it was much more difficult to document how well patients' symptoms of depression, fatigue, headaches, and decreased memory and concentration related to their thyroid hormone blood levels. Since how a person feels is hard to measure, some physicians may have assumed that the patients were fine when they and their tests looked fine, even though they **weren't** necessarily fine.

With the advent of thyroid blood tests, it became possible to guide therapy to the extent that death could almost always be prevented, and the symptoms of DTSF could frequently be greatly improved with few side effects. However, patients often still complained of severe symptoms of DTSF, even though they were not life-threatening, and their thyroid blood tests levels were within the normal ranges. Faced with the quandary and without any good approach to address such a problem, doctors were left with a couple of alternatives, both of which are used even to this day. They could acknowledge the patient's illness and admit to him that they are unable to find further sickness for which they can address treatment that might alleviate the symptoms of DTSF. Or, the doctor could ignore the patient's illness and deny that he may possibly have a physical problem based only on the available blood tests and the available literature (and even do so in a tone of voice that might imply that he believed the medical literature and his knowledge of it to be exhaustive— which, of course, is never correct). I emphasize the tone of voice only because of its potentially damaging effects from an authority figure on the unprepared.

Even in the case where a doctor feels that further pursuit of a medical cause of a person's complaint would be fruitless (because of the limitations of medical science and technology) and that the patient would be better off obtaining psychological help in learning to live with his complaints, I feel that it would always be preferable for doctors to arrive at the same bottom line with a different choice of words. For example: **"I can't find any abnormality that I am aware of that could explain your condition, and I am not very sure that currently anyone else can either. So your alternatives include: continuing to search for a possible explanation and solution; and taking measures to help you cope as well as possible until a solution can be found, when and if it can be found."** It is disappointing enough for one not to be able to find anyone who can correct the problem, without the matter being made much worse by it being said or implied that one also is a sissy, a faker, a complainer, a failure trying not to look like a failure, someone trying to find a socially acceptable excuse for their inadequacy as a human being, someone looking for pity, or someone who's crazy. If patients suffering from such a problem go to the doctor and the doctor cannot adequately recognize or treat it, that doesn't necessarily make that doctor a bad physician, and, it does not necessarily mean that the patient's complaints are all in his head.

To illustrate how the lack of a good rationale for treatment has helped Wilson's Syndrome to be overlooked, we can consider the following: Other sources of DTSF have responded well in the past to T4 or thyroxine therapy. However, if one gave a patient with Wilson's Syndrome T4 as treatment, the symptoms might improve temporarily, but it would be unlikely that they would remain persistently corrected after T4 therapy was discontinued. Giving a Wilson's Syndrome patient T3 as therapy in a non-specific way, wouldn't be expected to correct the patient's problem either. Even when T3 therapy is given to a patient with Wilson's Syndrome according to useful and specific guidelines, it is not always easy to correct the symptoms, because medicines aren't answers, they are tools. We all know what it is like to experience the surprise that comes from finding the unexpected value in something we are trying to use. For example, if we were looking into the wrong end of a pair of binoculars, we might conclude that binoculars are not useful in seeing far distances. However, if for some reason we turned the binoculars around so that we were looking through the correct lenses, then the surprising and impressive usefulness of the binoculars would be clear and we might be heard saying, "Oh-h-h-h, I see!" So in this way an inadequate rationale and guide for treatment has helped Wilson's Syndrome to be overlooked for a long time. The tools (thyroid hormone) that are important in the treatment of Wilson's Syndrome have been available for a long time (over forty years). **The difference is not in what is used in treatment but the important thing is how the tools are used.** Only when a condition responds predictably and reproducibly to a treatment is it most recognizable as a distinct condition. And only when the tools are used properly does Wilson's Syndrome respond predictably and reproducibly to treatment.

Another factor that has caused WS to be overlooked is that it is only natural for more obvious and definable problems to be addressed first. This has led to a great deal of resentment on the part of those people who are unfortunate enough to suffer from problems that affect the more fundamental levels of organization of the body. They sometimes view the limitations of the medical field and the medical professional as a lack of interest, concern, or respect. This sometimes causes them to perceive the medical profession has having a bad attitude. They may feel, "If I die tomorrow, that's **their** problem, but if I stay miserable for the rest of my life and nobody can show what's wrong with me, that's **my** problem."

Not All Medicine Is Scientific

Another set of conditions that has helped Wilson's Syndrome to be overlooked for so long, is the specialization and fragmentation of the medical field as well as the economic and legal aspects of the industry. In the beginning, there were no specialties in medicine. There was merely the field of medicine studied and practiced by doctors. However, as the scope of medical information expanded it became easier and easier for doctors to be jacks-of-all-trades and masters of none.

There arrived a time that the amount of information available in a fragment of the medical information, for example diseases of the lungs, was enough to occupy all of a physician's career. Not only did the medical information proliferate, but so did the number of doctors. And since doctors earn their living by practicing medicine there were also some economic considerations that helped encourage the specialization of medicine. Specialization also helped, in some ways, to better meet the needs of patients. By definition, specialization involves establishing some means to distinguish one specialty or group from another. So doctors having special interests formed clubs or organizations to identify themselves as having special interests. In other industries these are known as special interest groups.

Not everything in the human body can yet be measured, analyzed, or proven. Because of the unmanageable amount of available medical information, it is impossible for even one man to hold all of it in his mind at one time. Therefore, it is impossible for anyone to be able to adequately analyze the information to decide what is most important. For these reasons and others, medicine, in large part, is a matter of opinion. Hence the terms "second opinion," and "practice of medicine," and "art" of medicine. So, even though medicine is a scientific industry based on scientific facts, the interpretation and use of those facts is often a matter of opinion.

There are strong sociological, economic and political forces at work shaping the field of medicine. There are groups having special interests that organize themselves in an effort to promote their opinions on a national, state, and local level. To some extent, these arbitrarily and self-established groups have been able to obtain some support from associated industries (for example, health insurance and malpractice insurance companies and the legal system). Many people are aware of the increasing roles that malpractice and health insurance play in the way medicine is practiced (affecting how a doctor makes a living). These factors and influences work together to consciously or subconsciously encourage physicians to adopt similar practices espoused by various special interest groups and to do things because "that is the way they are done," and not necessarily because it is the best or most correct way. This has also influenced physicians to stay more strictly within the confines of their own special interest groups without addressing problems outside their "specialty."

Some people now have four, five, or six different specialists instead of one family practice doctor. They may go to a gastroenterologist for their stomach to find that he won't treat their skin problem; so they enlist the services of a dermatologist who is unfamiliar with breathing problems; which leads them to seek out a pulmonary physician, and so on. One can see that if more and more doctors specialize in more and more specific and narrow fields of practice dealing with more narrow ranges of symptoms, then there will be fewer and fewer physicians to address problems causing extremely wide ranges of symptoms. This would especially apply to a problem that can cause more than 60 symptoms which fall in all the different specialties.

The advances made in the problems affecting higher levels of organization of the body are responsible, to some extent, for the formulation of the different specialty fields of medicine. The problems that affect the lower levels of organization of the body, are harder to evaluate and measure. They generate a greater number of more generalized symptoms than do the problems that affect the higher levels of organization. With increased specialization, doctors are tending to consider much more specific and narrow areas of complaints, leaving the rest to others. So one can see how some quite difficult problems (those affecting the lowest levels of organization of the body) have tended to be left to be addressed by fewer and fewer doctors. **But we know that the lower the level of organization, and the more fundamental the level, the more important and far reaching it is.** What would have the greater effect, yanking out the bottom floor or the top floor of a 20-story building? If one removes the top floor, then one has affected one story, but if one removes the bottom floor then one can lose all 20.

There are different ways to approach problems.
1. We can consider the way it has always been done in the past.
2. We can consider the opinions of special interest groups.
3. Or, we can consider the possible causes and solutions; we can consider what resources may be brought to bear on the problem; we can consider the pros and cons of the various options; and we can do the best we can with what we have to correct the problems.

What's Important

What **Is** Useful In The Diagnosis Of WS

The following are some observations which have great predictive value in the diagnosis of Wilson's Syndrome:

1. What are the patient's complaints (when questioned carefully about the symptoms of Wilson's Syndrome)?
2. In what way did the complaints come on (Separately? Together? After a stress? After successive episodes? etc.)?
3. What is the patient's average body temperature pattern?
4. What is the patient's nationality (See Chapter 6)?

Too much emphasis can not be placed on the answers to any one of these questions. However, when taken together they paint a very useful clinical picture. The first three questions are the most predictive and the fourth (nationality) can be considered icing on the cake. The four questions listed above can be useful in helping to predict whether or not someone has Wilson's Syndrome (the most common cause of DTSF) as a cause of his/her symptoms of MED. However, the best indicator that a patient's complaints are due to MED is if the symptoms disappear in two days or two weeks with normalization of the body temperature patterns. That's a pretty good indicator that his or her symptoms were temperature related. The best indicator that a person's MED was caused by Wilson's Syndrome is if all of the symptoms resolved in a short period of time (often within two days or two weeks) when the body temperature patterns were normalized by the patient taking the right kind of thyroid medicine (Chapter 10) in the right way, and if the symptoms remained resolved even after the thyroid treatment was weaned. That's a pretty good indicator that his or her abnormally low body temperature patterns were being caused by Wilson's Syndrome and that a persistent correction had been effected. This is what is commonly known as a therapeutic trial.

Getting Well

The fundamental goal of medicine is to alleviate and/or correct disease and to promote good health. Since this is the fundamental goal of medicine, the value of tests can be measured on how useful they are in accomplishing that goal. Some tests are used to aid in diagnosis of problems and some are useful in the monitoring of treatment of problems. The tests for diagnosis and monitoring medical problems are frequently the same. An abnormality on the test may show what the particular problem is, thereby being helpful in diagnosis. And the returning of that same test to normal might indicate when the problem has resolved during monitoring of treatment. A good diagnostic test should be able to predict whether or not a particular person has a particular medical problem with few false negatives (people who actually do have a medical problem who are told they are normal based on the test) and few false positives (people who are told that they have a disease based on the test when in actuality they don't). If the diagnosis is correct based on the tests, then they should be more likely to respond to the treatment of choice for that particular problem. The value of monitoring tests can be measured in how well they predict, with few false positives and false negatives, how well a patient will respond to treatment and what the eventual outcome will be. The more useful it is in predicting response and outcome, the more useful it is as a test.

As far as the diagnosis and treatment of problems involving the **glands** of the thyroid system, the thyroid hormone blood tests are quite useful and reliable. However, in terms of the diagnosing and monitoring symptoms of DTSF, thyroid blood tests are, and will be, **extremely low in predictive value**. This is especially true in terms of diagnosis of DTSF in general, as a cause of a patient's MED symptoms, having an enormous amount of false negatives (thyroid blood tests may indicate the patient does not have DTSF when they actually do, complete with severe and debilitating symptoms of MED that respond quickly and easily to proper thyroid hormone supplementation); and in terms of directing treatment, being extremely poor predictors as to how to guide treatment for the predictable and reproducible resolution of the patient's **symptoms**.

A patient's body temperature pattern and presentation of symptoms of MED have much greater predictive value than blood tests in terms of diagnosis of DTSF, and can much better direct proper thyroid hormone therapy. Therefore, the collection of these indicators can be used to predict positive and beneficial response to therapy in approximately 95% of cases, that is, if a patient has many of the symptoms of Wilson's Syndrome and these symptoms came on together after a severe mental, physical, or emotional stress (which is understandable, explainable, and predictable) and if the patient has a consistently low body temperature. This is true, especially if the T3 therapy is administered in such a way as to elevate the body temperature to 98.6 degrees, on average, and to stabilize the body temperature for optimal enzyme function. Normalization of body temperature patterns correlates extremely well with resolution of Wilson's Syndrome symptoms. So, whereas thyroid hormone blood tests have few false positives and enormous false negatives in the diagnosis of DTSF; the criterion of MED symptoms and low body temperature patterns brought on especially after periods of stress, have much fewer false negatives, have few false positives and are much more useful and are of much greater predictive value in the diagnosis and treatment of DTSF in general and Wilson's Syndrome in specific.

Chapter Five

5. HOW WILSON'S SYNDROME WAS UNCOVERED

One day, a patient I was treating handed me a book titled, **Hypothyroidism: The Unsuspected Illness**, written by a doctor Broda Barnes, MD, copyrighted 1976, published by Harper and Row. She suggested that I read the book saying that it was a very good book on thyroid problems. I thanked her and assured her that I really didn't need to read the book since I already had a good understanding of the thyroid system. Nevertheless, she left the book with me and it sat on my bookshelf for about three weeks when I decided it probably would not hurt to look it over. As it turned out, I found the book extremely interesting with its major contribution being the association of body temperature patterns with low thyroid function and the suggestion that this association be used as a useful guide to directing thyroid hormone treatment. **To my knowledge, Dr. Barnes was the first doctor to emphasize the correlation between low thyroid function and low body temperature as a guide to therapy.** He also pointed out the importance of being mindful of the many and varied manifestations of deficient thyroid function and that it can be important in an unsuspectedly large number of health problems.

After reading this book, I began asking patients that I was treating more specifically about their symptoms. If a patient would complain of being tired, I would ask him if he also noticed having headaches, depression, dry skin, dry hair, fluid retention, and all the rest of the complaints. When they complained of having headaches, then I would also question them about whether or not they also noticed having trouble sleeping, difficulty swallowing, itchiness, and the like. I was amazed at how frequently the patients' symptom came on together with a large group of other symptoms; and not just random symptoms, but the symptoms of low thyroid system function. When I requested the patients to take their body temperatures, I was also intrigued to discover that many times, if not always, they were low, on average.

Dr. Barnes also had a few pages on the treatment of hypothyroidism (one cause of DTSF) as diagnosed by symptoms and low body temperature patterns. By following his treatment recommendations, I noticed that many of the patients' symptoms improved dramatically as their body temperatures began to normalize. I could see evidence that there was an unequivocal relationship between the symptoms and the body temperature pattern. Unfortunately, the treatment results were not very reproducible and predictable, and when symptoms did improve, they frequently did not improve completely. This suggested that the treatment was not completely adequate, especially considering that the patients remembered how they felt prior to the illness that responded partially to the treatment.

A few months later I came across another source of information which was a review article from a medical journal: **Thyroidal and Peripheral Production of Thyroid Hormones**; Schimmel; Utiger; Annals of Internal Medicine, 87: 760-768, (December 1977). The significance of this article has been overlooked for a long time, like the proverbial **"needle in a haystack."** Its significance lies namely in the pointing out of the importance of the conversion of thyroid hormones that takes place, for the most part, outside the thyroid gland (peripherally) in the tissues of the body. This article makes it clear that the degree to which T4 is converted to T3 or to RT3 could have profound physiological consequences. The article suggests that the function of the system may not depend merely on how much T4 a patient's thyroid gland produces or how much T4 the patient's body is given, but may very much depend on what the patient's body does with the available T4. **New data reviewed in the article has forced a reassessment of long-held views on thyroid hormone physiology.** There was some speculation in the article that elevated RT3 levels resulting from a transient shunting of T4 towards RT3 and away from T3 could then secondarily inhibit T4 to T3 conversion. Not only can this happen, it does happen. The same article reviewed the well-known facts that T4 to T3 conversion can be impaired or decreased by fasting, illness, glucocorticoid, and in the fetus.

So then, in addition to just asking patients about their symptoms, I began asking them specifically when their symptoms began, to see if they could identify their onset with any obvious stress, illness, or injury. To my amazement, patients suffering from symptoms of DTSF, while having normal thyroid blood tests, could, in almost every instance (greater than 90%), identify specific stresses which marked the onset and/or worsening of their symptoms.

The scientific information printed in the Annals article (after Dr. Barnes' book was published) made it possible to understand how a person could have symptoms of DTSF even with normal thyroid hormone blood tests. And it led to the finding that symptoms of DTSF can come on after a stress and persist inappropriately even after the stress has passed. It helped also in understanding why patients' symptoms of DTSF don't always resolve completely, as some would expect, with the use of T4 preparations or T4/T3 preparations (medicines). It also helped pave the way for the development of new, better directed, more predictable, more reproducible, and more effective treatment for DTSF symptoms (especially symptoms of DTSF caused by Wilson's Syndrome).

The clinical information contained in Dr. Barnes' book helped provide the basis for the all important guides (especially symptoms and body temperature patterns) to therapy. Without this information, the scientific data could not effectively be put to use. Without the scientific understanding provided by the review article, the information presented in Dr. Barnes' book alone could not explain why some patients responded satisfactorily to his suggested treatment, while a number of them did not.

Since then, I have performed computer searches of all the available medical literature on the subject. Although I have found many articles supporting the information found in the first two sources, I have found very little that adds to the information, and I haven't found any sources that could substitute for the first two sources. When taken together, they formed the embryo that has been developed into the information contained in this book. I had stumbled on to extremely simple, yet important information. Simple, because of the few number of variables involved; and important, since it involved one of the most fundamental processes of the body, namely thyroid system function.

Surprisingly Reproducible And Predictable Patterns

Since then I have spent my full time working in this area of medicine. Since I have been dealing with patients suffering from symptoms of MED (again, in the thousands), I have seen surprisingly reproducible and predictable patterns. These patterns become quite obvious when one has the two sources of information just referenced above and when one works with the same problem day in and day out, month after month, year after year. Some of these patterns are only easily seen when one deals with a large number of patients, because some of them are subtle. Since most doctors probably think about the thyroid system only three or four times per month while treating patients in their practice, their observations might be so few and far between that the pattern might not be as evident. So, it really is not too difficult to see how Wilson's Syndrome has been overlooked for so long. **The best indicator that patients' symptoms are being caused by Wilson's Syndrome are when their symptoms resolve together and completely when proper therapy is given.** By treating so many patients and carefully analyzing their responses, an extremely effective treatment has been developed. In addition, when a doctor is treating a large number of patients with a treatment that very effectively resolves their symptoms, patients sometimes make comments or observations that the doctor might not have been particularly listening for. But if one hears the same comments often enough, a particular pattern might gain one's attention. By exploring these patterns more fully, it is possible to find that they are quite reproducible and predictable. The patterns may contribute to changes which make the treatment even more predictable, reproducible, and effective.

This process has also made it possible to see the effect of the thyroid system on many symptoms and complaints that previously seemed unrelated. All these relationships can be very useful in recognizing the clinical picture of a patient suffering from Wilson's Syndrome. In fact, the clinical picture can be so recognizable that it is sometimes obvious just by looking at someone that they are likely to be suffering from Wilson's Syndrome. With a little experience, one could probably recognize several likely sufferers while walking through the mall. Many of the varied manifestations of Wilson's Syndrome will be discussed in Chapter 9.

Tools Of Problem-Solving

Perhaps the greatest value of medical learning is its usefulness in the treatment of patients' problems. Learning is obtained by reading and studying what is already known or believed to be true. Then it may be applied. By applying medical information one can gain experience. There are some things that aren't written yet, and some of the things that are written are incorrect, and that's what experience is for. As we gain experience, we can employ common sense postulates of problem solving that are used by all doctors in approaching medical ailments. Since there are still far more things in medicine that remain unknown than are known, it is better to use words like could, should, probably, maybe, possibly; and less often words like definitely, always, never, etc.. All we can do is the best that we can with the tools that we have available. The usefulness of tools certainly depends on how well they are used. **The following are some common sense postulates:**

1. When a cluster, group or multitude of characteristic symptoms appear or worsen at the same time, it is more likely that they are related.

2. If such a group of symptoms begin and end together at identifiable times, it is more likely that they are related.

3. If the onset of a group of symptoms was closely related in time to a particular event and the resolution of that cluster of symptoms was closely related in time to a particular treatment,

it is more likely (although not definite) that the event was the cause and that the treatment was correct.

4. If the symptoms appear after a particular event, resolve after a particular treatment, remain resolved after that treatment has been discontinued for a time (for example 10 months), return after a particular event extremely similar to the first, and resolve again after the same treatment and remain resolved after the treatment has been discontinued again, it is even more likely that the events were causes and that the treatment was correct.

5. If the symptoms appear after a particular event, then resolve after a particular treatment and remain resolved after that treatment has been discontinued, then it is more likely that a persistent correction has been effected.

6. The fewer the variables involved in a particular problem, the easier the solution.

7. The more predictable a patient's response to a particular treatment, the fewer unaddressed or unanticipated variables present.

8. The fewer the treatments the better, so there is less chance of drug interaction and also better chances of good compliance (patients following instructions as prescribed).

9. The more instances in which certain clinical observations are found, the more reliable are those observations.

These common-sense postulates have been useful in helping to uncover Wilson's Syndrome and to provide the information contained in this book. They have helped in generating certain criteria useful in the recognition and treatment of Wilson's Syndrome. **It is easy to predict whether a person will or will not respond to proper T3 treatment.** Many times patients will receive treatment and they will have their symptoms corrected and they will stay corrected for long periods of time, even years after the treatment has been discontinued. In such cases, the same symptoms may return again after another physical, mental, or emotional stress.

Wilson's Syndrome follows very predictable and recurrent patterns, and is based on a particular model, or theory. Considering how predictable and reproducible patients' responses are to treatment, monitoring, diagnosis, etc., it stands to reason that the model, or theory, upon which the treatment is predicated is very close to being correct, with there being few unaddressed variables. For example, when something happens 95 times out of a 100 just the way one would expect it to happen; the principles, ideas, or premises which caused one's expectations are likely to be very close to correct.

Adages From Medical School

There were some additional principles of common sense that we were taught in medical school to help us reason through medical problems and the various alternatives that can be used in addressing those problems. **Some of these adages follow:**

"It is better to treat the problem, not the symptoms." Patients with Wilson's Syndrome, suffering from a multitude of complaints, frequently find themselves being treated for their symptoms to varying degrees in varying ways. It stands to reason that it is always best to treat the underlying problem rather than treating the symptoms. However, with no obvious cause in sight, sometimes we are left to handle the symptoms as well as we can until a cause can be uncovered. For this reason, patients who present to doctors with symptoms consistent with Wilson's Syndrome will frequently be treated with a number of symptomatic treatments pointed toward handling the symptoms. The characteristic thing about symptomatic therapy is that when the treatment is discontinued, the symptoms return or persist.

I compare this to the problem of a ship that is taking on water. One can turn on a pump to get water out of the ship, or one can plug the hole through which the water is entering. If the pump is effective enough, it may be able to remove the water. However, if the pump is turned off and

the ship continues to take on water, it is unlikely that the hole has been plugged.

One saying that I really like, was told to me by an old professor. **"If you listen to your patients long enough, they'll tell you what's wrong with them, and if you listen longer still, they'll tell you how to fix It."** This saying underscores the point that the patients are the ones that live in their bodies 24 hours a day, 7 days a week, 365 days a year. After spending so much time with their own bodies, they frequently become quite well acquainted with their own bodily functions. In many ways, they know their own bodies better than anyone else does. When patients' symptoms of Wilson's Syndrome have resolved after proper T3 therapy they sometimes remark, "It's great to have all these symptoms gone, it's great to feel normal again, I knew I wasn't crazy. I had been told so many times that there wasn't anything wrong with me and I was even told that it was all in my head. But I knew my own body well enough to know that there was definitely **something** wrong. I knew that something, somewhere was not quite right. I could tell that something was out of balance."

It is interesting to watch, however, peoples' attitudes towards their symptoms and the resolution of those symptoms. I have a distinct vantage point because I see patients who are complaining with a large number of generalized complaints, and I have the opportunity to watch many of those complaints resolve quickly and completely, with the patients often experiencing a dramatic difference from before to after. Some people will say, "I was beginning to wonder if I was a hypochondriac." Others will say, "I **knew** I wasn't a hypochondriac." And most interestingly, some will say, "I'm sure you see a lot of hypochondriacs, but I knew I wasn't one of them."

Before treatment, certain patients sometimes seem to think that only they, of all the patients that I see, are not hypochondriacs. It seems strange, because of all people, it would seem that those who have been through it would be less likely to be prejudiced against others who may be unfortunate enough to be suffering from medical science has not yet been able to easily recognize or correct. Especially, when they have gone through the frustration and know what it is like to have their friends, neighbors, and doctors look at them as if they are complaining because they **enjoy** feeling bad; as if they are looking for sympathy or excuses; and as if they have ulterior motives. But sometimes even **they** seem to imply that they feel hypochondria is a prevalent condition.

Another adage states, **"When you hear hoofbeats, think of horses, not zebras."** This saying emphasizes that it is best to think of common things first, because common things are more likely to happen than rare things. By far, is abnormal body temperature is the most common cause of the symptoms of MED. We have already discussed that abnormal body temperature patterns could, theoretically, be caused by adrenal hormones, female hormones, and thyroid hormones as well as by other factors. I feel that DTSF is by far the most common explanation or cause of abnormally low body temperature. Since the thyroid system normally adjusts up and down in response to stress and other conditions, it seems reasonable that the thyroid system is the most likely to get stuck in a position that causes inappropriate body temperature patterns. This is a little like a man who often travels back and forth between two cities that are separated by a certain forest of trees. Suppose that through the middle of the forest runs a paved highway. Through other sections of the forest can be found two narrow and unpaved paths that wind through the forest from one city to the next. If the man called me asking me to bring him a can of gas because he had run out of gas halfway between the two cities, and hung up before he told me exactly where he was, the first place that I would look is on the paved highway. I would check the highway first because I know that even though the two paths also connect the two cities, they are both barely manageable with ordinary vehicles and they are used mainly for recreational purposes. I would reason that it would be much more likely that the man would run out of gas on the highway because he more commonly uses the highway for traveling.

"Treat the patient, not the tests." This adage underscores the important of remembering the shortcomings of our medical technology. The physical and emotional manifestations of patients suffering from DTSF resolve far more quickly, predictably, reproducibly, and completely with normalization of body temperature patterns than with normalization of thyroid hormone blood tests

Another saying that I remember hearing in medical school that I find quite useful is, **"Everything in medicine is a therapeutic trial."** This saying underscores the importance that we constantly reevaluate the clinical course of a patient. Because nothing in medicine is absolute, one can never be absolutely 100% sure of the diagnosis or 100% sure about how a patient is going to respond to a certain therapy. Subsequent therapy should always be based a patient's response to initial therapy. In other words, the plan of management should be continually reevaluated based on a patient's response. This decreases the chance of overlooking any important developments because of tunnel vision. This is another way of saying that there is always a small chance that the initial diagnosis and plan of management might not necessarily be optimal. In medicine, how patients respond to therapy is always the bottom line. In some medical problems, especially in those that affect lower levels of organization of the body, how a patient's symptoms respond to treatment may be one of the only indicators available.

For example, it is practically impossible to measure the chemical imbalances in a person's brain that are causing him to be depressed. Yet, with careful questioning and with careful observations, doctors frequently diagnose patients as having clinical depression and will often prescribe antidepressant medication in an effort to alleviate the condition. If the patient responds, this positive response to treatment provides more reassurance that the patient was suffering from depression and that the treatment prescribed was effective.

Some might ask "How can one tell if a patient might benefit from antidepressants when the situation can't be measured?" Or, others might ask "You mean, it can't be known how one will respond to treatment until it is given?" Yes, one knows best how a particular therapy will go, and how correct the diagnosis is only after one sees a patient's response. This is true for every medical problem and every medical treatment (easily measured or not).

History, physical examination, laboratory tests, and other observations may provide important clues to a patient's diagnosis and likelihood of responding to a particular therapy; but one can never know for sure how a patient will respond to a particular treatment until that treatment is given and the response evaluated. So, even though there are no good tests to pinpoint exactly the chemical imbalance in any given person's brain that is causing them to be depressed, this does not prevent antidepressant medications from being used in therapeutic trials to bring about a great benefit in many lives.

I like to use, from time to time, an analogy of a circuit breaker to illustrate another principle. "If your lights go off in your house all at once, you don't check the light bulbs, you check the circuit breaker," not because it is the only explanation, but because it is the most <u>likely</u> explanation and also the easiest to address first. If you're fortunate enough to find that the circuit breaker has been thrown, you can simply restore your lighting with the flip of a switch. This saves you from having to check all the light bulbs, or calling the power company, an electrician, or a service man. This analogy points out the importance of trying "simple things first."

First, Not Last

If it cannot be determined precisely which possible solution is correct, then the determination might only be made by a series of therapeutic trials. One can consider the risks and benefits of each alternative, and try one alternative after another until the best solution is found. It makes sense that one should first try, alternatives that have the greatest amount of pros as opposed to cons (greatest benefit as compared to costs/risks). If one treatment had a much greater potential for resolving the symptoms than another, or if one was much more simple to render than another, then the simpler treatment with the greater potential for benefit would seem to be the alternative that should be considered first.

The following are points that make Wilson's Syndrome and low body temperature patterns one of the first of all medical ailments to be considered rather than the last.

1. It is extremely common and is becoming more prevalent every day because of changes in our society and because of changes in our population brought on, in part, by advancements in medical technology that have helped more people live long enough to develop this problem. Again, "When you hear hoofbeats, think of horses not zebras."

2. It is extremely important. The symptoms can be severely debilitating and getting it treated can make all the difference in someone's life. It is hard to imagine any other malady (which is not immediately life-threatening) that takes a greater toll on individuals and our society. It meets, in spades, what is sometimes called the "so-what" criterion.

3. It is an easy solution to a lot of problems. So, if Wilson's Syndrome is the underlying problem, there is a chance of killing many birds with one stone. It is always better to treat the underlying problem rather than just the symptoms. The potential for benefit is so great because the problem affects such a fundamental level of organization of the body and therefore can have profound physiological consequences.

4. There is a good chance that the problem can be remedied, staying corrected even after the medicine has been discontinued. Women with irregular periods are often helped by being "cycled" on birth control pills for a couple of months to regulate their periods. Once the menstrual cycle has been restored to a regular pattern, they frequently stay regular even after the birth control pills have been discontinued. In much the same way, one may "take control" of the thyroid system and restore it to an appropriate pattern with the symptoms resolving and often staying resolved even after the "cycling" has been discontinued. It's always preferable when someone does not have to take a medicine for life.

5. It doesn't take long for one to see if one is on the right track. Since the problem is so simple, if one responds, the response is usually dramatic, with improvement being seen many times within two days to two weeks. If a symptom responds, it is expected that many, if not all, of the symptoms would also respond at the same time.

6. It's not foreign. Unlike most other medicines, thyroid hormones were not designed by a man in a laboratory. They are substances that have been present in each person's body since birth. This fact decreases the potential of any unforeseen long term side effects to the body, and it decreases the potential for unforeseen drug interactions (but, of course, thyroid medicines are not candy and no medicine is completely without risk).

Now, if one could choose the characteristics of medical problems that should be among the first possibilities considered in addressing any ailment, one would choose:

1. Common or likely

2. Significant and having an impact (so-what criterion)

3. Easy to address

4. Having a potential for correction or "cure"

5. Rapidly responsive

6. Least invasive, being less likely to cause any tissue damage or long-term harm

Because Wilson's Syndrome affects such a fundamental level of organization, or "cornerstone" of the human body, there is something unbelievably strange about it. Of all **chronic** medical problems, I believe that Wilson's Syndrome is **the** most common, has **the** greatest impact, is **the** easiest to address, is **the** most likely to be remedied, is **the** most rapidly responding and has **the** most inherent or non-foreign of treatments. For these reasons, Wilson's Syndrome should be the first of impairments to be considered in the treatment of patients rather than the last.

If WS is so common, then how could it be overlooked for so long? Well, what if it was so common and so similar to a body's natural response to living conditions that it was overlooked as being "pretty nomal," in spite of the symptoms being recognized, even individually, as inappropriate enough to warrant all manner of symptomatic treatments.

I know as well as anyone that this scenario sounds a little far-fetched. But nevertheless, strange things do happen. Lets talk about strange: A 45-year-old patient has been suffering from severe depression, dry skin, dry hair, memory problems, fatigue, fluid retention, constipation, and panic attacks and has been to numerous doctors who have treated her symptoms with antidepressants, antianxiety medicines, and headache medicines continuously for the past 20 years. She remembers her symptoms beginning 20 years previously when she lost her job and had to move to another state. Since then, her symptoms have not relinquished or subsided. She subsequently divorced and has not been in contact with her children for the past 12 years because of the severe depression. Her symptoms are not mild. In fact, they are quite severe, so severe that she has been continually under doctors' care since the symptoms began. All of her tests are normal, yet her body temperature patterns are low. It seems almost inconceivable, yet the patient's symptoms begin resolving immediately once her body temperature begins to become more normal when she is started on proper thyroid hormone treatment. Within a month and a half, her symptoms are completely resolved, and she has been weaned off the antianxiety and antidepressant medications without difficulty. She feels, for the first time in 20 years, the way she used to feel. If one sees enough of such cases it can begin to affect one's point of view.

In Summary

Wilson's Syndrome is probably the most common of all chronic ailments and may take a greater toll on society than any other medical condition. Since it is easily recognized and treated, it should be one of the first medical ailments considered in the treatment of patients, rather than the last.

It is paradoxical to be discussing such a simple problem that has such profound implications and yet has been overlooked for so long when it is so easy to recognize and treat. It is also paradoxical because, how could the uncovering of such a significant problem have been so simple or easy? One would expect that something with such great ramifications should have come about only after millions and millions of dollars have been spent by teams of scientists, governments, labs, research hospitals, or pharmaceutical companies; and by having computers read, assimilate, and analyze 54 centuries worth of medical information.

However, as it turns out, developments in science and medicine frequently **don't** happen in that way. I have always been intrigued by stories about how significant scientific and medical discoveries have been made, and they almost always have one thing in common. That is, someone noticed something a little bit unusual or unexpected and out of the ordinary as compared to what one might have expected. Then, by looking more carefully into the unusual event, and by analyzing it, and by trying to figure out what factors or forces played a part in causing the unexpected event to come to pass; the scientists were able to identify previously unidentified factors of great significance.

For example, in 1928, British scientist Alexander Flemming was working with cultures of bacteria that he was trying to grow in petri dishes. One day he pulled his bacterial culture off the shelf and noticed that it was contaminated with a mold. He could have just discarded the bacterial culture as being ruined, but just before he did, he noticed that the bacteria was not growing within a certain distance of the contaminating mold. He wondered to himself, what was preventing the bacteria from growing near the mold? By analyzing the mold and by looking more closely, he was able to isolate penicillin. That discovery, needless to say, has had an immeasurable impact on the practice of medicine and the lives of millions of people.

Another example is when Madame Curie noticed that when she developed radiographic plates of the image of her hand, she was able to see the outline of her flesh, and she could also see the skeleton of her hand. She realized that the energy that had exposed the plate had passed more easily through the soft tissues of her hand and less easily through the bone, which provided the interesting image on the photographic plate. Such was the humble beginning of the entire field of radiology. This discovery also changed the world forever, and thus, strange things do happen.

6. WHAT IS WILSON'S SYNDROME?

Wilson's Syndrome is the cluster of often debilitating symptoms especially brought on by physical or emotional stress that can persist even after the stress has passed (due to maladaptive slowing of the metabolism), which responds characteristically to the special T3 therapy protocol described in this book, and defined in the Doctor's Manual for Wilson's Syndrome. It is characterized by a body temperature that runs, on average, below normal, and routine thyroid blood tests are often in the "normal" range. Now, let's go step-by-step through the definition so that we can more fully characterize Wilson's Syndrome.

A Cluster Of Seemingly Unrelated Symptoms

A cluster, because the symptoms tend to come on together in a group. All of us, when asked to describe what it feels like to have a fever, can give extremely similar answers, since elevated body temperature patterns can cause characteristic complaints. So, also, can low body temperature patterns cause characteristic complaints.

Since the body temperature is so fundamentally important in many of the processes of the human body, an abnormally low body temperature pattern can cause a multitude of different symptoms. Usually, but not always, patients suffering from Wilson's Syndrome complain of many of the symptoms (rather than just a few). Although they can come and go separately at different times, they frequently come on together in a group also. When the symptoms come and go together at the same time under the same circumstances, it is more likely that they are related.

It is extremely interesting that the symptoms don't always follow the same order of severity in every patient. For example, when I am interviewing patients I will always ask them which symptom or complaint is bothering them the most. Sometimes it will be fatigue, sometimes depression, sometimes migraines, sometimes PMS, sometimes fluid retention, etc., etc. In fact, almost every one of the symptoms listed in this book has been claimed by one patient or another as being their most significant complaint. So one can see how varied the presentation of Wilson's Syndrome can be.

Some of the symptoms can seem unrelated because it is hard for most people to understand how one problem can be the cause of so many different complaints. But when one understands the fundamental importance of body temperature patterns on the functioning of the human body, it becomes much less difficult to understand.

As we have discussed, body temperature patterns reflect the thyroid hormone/thyroid hormone receptors interaction and closely correlate with the resulting symptoms of decreased thyroid system function. So any thyroid hormone treatment that does not consider body temperature patterns may not adequately alleviate the resulting symptoms of DTSF. The treatment described in this book does take into consideration the body temperature pattern, as well as peripheral conversion of T4 to T3. Since this treatment more effectively addresses the underlying problem and is directed towards the root of the problem, it more effectively alleviates the symptoms of DTSF when they are present, improving the symptoms both more completely and more quickly. Because of this, it is more evident which symptoms improve together, and therefore, which symptoms are more likely to be related. It becomes apparent that there are many more symptoms related to DTSF than has been previously realized.

What is interesting is that these symptoms appear not to be just a little related, but very much related to DTSF. For example, dry coarse skin, impaired memory, constipation, hair loss, brittle nails, depression, and fluid retention are well known symptoms related to hypothyroidism. But other symptoms, generally not considered as being related, including panic attacks, premenstrual syndrome, migraine headaches, irritability, asthma, allergies, and others, have been found to be.

Brought On By Stress

The symptoms usually come on together, especially after significant physical, mental, or emotional stress. The symptoms cannot always be easily related to episodes of stress, because sometimes the onset of symptoms is more subtle. But when they come on together after a significant stress, they are easier to recognize as being related. As has been pointed out earlier, the body frequently responds to stress by slowing down the metabolism, by slowing down the conversion of T4 to T3. It does this to conserve energy. The only problem is that the impaired conversion of T4 to T3 can persist even after the stress has passed, causing a person to be inappropriately stuck in the conservation mode. This can prevent him/her from being as productive as s/he otherwise might be and may lead to inappropriately persistent symptoms.

If careful histories are taken, one may find that patients will go through a period of stress and will slow down. When the stress is over, they will usually come back up to normal. Later they may slow down and come back up to normal after another stress. Then finally, after one particular stress, a patient may slow down, develop symptoms of Wilson's Syndrome, and stay down even after the stress resolves. Subsequent stresses may further impair the patient's conversion of T4 to T3, and some of their persistent symptoms may worsen and they may also develop additional symptoms.

So really Wilson's Syndrome is a coping mechanism gone amuck, an adaptive response responding maladaptively. It is a condition that can persist for many, many years, even forty to fifty years. It is not an *immediately* life-threatening condition, but it may contribute to increased deaths over time from higher cholesterol levels and coronary artery disease. And it can affect, to an amazing degree, the quality of life and productivity of a person. But, if recognized and properly treated, it can often be easily remedied.

However, subsequent stresses can cause this problem to return. Typical episodes that can precipitate the symptoms of Wilson's Syndrome include childbirth, divorce, death of a loved one, job or family stress, surgery or accidents, smoking and then quitting, and others. It is quite common for patients to pinpoint the fact that after a certain stressful event in their life such as the death of their father, they identifiably, and unequivocally have not been the same since (even though it may have occurred fifteen or twenty years previously). Sometimes they attribute the way they feel to the loss being so great, they sometimes feel that it changed the whole condition of their lives. However, for some patients, even though their father did die, they feel they have bounced back fairly readily (being left without financial problems and still having plenty of loved ones and family members to whom they can relate), but they still cannot seem to return to normal. The patients themselves will often be perplexed as to why they should stay persistently symptomatic and never quite get over the traumatic experience, even though mentally and psychologically they feel that they have recovered. They may have been close to their father, but they know that their father would have them get on with their lives and they feel fully psychologically and mentally prepared to do it, but they still have significant physical problems which they cannot overcome. These patients frequently get their answer when they come to realize that their physical complaints and problems weren't psychological, or mental at all; when with proper thyroid hormone therapy their symptoms resolve with normalization of body temperature patterns and the restoration of their metabolism back to the productivity mode.

The Patient's Story

1. When patients with Wilson's Syndrome go to a doctor for relief, it is helpful to determine what complaint is bothering the patient the most. This is what is known as a **chief complaint**. Sometimes patients will offer only a chief complaint without volunteering any other symptoms. This may be because they don't realize that their other symptoms could possibly be related, or because they are not of a severity that concerns the patient, or perhaps because they are afraid to be labeled complainers or hypochondriacs. But, additional complaints, or

characteristics can provide important clues to the underlying ailment or condition.

2. It is also helpful to ascertain from the patient when the major complaint or **complaints first began**. Wilson's Syndrome is more obvious when the complaints come on together in a group after a major stress because the onset is more identifiable. However, some patients have more subtle presentations, having some of the symptoms for even all of their lives. Frequently, the symptoms will worsen after subsequent stresses becoming progressively worse and more pronounced, and may even increase in number. It is also helpful to inquire of the patient what situations or circumstances seem to make the symptoms worse and which seem to make them better. Patients may notice that under conditions in which they are not under as much stress, when they are able to get more regular exercise, and with certain eating habits such as a hypoglycemic diet (for example, higher in protein, lower in carbohydrates taken in six small meals rather than in three large meals per day), their symptoms will often improve greatly.

3. It is also helpful to find out from the patient **if these symptoms have responded to treatment of any kind in the past**, and if the patient has been treated previously with thyroid medication. The symptoms of Wilson's Syndrome often improve in a group when patients are given thyroid medication. However, when a patient with Wilson's Syndrome is treated with thyroxin (T4), the symptoms usually improve for a period of time (usually for about three months), and then will often go downhill again. If the dose of thyroxin is increased the patient's symptoms will, again, frequently improve for a short period of time (often the same amount of time as with the first dosage), with the symptoms then worsening again. This cycle may repeat itself several times, with the patient's symptoms improving for a time and then worsening again with each successive increase of T4 medication. Frequently, if the T4 dosage is increased one too many times, then the symptoms can worsen "right off the bat" without there first

being any improvement. This is generally an unfavorable sign that indicates that the patient's thyroid system is being pushed too far in the wrong direction, with the wrong medicine, because of the feeding of the vicious cycle of T4 to T3 conversion impairment rather than the reversing of the vicious cycle.

4. There are people who seem to have a **greater predisposition** towards developing Wilson's Syndrome. Their presentations of the symptoms of Wilson's Syndrome are generally less dramatically associated with precipitating events. They more often have had the symptoms for many, many years, possibly for their entire lives. So it is more difficult for them to be able to notice the onset of the symptoms since they don't really know what it feels like to be "normal."

5. When patients are asked about their past medical history, it is often found that they have been treated with many of the symptomatic treatments that are listed later in this chapter. They may even have been diagnosed as having a "thyroid" problem and told that they need to stay on thyroid medicine "for the rest of their lives." If DTSF goes widely misunderstood, and is commonly overlooked today, then certainly it has been misunderstood and overlooked previously, and thus, not all past thyroid diagnoses are necessarily correct. Patients who have been told they have a "goiter" may not have had a "goiter" (swelling of the thyroid gland due to stimulation of the thyroid gland by TSH, thyroid stimulating hormone). Patients may have been told that they had frank hypothyroidism when they did not. Especially considering the difficulty in actually measuring the thyroid hormone/thyroid hormone receptor interaction. **All previous thyroid system diagnoses should be taken with a grain of salt.** Because, even if the diagnoses are correct, they may not be the only thyroid system abnormality present causing the symptoms of DTSF (there are several causes of DTSF and more than one can be present at one time). There have been patients that I have treated who were diagnosed as having hypothyroidism twenty years ago. They were started on T4

medication and told that they were going to remain on T4 for the rest of their lives. Yet, even with T4 medication the patients' symptoms of DTSF remained inadequately addressed. With proper T3 therapy the patients' symptoms were relieved with the symptoms remaining persistently better even after all thyroid hormone medication had been gradually weaned. Patients diagnosed in the past as having hypothyroidism may actually have had Wilson's Syndrome. If the patient states that his "hypothyroidism" happened twenty years ago after he was involved in a major car accident or divorce, then the likelihood the patient actually had Wilson's Syndrome increases. This is because Wilson's Syndrome is more commonly brought on by a precipitating event or major life crisis than is hypothyroidism.

6. Of course, when a patient is taking thyroid hormone therapy, their own thyroid system function is suppressed temporarily. **It is interesting to see patients' thyroid gland function come up and function normally even after it has been suppressed for twenty or thirty years.** These patients may never have suffered from hypothyroidism in the first place, but rather from Wilson's Syndrome.

It is hard to imagine that such a simple problem can cause so many and such severe complaints and can stay in a person's body for so long when it frequently can be corrected so quickly and easily with proper treatment. It can be a very touching thing, because many patients that I see, when their symptoms resolve quickly with treatment, are often tearful when they realize that they don't have to spend the rest of their lives feeling unwell. It's sad when they realize that twenty or thirty years of their lives have passed, and once thirty years have passed. Those years can't be retrieved or relived. Although the burden may be lifted for the rest of their lives, it is sometimes bittersweet, because they sometimes can't help but look back and wonder how things might have been if the problem had been treated thirty years earlier.

Maladaptively Slow

Somewhere along the line a person decides when their complaints and conditions are normal and when they are abnormal. Doctors also make the distinction between normal or abnormal as they are deciding whether or not to treat a particular condition. The patients that I treat usually determine their complaints to be abnormal when they feel they are inappropriate under the circumstances. It is normal to feel bad when one is sick with a cold, sore throat or other ailment. And when one has lots of pressures and stresses, it is understandable when one doesn't feel on top of the world. People recognize they have a problem, however, when their feelings cease to be appropriate with the things that face them. Different patients may express this in different ways:

"I get plenty of sleep and I'm still tired."

"I can't understand why I am depressed and having these bad feelings because there is nothing that's going wrong in my life, everything is fine."

"I can't understand why I can't concentrate and why I can't remember things."

'I can't understand why I can't get anything done at work when I used to be extremely sharp, and my business isn't really that challenging right now."

"My business is not extremely difficult, but I'm still having trouble functioning and trouble accomplishing even the smallest things."

"I can't understand why I'm so irritable, mean, and abusive towards the people that I love the most, namely; my family, my spouse, and my children."

"It literally scares me to look at my child, who I love more than anything else, when five minutes earlier I exploded in a rage of temper towards him for no good reason."

"I am trying to understand how and why I could possibly have those feelings of anger, considering how much I love my children and my family."

"I can't understand why I'm so miserable and depressed because I really love my job."

"I can't understand why I'm so anxious, fearful, and overwhelmed now, because everything is fine."

"I can't understand why I can't get things accomplished. I know a sinkful of dishes is not a big deal. I know emptying the garbage is not a big deal. I know that going to the grocery store is not a big deal. That's why I can't understand why I cannot get enough motivation, ambition, resources, or whatever it takes, to get it done."

"I can't accomplish the smallest things. And I can't figure it out because I should have plenty of resources to do them. I used to be able to accomplish tasks with no problem, but now I can't."

These are typical concerns of Wilson's Syndrome sufferers. It apparently is not too difficult for doctors to determine when a patient's symptoms seem to be inappropriate because they frequently treat the symptoms of Wilson's Syndrome separately, which will be discussed later in chapter 8.

Low Body Temperature

Wilson's Syndrome is characterized by a body temperature that runs, on average, below normal. Dr. Barnes' temperature test involved taking an underarm temperature using a glass thermometer as soon as one awakens in the morning (before rising).

For optimal enzyme function, it is important that the body temperature patterns run neither too high, too low, nor too unsteady. It is well known that the body temperatures do vary at different times in different situations. For example, body temperature tends to run lower in the morning, rises as the day progresses, and decreases again towards evening on a daily basis. Temperature patterns are also seen to change with monthly menstrual cycles, and it is for this reason that women take their temperature while they are attempting to get pregnant to determine ovulation. I believe there can also be seasonal variations in body temperature similar to the hibernation response in animals. And, of course, the body temperature patterns can be affected by activity, diet, and other factors.

Since the body temperature often follows a daily cycle, I prefer to have my patients take their temperatures orally beginning three hours after they have awakened and every three hours thereafter, three times a day **(for example, if they awake at 7am; then take temps at 10am-1pm-4pm)**. There are several reasons for this:

I. It is understandable that people's body temperatures may be low upon rising each morning after having been asleep all night, considering the body temperature does tend to be a little bit lower during sleep. But if the body temperature patterns run significantly below normal even during the bulk of the day when they are supposed to be at their highest, then it is more likely

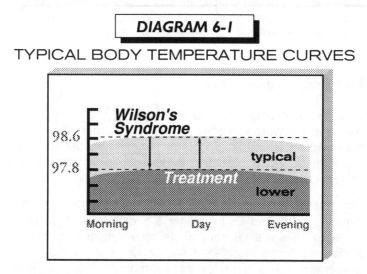

DIAGRAM 6-1

TYPICAL BODY TEMPERATURE CURVES

that the patient has abnormally low body temperature patterns (thus there may be fewer false positives with this test as compared to the morning temperature test) (see diagram 6-1).

2. Since body temperature pattern stability is also important and since body temperatures can fluctuate up and down within hours, I prefer three readings each day which can help one get an idea of the steadiness of the body temperature pattern as well as how high or low the average temperature is. Ideally, the body temperature should be at the proper level and also be steady. Digital thermometers can be more temperamental than glass thermometers, sometimes giving different values even seconds apart. **For this reason I prefer the accuracy of glass thermometers, even though they are less convenient.**

3. Oral temperatures are faster, and more convenient to take during the day than underarm temperatures.

From my experience, I would consider body temperature patterns that vary two or three tenths of a degree when measured several times during the waking hours to be relatively steady. I would consider body temperature patterns that fluctuate an entire degree or more to be relatively unsteady. This degree of unsteadiness, itself, is enough to explain adverse symptoms. I have seen patients that are not on any medicine, have their body temperature patterns fluctuate as much as two and even three degrees during the day.

Most commonly, the patients that I see who have symptoms of decreased thyroid system function, typically have body temperatures to average around 97.8 degrees. Some patients can be symptomatic with body temperatures of 98.2 degrees, on average. It is rare, but there are a few people who are symptomatic with body temperatures averaging 98.4 whose symptoms resolve when their body temperatures normalize to 98.6 degrees with proper T3 therapy. Again, most WS patients' temperatures average around 97.8 degrees, but frequently patients' temperatures may be found to average from the high 96's to the mid-97's. Sometimes there are patients who are found to have body temperatures averaging in the 95's. I have seen at least one patient with temperatures in the 93's. So, although there can be some variation in the body temperature patterns, patients with Wilson's Syndrome who are complaining of the symptoms MED generally have body temperatures that average about 8/10 of a degree below the accepted normal of 98.6 degrees. When they receive proper T3 therapy, normalizing their average body temperature to 98.6 degrees, their symptoms are most likely to resolve.

No, not everyone that has a body temperature that averages below normal has DTSF, Wilson's Syndrome, or MED. But a body temperature pattern that averages consistently below normal is more than enough to explain the complaints and symptoms of MED, and Wilson's Syndrome should be one of, if not the first, possible causes considered. Of all the characteristics of Wilson's Syndrome, body temperature patterns have by far the most predictive value in terms of diagnosis and monitoring of treatment. In fact, if a patient's body temperature pattern does not average below normal, then it is far less likely that he will respond favorably to T3 treatment.

Certain Nationalities More Prone To WS

A patient's family history may reveal that many people in his family have been diagnosed with "thyroid problems". Thyroid system problems, in general, tend to run in families. And Wilson's Syndrome, in specific, also appears to have a hereditary component.

It is interesting to me, considering Wilson's Syndrome is basically a starvation coping mechanism gone amuck that it seems to be more prevalent in patients who ancestors survived famine. Noting, that T4 to T3 conversion impairment is brought on by periods of starvation or fasting, I began questioning my patients carefully regarding their ancestry.

I was able to see a very definite pattern, namely, that there are some people who have a greater tendency towards developing Wilson's Syndrome than others. These people tend to have a

110

slightly different pattern of presentation than do people who have a greater resistance towards developing Wilson's Syndrome. Interestingly, the patients who seem to be the most predisposed towards developing Wilson's Syndrome (earlier in life with less provocation) seem to predominantly belong to certain nationalities such as, **Scotch, Irish, Welsh, American Indian and Russian** (as well as from other countries which have been plagued with famine). The greatest tendency of all is exhibited among those patients who are part Irish and part American Indian. But, people of any nationality can develop Wilson's Syndrome. Patients who have a greater tendency towards developing Wilson's Syndrome frequently have a light complexion with freckles, light-colored eyes, and red hair (or red highlights such as auburn colored hair). Irish and Scot people frequently have these characteristics of course, but there are people from other countries who also seem to have a tendency towards red hair, light-colored skin, and light-colored eyes who seem to be prone to WS (e.g. northern Italy). So there does seem to be connection to nationalities who have survived famine. There also may be an independent correlation with the genetic makeup that is consistent with people having light colored skin, freckles, red highlights or red hair, and light-colored eyes. Some days it seems as if half the people in the waiting room have red hair when I know that half the population does not.

It is not too difficult to understand how Wilson's Syndrome would be more prevalent among people whose ancestors survived famine, considering that people can compensate for starvation conditions by, among other things, decreasing the conversion of T4 to T3 in their bodies, which results in a conservational slowing down of the metabolism. As discussed previously, this impaired conversion is designed to return to normal once the starvation conditions have passed, so that the person might be able to return to a more productive and enjoyable life. It stands to reason that there may be some people who are able to compensate better than others, and one will not be among the survivors of a famine unless he is amongst the most adaptive to the conditions. The people who cannot slow down their T4 to T3 conversion (in response to starvation conditions) would be more likely to die. And those whose bodies can more readily adapt by slowing down T4 to T3 conversion are more likely to survive, and are more likely to pass this trait on to their offspring.

As it turns out, the more readily the T4 to T3 conversion can <u>slow</u> down, the more readily it can <u>stay</u> down causing people whose ancestors survived famine to be more likely to develop Wilson's Syndrome.

2 Classic Presentations

The presentations of those who <u>are</u> more predisposed to WS and those who <u>aren't</u> are typically different.

Patients who <u>are</u> more predisposed to developing Wilson's Syndrome tend to have more subtle courses. The symptoms tend to show up earlier in life, and with comparatively mild provocations. Sometimes they have Wilson's Syndrome even from birth (birth can be quite traumatic). Their symptoms are often less dramatic in onset. And although they will often worsen with stresses, they tend not to be as dramatically precipitated by stressful events as they are in patients who are less predisposed to WS. Sometimes, patients with a predisposition for Wilson's Syndrome might develop the condition at the age of 7 or 8 after they have their tonsils removed, when they start junior high school, after changing to a new school, after moving to a new town at age 5, and/or when there was any family discord in the patient's home such as divorce (which is not mild, of course, but often occurs early in a person's life). These patients frequently comment that they are not sure what it feels like to be normal, and they probably don't. Their symptoms sometimes increase in number gradually over the years, rather than all at the same time.

On the other hand, patients who are <u>less</u> predisposed often have a much more dramatic onset of their symptoms. They usually occur later in life, at least in the late teens or early 20's, frequently in the 30's and 40's, and sometimes in the 50's or 60's or older. They may go for 35 years without having any sort of problems whatsoever, then suddenly develop 25 or 30 symptoms coming on together at the same time after a major stress (such as a car accident or divorce), with the symptoms persisting long after the stress has passed. There is frequently a remarkable difference in their quality of life.

Through working with the large number of patients that I have seen with this condition, these two patterns of presentation call to mind the following analogy. It is similar to what happens when one considers the difference between a large dam and a small dike. In the event of a flood, rain water would build up and rise up against the resistance provided by a small dike and soon overcome its resistance and flood. So the difference before and after would not be that significant since the dike would do little to slow down the pressure exerted by the floodwaters. However, the large dam providing much more resistance, would hold back a much larger volume of water. As the days would pass and the heavy rains would continue, the water would build up against the wall of the dam. Over a period of weeks, the floodwaters would possibly even get near to the top of the dam. All the while the land on the other side of the dam would remain relatively dry. However, if the pressure were to become too much for the dam and it were to break, then tons of concrete and millions and millions of gallons of water would suddenly come crashing down on the other side of the dam. This would cause a dramatic onset of circumstances from before to after.

This can explain why people with a stronger predisposition towards Wilson's Syndrome seem to have a more subtle onset of their symptoms and complaints, while patients with a greater resistance seem to have a much more dramatic onset of their complaints later in life, usually developing a large number of symptoms at once after a significant physical, mental, or emotional stress.

As it turns out, patients who seem to have a greater predisposition towards developing Wilson's Syndrome initially, also seem to be more prone towards **relapsing** again after successful treatment has been weaned, and after a subsequent stress. However, patients with lesser

113

predisposition who stay well until later in life (35 or 40 years old) should be able to remain normal for a good number of years after treatment has been discontinued (unless they are pulverized by another subsequent stress). Of course, if the stress is severe enough (e.g., child abuse), even individuals with a great deal of resistance can develop Wilson's Syndrome in their childhood.

If patients with a history of Wilson's Syndrome do relapse, it is usually easier to correct a subsequent episode than previous ones if it is caught early enough. If a patient undergoes a significant stress, say, 7 to 8 months after treatment has been discontinued and begins to relapse, T3 therapy can be started to help prevent a full-blown relapse. Usually small doses for a couple of weeks (or until the stress has passed) are sufficient.

Some patients who are especially prone to Wilson's Syndrome, and who have gained enough experience to predict the degree of stress that can precipitate a relapse, can benefit from an extremely low **prophylactic** dosage of liothyronine (T3). For example, let's suppose you had a job such that once every 4 months it was necessary to make a large-scale presentation to your employers and to a group of hundreds of people. This might be quite a stressful situation. Now if this situation precipitates WS symptoms, then you may be able to prevent the symptoms by taking an extremely low dose of T3 therapy the day before, the day of, and possibly for a couple of days after your presentation. There are patients who find they have much less physical and mental problems with this approach, and they are frequently able to avoid relapses. Some patients who are, for example, part Irish and part Indian, and who are found to have a significant predisposition towards developing Wilson's Syndrome, may elect to be maintained on a small maintenance regimen of T3 therapy to help ward off a relapse. Usually, however, it is generally preferable to remain off medicine when possible.

Women More Than Men

About 80% of Wilson's Syndrome sufferers are women. Over the years, working with thousands of patients, I have
114

developed a certain perspective on the functioning of the human body. Of course, the human body is a complex and wondrous system. It has been discussed in previous chapters how the thyroid hormones, female hormones, and adrenal systems can be interrelated. I believe, of course, that nutrition, exercise, and environmental conditions also affect the functioning of the overall system. As mentioned previously, I picture these different influences and systems to be related like many different ropes tied to a single ring with pressure being exerted on the ring by the ropes in many different directions. The position of the ring, depends on the amount of tension in each of the ropes. So that if one rope develops an unusually large amount of tension, it can pull the ring out of position, thereby affecting the rest of the ropes as well. Depending on the various tensions in the rope, I believe the system can sometimes get "out of balance."

It seems that there are some people whose body is more flexible or adaptive than others with their "ring" being capable of a wider range of "positions." Sometimes this flexibility or adaptiveness can be quite important. The survival of the species may even depend on it.

Of course, **tremendous** system changes are required in the process of menstruation, ovulation, conception, pregnancy, delivery, and returning to normal after pregnancy. I remember being astounded in medical school when we first studied the physiological changes that take place in a women's body as she is carrying a child, even in terms of the values of blood tests, heart rate, respirations, glucose metabolism, hemoglobin levels, etc. It was amazing that these great changes could even be compatible with life. I have heard it said that there are three types of people in the world, men, women, and pregnant women. I can see the meaning of this statement, because the difference between a woman and a pregnant woman does almost seem to be as great as the difference between a man and a woman. Not in any derogatory sense, but I do remember thinking that the difference between a woman and a pregnant woman seemed to be as great as the difference between two different species. It was eye-opening, because again, in many ways pregnant women look much like non-

115

pregnant women in that they have two eyes, hair, teeth, skin, arms, legs; and in that they walk, talk, and function in a way that is quite similar to non-pregnant women. But if one wanted to compare the "position of the ring" of a woman during pregnancy as compared to that same woman prior to pregnancy, I think that most people would be extremely surprised by the huge difference. The difference would be due to the change in "tensions" in the many different factors that affect the function of the body including the amount of blood pumped per minute by the body, calories consumed, materials produced, oxygen consumed, carbon dioxide produced, female hormones, thyroid hormones, adrenal hormones, dietary intake, exercise, stress levels, etc. So it is not hard to imagine that the total body system of a pregnant woman can sometimes be "out of bounds" as compared to when she is not pregnant. Women demonstrate amazing hormonal and physical flexibility through the miracle of pregnancy.

Men do not as often demonstrate such great flexibility. Indeed, they may not **have** such flexibility. As we noted previously in the discussion of hereditary predisposition towards Wilson's Syndrome, some people are more flexible or adaptive than others and can more easily enter into the conservation mode in response to prevailing conditions. I feel that women naturally have a greater degree of flexibility and adaptiveness than men. It stands to reason that the more readily one can get "out of bounds," the more readily one can stay "out of bounds." So I feel that women are more likely to get out of bounds and stay out of bounds than men because they can (that is, they are more flexible). However, under periods of severe stress, since Wilson's Syndrome is nothing more than an aberration of an inherent stress/starvation coping mechanism and since this coping mechanism is present in every human's body, anyone can, under severe enough circumstances, develop Wilson's Syndrome. It can affect men and women of all ages and from all walks of life. It can happen to anyone. Careful histories should be taken in all patients. Even though the condition and symptoms tend to worsen in a step-wise fashion after subsequent stresses, the condition can sometimes worsen in one step and stay persistently low at that level, neither getting better nor getting worse even for years. In such cases the symptoms can be shown to be related when they resolve together in a group with proper T3 therapy.

Why Is WS So Prevalent These Days?

How can Wilson's Syndrome be so common? This is not a new condition, although it does seem to be on the rise. It may be argued that we live in one of the most stressful periods of time in history. With the advent of the telephone and the airplane and the computer, the world is becoming a smaller and smaller place. There is a great deal of political unrest, and many struggling national economies. There is more and more pervasive drug abuse, pornography, child abuse, dysfunctional families, divorce, crime, moral decay, and other significant problems. Though the world may be a wonderful place in which to live, not many would argue against these being challenging times.

Medical advances may be contributing. When in medical school studying genetics and also studying the vast explosion of medical knowledge and expertise that has taken place within the last 80 years, I marveled how so many people's lives have been <u>changed</u> and <u>saved</u> by the progress of medical science. With the advent of antibiotics many people that would have died from pneumonia, appendicitis, and even severe ear infections were saved by the elimination of the infection through antibiotic treatment. Babies that were born prematurely were able to be saved through the use of respirator machines, IV fluids, the development of special nutritional formulas, etc. Younger and younger premature babies were able to survive because of these advances in neonatology technology. Great advances have been made in the surgical field. New approaches and techniques have been developed, especially for critically ill patients and trauma victims such as those people injured in severe car accidents. These advances have also kept many more people alive who would have otherwise died. In addition, great advances have been made in pediatric medicine enabling doctors to save the lives of more and more critically ill children. Advances have also been made in the field of oncology, with treatment being able to extend life and even to cure the cancer in more and more people.

I wondered something while I was learning about these advances in medical technology. We are all different. And our physical differences sometimes manifest themselves in how we develop and respond to illness and injuries. Some of us are more likely to develop cancer, asthma, or to be overwhelmed by infection; while some of us are more likely to survive a premature birth, heart attack, or severe car accident. But if medical technology became able to alter how some people develop and respond to certain illnesses and injuries, would their physical differences then manifest themselves in how they develop and respond to **other** diseases and injuries? If the percentage of people dying from a certain cause decreases because of some advancement, then the percentage that die from another must increase, since we all have to die of **something**.

People who slip into conservation mode more easily than others, are more likely to be able to survive famine. Unfortunately, people who are more likely to slip into conservation mode are also more likely to stay in that mode inappropriately. This makes them more susceptible to infections, poor wound healing, poor recovery from injuries, and probably poor immune system function. I believe that over the centuries famines have left the population with a greater percentage of people who can slip more easily into conservative mode. However, this has been counterbalanced by the whittling down of this percentage due to decreased recovery from severe infections, illnesses and injuries. On the other hand, advancements in medical technology over the past couple of generations, have greatly increased this percentage's chances for surviving such health problems. This has made it possible for a greater percentage of people, who tend to slip inappropriately into conservative mode, to survive. More and more of them are living long enough to experience the persistent and debilitating symptoms of MED caused by abnormal body temperature patterns caused by Wilson's Syndrome. They are also living long enough to pass their

118

predisposition for WS to their children. With more of such people being born, more surviving, and with increasing stress in the world, more and more people will suffer from Wilson's Syndrome.

A Few Sample Stories

Next, we will explore some typical causes of Wilson's Syndrome. The symptoms in this book all have some things in common. They each have been seen to come on together with some of the other symptoms in a group, and to resolve together with some of the other symptoms with normalization of body temperature patterns.

Patients can usually relate the onset of their symptoms to an identifiable stress (usually within weeks, days or even hours after the precipitating event). With less insidious onsets, the symptoms surface gradually within two months of a particular stress. At other times a precipitating event cannot be identified at all. The stress correlation is much more obvious when the symptoms come on within days, if not hours after the stress. Through these obvious cases, it has been easy to identify typical **causes** of Wilson's Syndrome. Interestingly, emotional stresses seem to be as prevalent as, if not more prevalent than, physical stresses as causes of Wilson's Syndrome.

Considering the great flexibility and adaptivity of the female hormonal and physical systems, it is easy to understand why pregnancy and childbirth are the number one causes of Wilson's Syndrome. This same pattern has been seen during other periods of great hormonal system fluctuations, such as menarche (the onset of a young woman's first menstrual cycle), puberty, administration of birth control pills, hysterectomy, and administration of female hormone replacement therapy for menopause. It is not difficult to imagine how Wilson's Syndrome could be precipitated at these times of hormonal changes since changes in the "tensions" can affect the position of the "ring" (overall balance of body functions). When the overall balance of body functions is changing it's easier for it to be pulled off center. The further out of balance it gets, the more likely the overall balance is to stay out of balance. No wonder childbirth and pregnancy would be the number one causes of Wilson's Syndrome. It's difficult to imagine a time when there is a greater change in the overall balance of bodily functions. Bringing a child into the world is more than enough to explain how a woman might change in certain respects, never quite being the same. Fortunately, the condition can often be very much improved with proper T3 therapy.

Certainly stressful life-styles can predispose people to developing Wilson's Syndrome. Being raised in a dysfunctional family can frequently contribute to its development. Too often, patients can trace the onset of their Wilson's Syndrome to the time that they were abused physically, emotionally, or sexually as a child in their home. I recall the sad story of one patient in her late thirties or early forties. She could easily trace the onset and persistence of her symptoms to a time when she was in second grade. At that time, she was locked in a safe for a time as a punishment by a strict disciplinarian at school. Needless to say, she was quite frightened and uncomfortable. Not surprisingly, she has been panicky and claustrophobic in elevators and other types of places since then. Such a story certainly sounds psychological in nature, until the persistent symptoms begin to resolve quickly as a group with the administration of proper T3 therapy.

Difficult living conditions brought about by the alcoholism or drug dependence of a person's parents can also lead to Wilson's Syndrome. Sadly, patients will sometimes recount the onset of their symptoms to be the time they were raped in their teens, twenties, or thirties. Certain occupations can contribute to patients developing Wilson's Syndrome, especially

- Jobs that involve a great deal of stress, such as certain high pressure sales positions where the person is constantly under the threat of losing his job because of not being able to meet quotas, etc.
- Jobs that carry a lot of responsibility, especially in terms of being responsible for others, and where one is in a position where he or she is responsible for getting others to produce.

- Difficult job situations where there is a great deal of discontent, hostility, arguing, and great emotional pressure.
- Jobs that involve extremely long work hours and poor sleep habits, or that deprive a person of proper exercise and nutrition by encouraging the patient not to eat all day, but to eat one big meal at nighttime right before going to sleep.
- Certain work-related injuries with heavy equipment, such as back injuries.
- Emotionally punishing jobs seem to cause problems more often than physically punishing jobs, especially when there is no opportunity to relieve or counteract that stress with proper exercise and nutrition.
- Of course, large pay cuts or losing one's income because of being laid off, fired, or losing a business, especially when there are unexpected expenses.

Again, we see that the condition is most commonly caused when one's resources are perceived by the body to be inadequate for the challenges being presented. This may occur when the resources are significantly decreased (losing a job), or when the challenges are significantly increased (aged parent becoming ill and needing to be nursed back to health).

It is a continuous source of fascination for me to see the varied and unusual circumstances that can precipitate Wilson's Syndrome. Again, it is easy to identify the precipitating events when the symptoms are related to one another in onset and are very easily related to a significant change in a person's life, when no other obvious explanation can be identified, and especially when the symptoms resolve together at the same time when the body temperature patterns are normalized with proper thyroid hormone treatment.

As it turns out, tonsillectomy is also a common cause of Wilson's Syndrome. I'm sure all of us have wondered from time to time about the consequences of removing different parts of the body that have been with us since birth (tonsils, appendix, gall bladder, etc.). I have heard many patients say:

"I was fine until I was eight years old and had my tonsils out, and I have never been quite the same since."

"I was fine until I was eleven years old and had my tonsils out and I have never been quite the same since."

"I was fine until I was nineteen years old and I had my tonsils out and I have never been quite the same since."

This is a reproducible presentation with the patients developing classic signs and symptoms that respond well to proper T3 therapy.

Because of the many classic and obvious cases I have seen, I have also been able to see the same pattern of onset in more subtle presentations and cases. One patient I treated in her early fifties, responded well to proper T3 therapy and enjoyed a persistent resolution of her Wilson's Syndrome symptoms for ten months, even after thyroid hormone treatment had been weaned. She was fine until one day she was walking down the sidewalk and accidentally bumped her head on a tree limb. She was not severely injured and the incident startled her more than anything else, yet she noticed, especially the next day, the relapsing of some of her symptoms. I am convinced that this small incident caused her symptoms to relapse since she could think of no other unusual circumstances, and since she recognized the symptoms coming on together, and responding together in the same way they did with the first occurrence.

Over the years, having treated thousands of patients with these types of problems, I have certainly been able to see amazingly predictable and reproducible patterns. And I have seen a number of interesting cases. One unusual case is that of a young woman in her early thirties who had been recently married. She identified the onset of her symptoms to be the weekend she and her husband flew up north to stay with her in-laws for the first time. She remembers his family as being quite odd, if not certifiably crazy. Since that fateful trip a year and a half prior to treatment, the patient had not been quite the same.

More long-term living conditions can also contribute, in huge measure, to a patient developing Wilson's Syndrome. For example, when there are problems in the home that lead to contention, alienation, and decreased cooperation, these problems can lead to arguments, divorce, strained parent/child relations, and Wilson's Syndrome.

Doing The Best We Can With What We Have

As mentioned previously, the symptoms of Wilson's Syndrome (more than 60 of them) are actually symptoms of Multiple Enzyme Dysfunction (MED). The symptoms of MED are most often caused by abnormal body temperature patterns, which can arise from a number of causes. However, we are most concerned with the abnormal body temperature patterns that result from an impairment in the conversion of T4 to T3.

This impairment is perpetuated, in part, by the inhibition of T4 to T3 conversion due to **RT3**. The treatment of Wilson's Syndrome has been designed to **"reset"** the pattern of peripheral conversion by altering, for a time, levels of RT3. This is done in an effort to re-establish normal T4 to T3 conversion patterns, normal body temperature patterns, and to resolve the symptoms of MED.

This approach has proven to be very successful. In many cases, patients are able to be weaned off the medication with their body temperature pattern remaining more normal even after thyroid hormone supplementation has been weaned.

If a patient responds favorably to treatment for a suspected problem, then it is more likely that the patient did in fact, have that problem and that the treatment prescribed was correct. Since so many people respond so well to treatment designed to correct persistently impaired peripheral conversion of T4 to T3, then it is more likely that is their problem, and furthermore, that the treatment is correct. The characteristics that help predict who will respond favorably to the treatment, then, are likely to be characteristic of a medical problem the treatment corrects.

The presence or absence of one or more of the characteristics and patterns of Wilson's Syndrome discussed in this chapter does not necessarily mean that a patient is or is not suffering from an impairment in the conversion of T4 to T3 or Wilson's Syndrome. But these characteristics or patterns should instead be considered to be predictive, in that the **more** characteristics of Wilson's Syndrome a particular person has, the more likely it is that he is suffering from Wilson's Syndrome and the more likely it is that he will respond favorably to treatment. And, as was mentioned earlier, everything in medicine is a therapeutic trial, and nothing in medicine is absolute.

Some people may have characteristic symptoms that are not necessarily caused by low body temperature patterns. Not everyone that has low body temperature patterns has Wilson's Syndrome or symptoms consistent with it. However, if a person does have the symptoms of Wilson's Syndrome and if he has a persistently low body temperature, then the low body temperature pattern is more than enough to explain the patient's symptoms. So, it is important that we consider carefully what is and is not being said so that the information in this book is not used unwisely. As has been mentioned previously, faulty assumptions and faulty conclusions have caused Wilson's Syndrome and probably many other important problems to be overlooked for a long time.

The important point is that this information is incredibly useful and has a tremendous amount of predictive value in alleviating or correcting a great amount of debilitation and suffering in a large percentage of people who are currently unable to find relief.

In each case, the doctor and patient must decide whether or not the patient's complaints and presentations are or are not inappropriate (decide if the patient is sick). Patients suffering from the symptoms of Multiple Enzyme Dysfunction and their own doctors often agree that their complaints are inappropriate and undesirable to the extent that their doctors often prescribe all manner of symptomatic treatments in an attempt to address those complaints. The characteristics of WS discussed in this chapter are useful only to the extent that they help in evaluating such complaints. Of course, the more characteristics, the greater the likelihood that the patient will respond well to treatment. The less characteristics, the less chance a patient has of responding to treatment. Always the various alternatives, the pros and cons, probabilities, and likelihoods must be weighed on a case-by-case basis.

Because not all things can be determined exactly does not mean that efforts cannot be made to predict likelihoods based on certain observations. This process is similar to what you might do if someone gave you a birthday present and wanted you to guess what it was. It might be easier to guess if the wrapped present was in front of you, judging by the size you might be able to narrow down the possibilities. Picking up the present to see how heavy it is, and squeezing the wrapping with your hands and fingers may also help you determine its shape. Shaking the present gently, listening for the sound that it makes, or smelling it, may help further characterize the gift. All of these observations are helpful, but can't always be relied upon completely, as all of us know who have ever received a small gift packed in a large box with a lot of filler paper.

It's a little like trying to determine the contents of a large black box that we cannot see into. We can shake it, prod it, poke it, smell it, listen to it, cool it, warm it, etc., in an attempt to determine the contents. If one hears a meow, then most of us would have a pretty good guess as to the contents of the box, because there are few things in the world that make such a sound. So based on the suspicion that the animal inside is a cat, then certain things can be done to see if there is a predictable and reproducible response. For example, if the animal inside eats cat food like a cat, knocks a ball of yarn around the box like a cat, leaves droppings like a cat, shreds a scratching post like a cat and sheds hair like a cat, then it is more likely that the animal inside the box is a cat. This information would prove useful if it were important to preserve the contents of the box. One might choose to supply the box with services that would be directed to the proper care and feeding of a cat. So, even though we can't see **exactly** what's inside the black box, a lot of good can be done by doing the best we can with the information that's available. In this process one might be able to preserve the contents of a lot of boxes that might otherwise be lost.

Just as it may be characteristic for a cat to eat certain things, to behave in a certain way, to make certain noises, to make certain droppings, and to have certain smells, different medical problems and conditions also have characteristics that can aid us in distinguishing one from another and therefore in helping us to direct therapy. The more predictably a condition or complaint behaves, the greater the predictive value its behavior has. As it turns out, Wilson's Syndrome is extremely predictable and reproducible in its behavior and responses.

It must be remembered, however, that not all cats will eat certain kinds of cat food, and not everything that will eat cat food is a cat. Not all cats scratch scratching posts, and not everything that scratches a scratching post is a cat. Whereas all cats may have droppings, some animals may have droppings similar to cats. There are, however, few animals that make meow sounds. The point is, that some observations have more predictive values than others. Some observations have less predictive value, but nevertheless, they are important and may add to the overall picture, so that all the observations can be taken together to help us do the best we can with what we have.

7. EMOTIONAL AND SOCIAL IMPLICATIONS

Certain emotional tendencies are typical in characterize Wilson's Syndrome. These tendencies, along with the fact that Wilson's Syndrome may not be immediately obvious to the observer, can frequently lead to serious problems.

Insufficient Resources

All of us can feel overwhelmed at times. However, in Wilson's Syndrome the associated emotional and physical manifestations persist inappropriately, even after the adverse conditions have resolved. There is a good physiological reason why these people often suffer from inappropriate feelings of frustration, disappointment, discouragement, inadequacy, weakness, anger, irritability, hostility, defensiveness, moodiness, depression, anxiety, panicky feelings, selfishness, guilt, low self esteem, and feeling overwhelmed or out of control. They can even have more severe emotional problems, including difficulty in controlling one's actions (which can erupt into inappropriate violent behavior and abuse).

Sufferers may tend to be on the selfish side because they have a pervasive feeling of not having enough resources for themselves, much less enough to make the lives of other people any better. They can be extremely short-suffering and feel that they are at the end of their rope. They can have severe mood swings, especially prior to the menstrual cycle. They can suffer from lack of motivation or ambition and find it difficult to accomplish even simple tasks, such as washing dishes, driving to the store, giving the kids a bath, or changing a diaper. They sometimes just can't gather themselves up in order to scrape off a few plates after dinner, wash them, and put them on the shelf. They just can't picture being able to go to the grocery store to pick up a few groceries or even take out the garbage. They sometimes tend to be cranky, abusive, stingy, critical, judgmental, and have a whole host of other exceedingly undesirable tendencies.

The patients know that their feelings and behavior are quite inappropriate. They often feel very frustrated, because in spite of their best efforts, there doesn't seem to be much they can do to control these feelings, especially when the symptoms worsen during times of stress or just prior to the menstrual cycle. For instance, if someone drops a spoonful of oatmeal on the floor, the WS sufferer might very well go through the ceiling.

It's often hard for them to find enjoyment in activities. They have a tendency to not feel like doing anything. They don't feel like going to the beach, to the movies, or to the park. "There's no sense in going to the beach because it's not going to be any fun anyway." They frequently can no longer find enjoyment in the things that they used to find quite interesting and enjoyable. For them molehills frequently seem like mountains.

Many patients I treat are concerned about their relationships with their children. Especially during difficult times, feeling overwhelmed and frustrated by the actions of their children, the patients can often feel that they are at the end of their ropes. It can be very difficult, because although they have great love and concern for their children and want them to have the best, they so easily and quickly become impatient that they are concerned about what they might do in a moment of anger. They frequently walk in fear of those times, feeling guilt, and loss of control. The impact of this condition on society is enormous and can lead to dysfunctional family units, and less than ideal work-place performance.

Of course, we all have had these types of feelings at one time or another. But, there are times when people know intuitively that the emotions with which they struggle are inappropriate. It is especially obvious when the feelings disappear rapidly with normalization of body temperature patterns from proper thyroid hormone therapy.

One way normal people can imagine what it feels like to have a severe case of Wilson's Syndrome is by imagining that they

128

have lost their job, their home, their wife and family, have become paralyzed and unable to walk, and have had to move to another state where there are no family or friends. What's so difficult is that Wilson's Syndrome sufferers may be troubled with such severe emotions persistently, even when the adverse conditions are long gone.

With proper T3 therapy patients sometimes use phrases like, "It feels as if someone has turned on a switch," "It's like looking through a new pair of glasses for the first time and seeing the world differently," "It feels like a great burden has been lifted off my shoulders." It is unlikely that the inappropriate feelings were completely psychological when the patients' emotional manifestations resolve quickly, even within two days or two weeks of proper thyroid hormone therapy, especially when they have the same house, the same job, the same husband, the same children, the same family, the same parents, the same brothers and sisters, etc.

Many times one of the first things that happens to a patient with proper thyroid therapy, is that people around them (their husbands, their children, and their coworkers) notice that they seem nicer. They can be much more calm, resourceful, cooperative, patient, easily pleased, and less easily provoked. It is amazing how many of the feelings that we take for granted as being completely mental or psychological, can actually have a tremendous physical component. The real eye-opener comes when patients who have been suffering from debilitating, emotional problems, such as depression, anguish, sorrow, irritability, and confusion for years, have their symptoms resolve with proper thyroid therapy, even though their lifestyles and other factors haven't changed at all. It makes one realize that the roller coaster emotional problems with which many of these patients must cope, can indeed have a physical basis and can be closely related to their body temperature patterns.

While this doesn't explain all emotional problems, it certainly can explain some of them. This is especially true when a person's feelings of inadequacy or other emotional problems can be traced, upon careful history taking, to a major life stress, and when these feelings resolve quickly with proper T3 therapy and there are no other changes in life style. Again, extremely obvious cases make more subtle cases easier to recognize.

When The Cause Is Not Immediately Obvious

We know that the emotions and the mental processes come from the brain, which is an organ made up of chemical (physical) processes. It can be argued that all that is emotional and mental is a result of that which is physical. Of course, neither I nor the patients who suffer from this condition are wanting Wilson's Syndrome sufferers to be given excuses, or to be patronized, legitimizing their falling short of their potential. To the contrary, they want to get better so that they can more fully realize their potential. These people don't want to be sick so they can be excused from life. They want to be helped so that they can return to normal, productive lives. Of course, it is best for the tough to get going when the going gets tough, especially if they can. For example, not many people would encourage a marathon runner on the streets of a large city to get up and finish the race if they saw him struck by a car causing both his legs to be broken. But, if he is taken to the hospital and treated for his fractures and given proper support and nutrition for his legs to heal properly, some might encourage him to begin training again for the sport he loves so much. He might some day win the Boston Marathon.

Again, the difficulty with Wilson's Syndrome is that the impairment is not so obvious to outside observers. Once patients themselves and the people around them see the dramatic difference that can take place when a patient suffering from a classic case of Wilson's Syndrome is properly treated, then it becomes more obvious to them that criticizing and condemning people with the inappropriate emotional manifestations of Wilson's Syndrome is a little like criticizing a blind man for not being able to see. Perhaps only after you have been through the experience yourself can you easily recognize others around you suffering in the same way.

It must be remembered that the emotional manifestations of Wilson's Syndrome; short suffering, impatience, irritability, selfishness, and others, are not held by Wilson's Syndrome sufferers out of strength, but out of weakness and out of a lack of resources. People usually don't try to be miserable for the fun of it.

Some people might think that if a person did have such a severe impairment, then it should be more physically obvious like the blindness of the blind man or the fractured legs of the marathoner. They might think, "You **can't** be feeling that badly because you **look fine**." It can be especially difficult for a WS sufferer when her doctor sees that her blood tests also look normal. Such patients sometimes get the feeling that their doctors think the tests are telling "the truth" and that they, the patients, are lying.

Relationships Suffer

When too much emphasis is placed on medical knowledge and tests that are incorrectly considered to be conclusive, relationships suffer.

Wilson's Syndrome is most easily recognized when it disappears quickly and easily with proper thyroid hormone treatment. As I mentioned, for patients and their families who have been through the experience, it is easy to recognize the condition in other people. Many of them describe it as if blinders have been removed from their eyes and they are able to see it almost all around them. WS is not difficult to recognize, and when people become aware of the condition, it will be, together with the body temperature, one of the first things to come to mind, rather than the last. While not everyone has Wilson's Syndrome, I would say that almost everyone knows someone whose life is being greatly affected. People have been blinded to the existence of this condition because of over-reliance on indirect and therefore inconclusive measurements (thyroid hormone blood tests with large numbers of false negative results for DTSF). This blindness often leads harsh and unfounded criticism of those suffering WS.

Of course, one of the biggest ramifications to which this problem can contribute is divorce. It is very common for patients with Wilson's Syndrome to have their marriages end in divorce because it is hard for WS sufferers to live with other people. And it is hard for other people to live with them because of their physiological predisposition to be short suffering, irritable, and difficult to please. One of the saddest and most ironic aspects of this problem is that they often inadvertently alienate the people they love the most and, who are the only people that are really in a good position to be of support to them.

As we have discussed, Wilson's Syndrome is characterized by a person being stuck in the conservation mode, which is a physiological state in which the body feels that it does not have sufficient resources to meet its challenges. Of course, in such a situation it would helpful to be able to obtain more resources and/or reduce the challenges for a time. However, when the resources are down it is easy to be irritable, frustrated, and selfish. This may further decrease available resources by alienating those in a position to help, for example; parents, spouses, children, friends, neighbors, coworkers, etc. If this process continues too long, it may lead to an even larger drop in available resources such as being fired, getting a divorce, or alienating parents and children, which only adds to the predicament. It would then be even more difficult for them to leave the conservation mode and enter back into the productivity mode.

Wilson's Syndrome sufferers may have terrific difficulty with their sex drives which can further impair marital relations. The spouse may become insecure about his or her own desirability when the patient's sex drive drops off dramatically, especially during difficult marital times. This problem can be hard to address, especially when the patients themselves can't explain it adequately, maybe not even to themselves. They begin to wonder what could be wrong with their sex drive and why they don't feel the way they used to towards their spouses. This can result in further difficulties in a family, which can lead to further complaints of Wilson's Syndrome, thereby stating a vicious cycle that frequently ends in divorce. It seems that the

132

incidence of divorce in Wilson's Syndrome sufferers is much higher than that of the normal population, especially in those patients in which the condition has been long-standing. It is sad because when patients' resources are down and they are feeling inexplicably overwhelmed, confused, and tired, they and their families may strike out in frustration, saying things to each other that are difficult to take back.

Patients often relate to me that they are putting up fronts at work and at home in an attempt to keep their problem from being easily noticed by others. This is true especially of executives in high pressure positions who have to work up schemes and methods to disguise their impairment and shortcomings at work. They live in fear that their employer, subordinates, or clients might discover their impairment and their inability to remember, concentrate, or function properly at work.

The fatigue of Wilson's Syndrome, unlike the fatigue resulting from other causes, can frequently be overcome for short periods of time. It's not as if the patients have absolutely no resources. It's just that their resources are easily depleted. They can put on fronts at work, being able to function behind the façade of being halfway normal. Then if they don't fall asleep on the road, they might collapse in a heap once they are home and be worthless for the rest of the night. They can muster their resources for a time, but when they are gone, they are gone. In the worst cases, their disability is so severe that it can't be overcome and they simply can't function at normal levels, making their disability obvious to all.

Interestingly, Wilson's Syndrome sufferers are sometimes over-achievers. Because they push themselves so hard to overcome the feeling of fatigue, they can develop strong determination and frequently end up accomplishing a lot, even though it is difficult. If the condition is long-standing, the sufferer may have an unsteady job history being unable to function well in the work place.

I remember one person who was having an extremely difficult time passing her real estate license exam. Although she had previously been an excellent student and adept at taking tests, since she had developed Wilson's Syndrome, she found it very difficult to study. She found herself reading the same page over and over and unable to remember what she had read. She had the opportunity to take the test only three times and had failed the exam on her first two attempts. With treatment, her body temperature was normalized with a gratifying resolution of her symptoms and she was once again able to retain what she read. She was happy to report that she had passed the third and final try without difficulty. It is staggering to wonder how many other people's test scores and lives are being affected by their body temperature patterns.

Typical Treatment Received By Medical Field

Let us now explore briefly how Wilson's Syndrome sufferers have been typically handled by medical doctors. They will usually come to the doctor complaining of their worst symptom or possibly a combination of the worst two symptoms (again, either being unaware that more symptoms are related or out of fear of being considered a hypochondriac). If they are not severe, but only bad enough to bring the patient to the office because he or she is not feeling well, they may be told that there is no need for alarm, that it may simply be a matter of getting older, and that they may need to learn to live with the symptoms. If the patient does recount enough of the symptoms or if they are severe enough, the doctor might order routine multichemistry blood tests. Such tests generally check for 24 to 26 blood chemistry values including sodium, potassium, glucose, cholesterol, triglycerides, liver enzymes, kidney function tests, and others. With this screening, he may also order a complete blood count or CBC. The blood chemistry tests and CBC tests look primarily for evidence of any obvious abnormalities that could explain the patient's complaints, such as kidney impairment, liver derangement, anemia, leukemia, electrolyte abnormalities, diabetes, infection, and other possible explanations for the patient's complaints. Thyroid blood tests are frequently not tested on a screening (routine) basis. When they are tested, they are frequently normal, even in patients who are suffering from DTSF.

If the person's description of their own problem does not lead the doctor to think of any specific problem and if the blood tests show no significant abnormality, the physician will often conclude that there is nothing significantly wrong with the patient and that they should get more exercise, more sleep, start eating better, and stop certain bad habits, such as excessive alcohol consumption, or smoking. If the patient's complaints are specific enough and reminiscent enough of thyroid hormone deficiency, the physician may think to order thyroid blood tests. However, if these blood tests come back within normal limits, the physician will frequently incorrectly conclude that this necessarily means that the thyroid system is functioning adequately, and the patient might be given the same instructions as above.

If the symptoms are so severe and debilitating that the patient and doctor would consider the above advice to be obviously insufficient, if not ludicrous, and, if it appears to both the patient and the physician that there is definitely something seriously wrong; then the patient may be sent to a hospital, and/or multiple specialists in an attempt to isolate the problem. The patient may be referred from their family practitioner to an internal medicine specialist who may perform extensive blood tests looking for some other possible explanations for the complaints. Patients are often referred to neurologists, gastroenterologists, gynecologists, ENT (ear, nose and throat), infectious disease, endocrinologists, and psychiatrists. In some cases patients are given virtually every test in the book (brain scan, EEG, liver spleen scan, all manner of blood tests, thyroid scan, gall bladder scan, chest x-ray, upper GI, lower GI, etc.). Their bills can run in the tens of thousands of dollars in less than a month. At the end of all the tests and evaluations, there is often still no clear diagnosis. There is no treatment recommended and the patients are discharged from the hospital with all the currently known health problems being pretty well ruled out as causes of the symptoms. These evaluations aren't always confined to a one month period of time. It may take place over a period of many years in a lifelong search to feel well.

With careful history taking, physical exams and laboratory tests (to rule out other obvious causes), such patients can often be recognized as having classic presentations for Wilson's Syndrome. Although it is not extremely expensive, there is a test that is very useful in helping to predict the likelihood of such a patient responding favorably and quickly to proper thyroid hormone therapy—<u>body temperature measurements</u>. Although the evaluation does not take weeks or tens of thousands of dollars, the findings can be more than enough to explain a long list of annoying and even debilitating complaints.

Chapter Eight

8. HOW THE SYMPTOMS ARE TYPICALLY TREATED, INSTEAD OF THE PROBLEM

It is commonly assumed that generalized complaints are not very serious, or that if a patient complains of a multitude of complaints, then no single complaint must be bothering him very much. Neither of these assumptions is necessarily correct. As mentioned in previous chapters, medical problems that affect lower levels of organization of the body tend to be more difficult to measure with our current technology and tend to cause more generalized complaints. So, some might assume that because a condition is difficult to quantitate or measure exactly with available technology, the resulting generalized complaints can't be very severe. But, it must not be assumed that the symptoms of Wilson's Syndrome are mild and insignificant. They are severe, inappropriate, and undesirable enough for WS sufferers to be given all manner of symptomatic therapies in an attempt to address them.

Sometimes patients will come to my office on five or six different symptomatic medicines for five or six different symptoms that are related to Wilson's Syndrome. These medicines can often be discontinued when the body temperature patterns have been normalized without return of the symptoms even after proper T3 therapy has been weaned. Of course, not every symptom of which a person complains is necessarily due to thyroid hormone deficiency. But we have discussed in previous chapters, why DTSF especially due to Wilson's Syndrome, should be one of the first possibilities considered. It is very common, very easy to recognize, very easy to treat, and getting it treated can make all the difference in a person's life. Considering the pervasive influence of thyroid hormones on the body, and considering thyroid hormone function can affect all aspects of life including recovery from illness, emotional make up, productivity, and overall good health, it stands to reason that special attention should be paid to the possibility of DTSF—especially since it can affect the way a patient responds to treatments for other medical problems that may also be present. Finally, Wilson's Syndrome and other causes of DTSF should always be considered in patients suffering from symptoms of MED since it is better to treat the underlying problem rather than just the symptoms.

I will now review symptomatic treatments that are commonly implemented by doctors to treat the symptoms of Wilson's Syndrome. There are a few things that the following treatments have in common. I have seen each of them used in the treatment of symptoms of Multiple Enzyme Dysfunction in Wilson's Syndrome sufferers prior to their being treated with proper liothyronine therapy. When the symptom a certain treatment is managing returns after the treatment is discontinued, it is more likely that the treatment is symptomatic. It has also been seen in some cases, that the patients' symptoms responded at least as well if not better to proper thyroid hormone therapy as compared with the symptomatic treatment; with the symptoms remaining persistently improved after the symptomatic therapy had been discontinued and even after the thyroid hormone therapy had been weaned. So proper liothyronine treatment can be a symptomatic treatment (managing the symptoms during treatment), and even a therapeutic one (effecting a persistent "cure").

We will now discuss symptomatic treatments commonly given for the symptoms of Wilson's Syndrome which often respond better to proper thyroid hormone treatment. The following are common symptomatic treatments:

Allergy shots, antihistamines, and decongestants

Given for the treatment of allergies, hay fever, sinus congestion, and other associated complaints. Again, when one finds out through careful history that the patient's hay fever or allergies came on together in a group after a major stress several years ago, and its onset correlated with that of several other symptoms of Wilson's Syndrome, it is possible that the complaints are related to DTSF and low body temperature patterns. This is especially true when the allergy and hay fever symptoms resolve together with the other symptoms of Wilson's Syndrome quickly and predictably after normalization of body temperature patterns with proper T3 therapy.

Antacids, Histamine Blockers

Given for acid indigestion and ulcer formation that develop secondary to decreased bowel motility which caused decreased stomach emptying and greater build up of acids in the stomach. Many times patients can be easily weaned off ulcer medication, and enjoy resolution of their heartburn and indigestion problem once their body temperature and bowel motility have been returned to normal with proper thyroid hormone treatment.

Anti-dizziness Medicines

Given for the lightheadedness, clumsiness, and sensation of being "off balance" that frequently resolve better with proper thyroid hormone treatment.

Anti-inflammatory Medicines

Patients frequently take prescription and over-the-counter anti-inflammatory medicines for menstrual cramps and arthritis that can be associated with Wilson's Syndrome. The menstrual cramps are often easily resolved with proper thyroid hormone treatment.

Antibiotics

Given for the respiratory, urinary, skin, and yeast infections that are commonly associated with Wilson's Syndrome. Recurring and difficult to treat infections such as acne, yeast infections, skin, and wound infections can frequently be eliminated with proper thyroid hormone treatment and normalization of body temperature patterns.

Antidepressants

Given sometimes for the depression that is related to Wilson's Syndrome. They are also sometimes given with the intention of treating the muscular aches or fibromyalgia that is sometimes associated with WS. The antidepressants are also sometimes prescribed in an attempt to address the associated anxiety and panic attacks.

Appetite Suppressants, Liquid Diets, Gastric Bypass

Inappropriate weight gain has long been recognized as a characteristic of hypothyroidism (one cause of DTSF). This symptom of DTSF can present in the same fashion as other DTSF symptoms caused by Wilson's Syndrome. It can appear or worsen after a major stress, be related to one or many of the other symptoms of Wilson's Syndrome; and be well correlated with a consistently low body temperature pattern. A patient's weight can depend on their diet, exercise, female hormones, adrenal hormones, and thyroid hormones as well as body shape and stress levels. Of course, not all of these factors can be controlled with thyroid hormone medication. However, it has long since been made clear that decreased thyroid system function can greatly affect a patient's ability to maintain normal weight. If a person's DTSF is overlooked when approaching their weight problem, the approaches taken may not fully address the underlying problems. Such approaches, therefore, often result in the gaining back of the patient's weight after the approaches have been discontinued. Since Wilson's Syndrome is essentially a starvation coping mechanism gone amuck, severe dieting can actually make the problem worse causing the patient to gain all the weight back and then some. If people are having a problem maintaining their weight, it would be worth taking a careful history to see if the patient's weight problems came on after a major stress together with other symptoms of Wilson's Syndrome and a low body temperature pattern (WS?).

Artificial Nails, Wigs/Repeat Perms

Even though these are cosmetic issues, they deserve to be mentioned because of the impact that they can have on a patient's life, financially and emotionally. Many, many of the female patients that I treat for Wilson's Syndrome have artificial nails because of the splitting, breaking, peeling, and lack of growth of their own nails. Patients will often wear wigs or toupees due to hair loss. Patients may sometimes require a repeat perm after their permanent falls out within two weeks, when their permanents usually stay in for months (before Wilson's Syndrome). Sometimes the perm may not take at all. This problem is often corrected with proper thyroid hormone treatment. Interestingly, the dry and brittle hair problem that is frequently associated with Wilson's Syndrome sometimes begins to clear up in a manner of days, even two to fourteen days. Since the hair certainly has not had time to grow out completely within a period of two weeks, it appears that the condition and quality of the hair must have something to do with the oils that are secreted from the scalp. Frequently, with proper thyroid hormone treatment the change in the hair can often be dramatic and noticeable leaving it more manageable even within a period of two weeks. Some of the changes come over time as the hair grows out but it is interesting that some of the hair complaints improve in such a short period of time. (See PIGMENTATION, SKIN AND HAIR, CHANGES in Chapter 9).

Asthma Medicines

Asthma is not commonly considered to be related to DTSF. However, that it can be related has been seen to the extent that the asthma associated with Wilson's Syndrome frequently follows the pattern of onset and resolution of the other symptoms of Wilson's Syndrome (coming on together in a group after a stress and resolving with that group with proper thyroid treatment). The asthma, when untreated, can be quite severe at times with some patients even being hospitalized and requiring maintenance asthma medicine therapy to control their symptoms. Again, careful history can provide clues that a person's asthma may be related to Wilson's Syndrome. Asthma is frequently a disease of childhood that people outgrow, but Wilson's Syndrome patients sometimes first develop asthma in adulthood. Whether the symptoms of asthma begin in childhood or adulthood, the patient should always be asked if they presented after a major stress and if they came on in association with any of the other symptoms of MED caused by low body temperature patterns, to see, if by chance, the asthma may be related to Wilson's Syndrome. Many times these patients respond much better to thyroid hormone treatment than they do to asthma medicines, especially in the sense that their asthma sometimes stays persistently improved even after treatment has been discontinued. I have seen many patients who, when I first saw them, had been taking asthma medicine for years (even 10 to 20 years). Upon careful history one sometimes finds that these patients' asthma began after they were having a period of severe marital problems, financial collapse, or other severe stress, with their asthma persisting even after the stress had passed. Many of these patients have been able to wean off their asthma medicine (beta-agonist pills and bronchodilator inhalers) even completely. Their asthma sometimes even remains persistently improved even after the thyroid hormone treatment has been gradually tapered off and discontinued.

Birth Control Pills

Frequently given to help regulate irregular periods or to treat heavy menstrual periods. In this setting, the birth control therapy frequently does help. The irregular periods and heavy menstrual cycles can sometimes be corrected to such an extent that they even remain corrected even after therapy has been discontinued. Sometimes, however, the irregular menstrual cycle and heavy periods resume once birth control pill therapy has been discontinued. Proper thyroid hormone treatment can often be used in Wilson's Syndrome patients to treat the irregular periods and heavy menstrual cycles with there being persistent improvement even after the therapy has been discontinued. So, in cases where irregular menstrual cycles and heavy periods do not remain persistently improved after birth control therapy has been discontinued, persistent improvement might be accomplished through the use of thyroid hormone therapy (in Wilson's Syndrome sufferers).

Carpal Tunnel Syndrome Surgery

Sometimes patients with Wilson's Syndrome have scars on their wrists where they have undergone surgery to release the ligament that overlies the carpal tunnel. The carpal tunnel is the bony tunnel at the base of the hand through which many of the hand's most important blood vessels, nerves, and tendons pass. The Carpal Tunnel Syndrome surgery is done to release the pressure that results from fluid retention in the tissues of the confined space that causes pinching of the nerves, and numbness and tingling of the hands. Carpal Tunnel Syndrome has long been associated with hypothyroidism. Again, however, DTSF is commonly overlooked because of over reliance on thyroid hormone blood tests. A patient presented to my office with a scar on her right wrist and numbness and tingling of her left hand. The scar on her right wrist was from the successful Carpal Tunnel Syndrome surgery that had relieved the numbness and tingling of her right hand which she had had previously. When I first saw her, she was having the identical problem with her left hand. She had already been scheduled for surgery that was to be done thirty days after our first meeting. Since her related symptoms, signs, and story were so characteristic of Wilson's Syndrome, it was recommended to her that she postpone her Carpal Tunnel Syndrome surgery until after a therapeutic trial on thyroid hormone treatment. Within the month the numbness and tingling of her hand resolved with normalization of her body temperature patterns and she canceled her Carpal Tunnel Syndrome surgery.

Cholesterol lowering Drugs

Because patients are sometimes unable to get their cholesterol levels down to a normal level in spite of diligent dieting and exercise.

143

Cortisone

Wilson's Syndrome patients are sometimes treated with cortisone for arthritis, asthma, and hair loss. Low body temperature patterns frequently can lead to fluid retention or swelling that can result in aches and pains of the muscles and joints; for which patients are sometimes treated with cortisone. It is interesting that cortisone is well known to inhibit 5'-deiodinase (the enzyme that converts T4 to T3) directly. Understandably then, cortisone therapy has been seen to precipitate or bring on cases of Wilson's Syndrome as well as worsen existing cases. Cortisone therapy can often be quite useful in the treatment of arthritis, asthma, and hair loss (frequently given by injection into the scalp). However, sometimes these problems can respond much better to thyroid hormone therapy than to cortisone therapy as can the other related symptoms of Wilson's Syndrome. Careful history can frequently correlate the onset of these symptoms with the clinical picture of Wilson's Syndrome (beginning after a major stress, associated with low body temperature patterns, and responding very well with normalization of the body temperature patterns).

Diuretics

Frequently given for fluid retention.

Evaluation For Ringing In The Ears

Wilson's Syndrome sufferers sometimes develop ringing in the ears that begins or worsens after a significant stress. Ringing in the ears typically gets worse with the onset of fluid retention symptoms and gets better with the resolution of fluid retention. These patients frequently have undergone a number of evaluations and sometimes treatments for their ringing in the ears without success. In several cases that I have seen, these patients can have very disturbing, almost maddening ringing in the ears that responds quite well to proper thyroid hormone treatment, even with complete resolution of this disturbing complaint.

144

Fertility Drugs

It is well known that one of the first things that should be checked in a patient being treated for infertility is their thyroid function. Unfortunately, too much attention is often focused on the thyroid **gland** rather than the thyroid **system**. The possibility of decreased thyroid system function is often dismissed if thyroid hormone blood tests are normal even in the face of classic DTSF symptoms. Sometimes fertility drugs can even worsen the situation in Wilson's Syndrome, causing initiation or worsening of the symptoms of Wilson's Syndrome; sometimes, with the symptoms remaining persistently worse even after the fertility medicine has been discontinued. Quite a few patients I have treated have conceived easily when they had previously had difficulty getting pregnant. Of course, Wilson's Syndrome patients often have a history of one or more miscarriages. Proper thyroid hormone treatment is sometimes necessary to enable these patients to conceive and maintain a pregnancy.

Hypoglycemic Diets

Since patients with Wilson's Syndrome frequently have hypoglycemia, they are frequently advised to eat six small meals per day (rather than three) that are a little higher in protein and a little lower in carbohydrates. Indeed, this is good advice since it does alleviate fairly well the symptoms of hypoglycemia and it does decrease the body's incentive to slow down further into conservation mode. The less time the stomach is empty, perhaps the less inclined the body is to perceive itself as starving. I remember one case in particular when a patient developed the symptoms of Wilson's Syndrome (including hypoglycemia) and a low body temperature pattern after a major stress. Upon discussing the pros and cons, risks, and benefits of the alternative treatments, it was decided that the patient should employ a hypoglycemic diet initially. Interestingly, she was able to bring herself out of the conservation mode and back into the productivity mode through the use of her hypoglycemic diet, which is possible in some cases. However, in the many cases that hypoglycemic dieting and proper exercise alone are unable to reverse the patient's tendency for hypoglycemia (due to Wilson's Syndrome), normalization of body temperature patterns through the use of proper thyroid hormone treatment frequently will.

Laxatives, Antispasmodics, Hemorrhoid Preparations

Decreased thyroid system function and resulting low body temperature patterns can cause decreased bowel motility which can manifest itself in several ways. It can lead to constipation, which constipation is frequently treated with various types of laxatives, including bulk-forming laxatives and suppositories. Patients can frequently go three to five days without a bowel movement and sometimes as long as three weeks. This constipation is often treated with high fiber diets, bulk-forming laxatives, and stool softeners. The constipation can also lead to straining-at-the-stool and consequent hemorrhoid formation which is often treated with creams and other preparations. The abnormal bowel motility and constipation sometimes leads to reflexive spasms, abdominal pain, cramping, gas, and even diarrhea. This situation is commonly referred to as Irritable Bowel Syndrome or Spastic Colon. Patients with Wilson's Syndrome often have constipation and/or diarrhea with gas, bloating, and cramping. I remember one patient who was suffering from acid indigestion, constipation, and hemorrhoids because of his decreased bowel motility. He was taking histamine blockers (ulcer medicine) for his acid indigestion. He was on a bulk-forming laxative to prevent constipation, and he was requiring a steroid hemorrhoid cream for his hemorrhoids. With proper thyroid hormone treatment, his bowel motility returned to normal. His tendencies for constipation and acid indigestion also resolved. And he was no longer bothered with hemorrhoids. He was able to wean off his ulcer medicine, laxative, and hemorrhoid medicine as well as the thyroid hormone treatment.

Antispasmodic medicines are frequently given for the spastic colon symptoms to help patients with gas, bloating, and sudden episodes of diarrhea. One such unfortunate patient can remember, to the day, when his case of severe spastic colon began (a day of severe job stress). From that day, he had symptoms of Irritable Bowel Syndrome so severe that he had been unable to enjoy some of his favorite pursuits (piloting an airplane and scuba diving). Doctors were unable to find the cause of his Irritable Bowel Syndrome and were treating him with antispasmodic/anti anxiety medications, which improved his situation but did not correct it. With proper T3 therapy, the patient's symptoms of spastic colon resolved quickly (several weeks), and dramatically, with normalization of his bowel motility. His situation was far better treated with proper thyroid therapy than with the less successful antispasmodic therapy.

Marriage and Family Counseling

Wilson's Syndrome patients often benefit from marriage and family counseling for the interpersonal relationship problems that can sometimes result due to the symptoms of MED caused by low body temperature patterns. However, this counseling can sometimes be disappointing in that it cannot always get to the underlying problem. I have seen cases where proper thyroid hormone treatment resulted in such an improved level of well-being and restored emotional resources that the patient and patient's family were able to enjoy much more appropriate interpersonal relationships—so much so that the need for marriage and family counseling was obviated. It is truly amazing to see how much Multiple Enzyme Dysfunction resulting from low body temperature patterns caused by Wilson's Syndrome can affect the attitudes of people, the way they feel about themselves and other people, and the way they interact and get along with other people. It can literally be as great as the difference between night and day.

Migraine and Headache Medicines

Patients are frequently treated with long lists of different headache medicines for the troublesome and debilitating headaches, and even severe migraines that can be associated with Wilson's Syndrome. These medicines include aspirin, acetaminophen, ibuprofen, and an assortment of migraine headache medicines (beta-blockers, calcium channel-blockers, ergotamines, and narcotic pain medicines). One dramatic case that I remember involved a woman who was diagnosed as having severe basilar artery migraine headaches that would cause severe headache pain, nausea and vomiting, and even neurological changes that would cause numbness and/or weakness of her face, mouth, and hands. Her migraines were so severe at times they would leave her almost unresponsive. During such episodes she would often be taken to the hospital and given oxygen therapy which would sometimes help. Since her headaches were so frequent and so severe, she actually was given a prescription for oxygen tanks that she could keep at home for this purpose. When the migraine headaches became very severe she would sometimes use oxygen at home to provide her brain with sufficient oxygen. She has undergone every available migraine headache treatment from pain medicines, to the blood pressure medicines that are frequently used for migraine headaches (beta-blockers and calcium channel-blockers). She has even been given an experimental treatment involving a blood thinner. She was given a treatment wherein a blood thinner was aerosolized into a fine mist which she would then inhale in an attempt to alleviate the migraines. This treatment would help but it would not correct her severe migraine headaches. To the patient's utter dismay her migraine headaches responded quickly and dramatically to proper thyroid hormone treatment and body temperature pattern normalization. She has not had a severe headache since the time she was started on thyroid hormone therapy, when she was to the point of having these headaches every several days if not every day. Not only has she not had a severe headache but she hasn't had any (other than those easily relieved with very mild analgesic medicine, such as aspirin). In this patient's case, and in many others, the thyroid hormone treatment wasn't just helpful in the treatment of migraines -- but essentially eliminated them.

Orthopedic and Chiropractic Therapies

Wilson's Syndrome can result in muscle and joint aches, poor healing of musculoskeletal problems, and pinched nerve syndromes. Many things can cause muscle and joint pain, and pinched nerves. Thyroid system impairment is not an exception. The musculoskeletal complaints associated with Wilson's Syndrome often seem to be related in some way to fluid retention. Since Wilson's Syndrome is so easily treated and can have such a profound affect on the musculoskeletal system, it is a condition well worth considering. It can explain why some patients recuperate much more slowly than others from surgeries or accidents because of significant fluid retention and inflammation which can impair proper healing. The presence of Wilson's Syndrome can also explain, therefore, why some patients do not respond as favorably to orthopedic physical therapy and chiropractic therapy as well as others.

Progesterone and Female Hormones

Frequently given for premenstrual syndrome symptoms and for symptoms that are suspected to be menopausal in origin. PMS symptoms will frequently respond, to an extent, to progesterone therapy since progesterone can affect body temperature patterns as can thyroid hormones. Frequently, however, the symptoms will not thoroughly respond to progesterone therapy and do not often remain persistently improved after that therapy is discontinued. One major difficulty with female hormone therapy is that there are a great number of variables to be considered. Usually, the greater the number of variables, the more complicated and the less predictable a certain treatment is. For example, it would be hard to direct therapy, since the female hormone system has a cyclical (monthly) influence on the body temperature pattern and it would be hard to predict when it should go up and when it should go down. And, there are both progesterones **and** estrogens which can be given in many different combinations and it is hard to predict what influence those combinations will have. There are also many different brands and forms of

149

estrogens and progesterones, some of which are not found in nature. When the symptoms return after the progesterone therapy has been discontinued (even if the symptoms were improved with progesterone therapy), it makes it more likely that the treatment was affecting the symptoms rather than the underlying problem. PMS resulting from Wilson's Syndrome will frequently remain improved even after treatment has been discontinued.

Sleeping Pills

Paradoxically some patients with Wilson's Syndrome who suffer from fatigue during the day also complain of insomnia or difficulty sleeping at night. These patients are often treated with sleeping pills that control the insomnia with varying degrees of success, sometimes not working at all. Many of these patients return to having normal energy during the day and sleeping very soundly at night once their body temperature patterns are returned to normal.

Surgical Revision

Wilson's Syndrome patients can be more susceptible to poor wound healing and infection. In severe cases, they may report having had to undergo a surgical revision of a surgical wound several days or weeks after a previous surgery due to poor wound healing or infection. Sometimes the wound healing is so poor that the wound may literally fall apart and/or tear open again. Patients who have had to undergo these revisions often relate classic histories consistent with Wilson's Syndrome. Of course, surgery itself can precipitate the onset of Wilson's Syndrome. So a person might undergo a surgery so physically stressful that it precipitates Wilson's Syndrome, making it difficult for the patient to heal and recuperate properly from the operation. With proper thyroid hormone treatment, wound healing often improves tremendously, as well as one's ability to fight off infection. It is easy to understand how Wilson's Syndrome sufferers might have greater complications and longer hospital stays after surgical procedures than are typical and expected. This single problem accounts for a huge amount of cost in terms of longer hospital stays, very expensive antibiotics, and repeat surgeries. Not only can it be disappointing and unfavorable to the patient's physically, but financially as well.

Thyroid Hormone Medicines (T4 Preparations and T4/T3 Preparations)

I am including thyroid hormone medications as symptomatic therapies (as opposed to therapeutic) frequently given to patients with Wilson's Syndrome who would frequently respond better to proper thyroid hormone therapy (especially T3 therapy). This is to underscore the fact that the choice of thyroid hormone medication must, in every case, be based on the underlying cause of DTSF suspected in each individual patient. As we discussed previously, there are different causes of DTSF and they are not all best treated in the same way. Even patients having the same cause of DTSF, should be treated on a tailored individual case basis. For example, even though three different people each drive separately from the same apartment building to the same grocery store by car, their paths should be individualized depending on red lights, green lights, roads taken, curbs, pedestrians, traffic, lane changes, and other important factors. Some patients may be suffering from two causes of DTSF at the same time. Patients suffering from DTSF frequently do not respond completely to the thyroid hormone regimen they are being prescribed because it may not be adequately addressing the underlying cause or causes. Likewise, if the symptoms do improve to an extent, they may return after treatment has been discontinued; whereas, they might remain persistently improved if the proper thyroid hormone treatment is prescribed.

One such example is the frequent situation that occurs when a patient suffering from Grave's Disease (hyperthyroidism) undergoes complete removal or destruction of the thyroid gland in order to correct this, sometimes life-threatening, over-active thyroid gland problem. After the removal or destruction of the gland, the patient will be dependent on thyroid hormone medication for life. Such patients are frequently started on T4 preparations. As one might imagine, however, developing a serious illness which results in the removal of one's thyroid gland can be a rather stressful experience. Consequently, such patients may not satisfactorily convert the T4 medication they are given which can leave them with some very disturbing complaints of DTSF. Prior to developing Grave's Disease such a patient may have been completely healthy without any problems or health complaints of any kind, then the patient develops symptoms of an **overactive** thyroid system for which the patient requires treatment. After treatment, the patient may be left with symptoms of **underactive** thyroid system function in spite of being treated with thyroid hormone medication. So, in spite of treatment, the patient is left with disturbing symptoms of DTSF which were not present before the patient's development of Grave's Disease. However, with proper T3 therapy, the former Grave's Disease patient's DTSF, due to Wilson's Syndrome (impaired conversion of the T4 medication prescribed), may be corrected. Once the T4 to T3 conversion impairment is corrected with proper T3 therapy, the Grave's Disease patient can frequently be switched back to T4 therapy and enjoy persistent correction of the symptoms of DTSF, and once again return to feeling much the way he or she felt prior to developing Grave's Disease.

Tranquilizers and Antianxiety Medications

Wilson's Syndrome can sometimes lead to feelings of anxiety and even panic attacks. Some patients present to my office being treated with tranquilizers and antianxiety medications. These medicines are often extremely helpful to control the symptoms, but do not treat the problem, when the problem is impaired T4 to T3 conversion with resulting low body temperature patterns. One such patient had developed anxious feelings and quite severe panic attacks that would greatly hinder her normal daily functioning. Her symptoms, characteristically, came on together with a group of other related symptoms after a major physical and emotional stress. She had been plagued with these attacks for years and within two weeks of proper thyroid hormone therapy, her panic attacks resolved completely to her astonishment and delight.

Vitamins

Patients with DTSF often find their symptoms to be improved with vitamin supplementation and these patients can often be quite knowledgeable on vitamins. Although they sometimes feel much better with vitamin therapy, they do not always return completely back to normal; nor do their improvements generally persist after vitamin therapy had been discontinued. These patients will frequently respond better to treating the underlying problem with proper thyroid hormone treatment. It may be that Wilson's Syndrome affects intestinal absorption or body utilization of vitamins, so supplementation with vitamins is often quite helpful. However, after body temperature patterns have been normalized the patients' symptoms of fatigue, depression, dry skin, dry hair, brittle nails, etc., frequently remain improved even after vitamin therapy and thyroid hormone therapy have been weaned.

9. SIGNS AND SYMPTOMS AND HOW THEY MADE THE LIST

In the preceding chapters I have tried to lay the foundation to prepare the reader for what follows -- **symptoms, treatments, and significance of Wilson's Syndrome.** The present chapter deals with the symptoms of Wilson's Syndrome. We have talked previously about how it is better to treat the underlying problem rather than just the symptoms. When the underlying problem is treated, not only do the symptoms respond more completely, but they frequently remain corrected even after therapy has been discontinued. An effort has been made to prepare the reader for that which is very difficult to imagine. I am continually amazed by its ramifications. There are many days in which I will see several patients that I would feel comfortable putting in the "miracle" category. Miraculous because their severe and debilitating symptoms, some of which have been treated by some of the best doctors in the world for years without much success, have resolved quickly and easily with proper thyroid hormone treatment. Of course, many of the symptoms in this chapter are normal for anyone to have at times, but they are especially problematic when they are inappropriate and persist.

There are at least two things that are difficult to imagine about the unprecedented impact and significance of Wilson's Syndrome.

1. **How can <u>one</u> problem cause so many complaints?** It is because it affects such a fundamental process upon which so many other functions are dependent (like removing the one card from the bottom of a card house that cannot be removed without the whole house of cards collapsing).
2. **How can so many different symptoms respond so completely to the same treatment?** Because in so many cases the treatment is addressing the problem rather than the symptoms.

We have also mentioned previously why Wilson's Syndrome should be considered first in addressing many of the associated symptoms for several reasons: Very few, if any, non life-threatening conditions can affect a process so fundamental so as to easily explain so many different symptoms; it is extremely common; it is easily recognized; it is easily treated; response to treatment is rapid; the medicine is found in nature and is not foreign to the body; and there is a chance for "cure". The symptoms listed in this chapter all have certain things in common. They have all been seen to follow the typical pattern of presentation and response of Wilson's Syndrome. Namely, they each have been seen to come on together with several or many of the other symptoms listed. They many times occur after a major mental, physical, or emotional stress. They have each been seen to be correlated in many cases with a low body temperature pattern. They have each been seen to respond together with other presenting symptoms upon normalization of body temperature patterns with proper T3 therapy. And finally, they each have been seen to, in certain cases, remain persistently improved even after T3 therapy has been gradually weaned.

I feel that proper T3 therapy is not only a treatment for many of these symptoms is also the best available treatment in many cases, for many of the symptoms (when persistent and inappropriate), including fatigue, migraines, PMS, decreased memory, insomnia, anxiety, panic attacks, depression, constipation, and irritable bowel syndrome.

Proper T3 therapy for Wilson's Syndrome is not a panacea or "cure-all" and I don't mean to imply for a moment that it is. But there is no reason that it should be overlooked any longer. Time will tell if Wilson's Syndrome accounts for more cases than other causes of migraines, PMS, fatigue, depression, insomnia, anxiety, panic attacks, constipation, and irritable bowel syndrome. Therefore, time will tell also if proper T3 therapy proves to be more effective than other treatments in more cases of migraines, PMS, fatigue, decreased memory, insomnia, anxiety, panic attacks, depression, constipation, and irritable bowel syndrome.

The following are descriptions of the most common pervasive effects of Wilson's Syndrome:

156

Acid Indigestion

Decreased bowel motility secondary to WS can result in the backing up of stomach acids. This can lead to heartburn, esophageal acid reflux, and even ulcers. As mentioned previously, this acid indigestion and predisposition for reflux and ulcers often responds quite easily to proper T3 therapy, even when not well controlled by other medicines.

Allergies

Not uncommonly, Wilson's Syndrome sufferers relate the development and/or worsening of allergy symptoms such as stuffy nose, sinus drainage, hay fever, etc., to a major stress. When the allergies come on together with other signs and symptoms of Wilson's Syndrome, it is more likely that they are related, particularly when they become worse after a significant mental, physical, or emotional stress. As will be discussed later, other allergic type responses can also be associated with Wilson's Syndrome such as asthma, itchiness, and hives. I suspect that body temperature changes can affect histamine physiology, possibly by causing enzymatic changes that result in an over production of histamine or resulting in decreased breakdown of histamine by the body. The symptoms of allergy, asthma, itching, and hives also seem to be related to the balance of fluids in the body (the degree of fluid retention and degree of fluid fluctuations). Interestingly, histamine among other things mediates changes in fluid balance to a certain degree in certain areas. It may be that histamine and body temperature patterns play a role in the symptoms of allergies, asthma, itching, and hives to the extent that they influence fluid balance in certain areas of the body.

It may be that with lower body temperature patterns, the blood vessels of the sinuses dilate resulting in increased transudate (which is fluid that seeps from the blood vessels into the tissues), thereby resulting in tissue swelling, congestion, and increased sinus drainage. Regardless of the mechanism, it is clear that allergies can be related to low body temperature patterns and can follow the behavior of other symptoms related to Wilson's Syndrome. Allergy manifestations can present together with other symptoms of Wilson's Syndrome especially after a significant stress, and can resolve even completely (together with the other presenting symptoms of Wilson's Syndrome) upon normalization of body temperature patterns with proper T3 therapy.

Anxiety, Panic Attacks

Panic attacks are acute episodes of anxiety. They can be accompanied by overwhelming feeling of fear and dread. They can be associated with palpitations, breaking out in sweats, and even chest pains. Panic attack sufferers commonly say that they sometimes feel as if they are going to die during some of their attacks. Panic attacks are one of the most interesting manifestations of Wilson's Syndrome. They are somewhat the way one feels when one awakens thinking that there might be a burglar in the room. When faced with such a threat, feelings of fear and dread are appropriate and the surge of adrenaline is useful in helping one prepare to react to threatening situations. This is what is sometimes referred to as the "fight or flight" response. This response can be quite inappropriate, however, when it takes place with very little or no provocation. Common settings in which WS sufferers will find themselves having pain attacks include shopping (especially in grocery stores, for some reason), driving over bridges, driving in heavy traffic, or flying in an airplane.

Wilson's Syndrome is characterized by the body being stuck in conservation mode wherein it feels its resources are being threatened even when such feelings may be inappropriate. In a similar way, panic attacks are characterized by the body responding dramatically to inappropriately small challenges. All of us know what it feels like to panic, however, most of us would agree that such feelings would be inappropriate if they occurred out of the blue with little or no provocation.

The "fight or flight" response is mediated by adrenaline produced in the adrenal gland, which causes an increase of blood supply to the extremities and muscles, increased heart rate, enlarging of the air passageways, etc. The adrenal gland is stimulated to release adrenaline during threatening circumstances. The adrenal gland secretes adrenaline also during normal maintenance of proper blood pressure levels. When the blood pressure is detected by the body as being too low, a signal will be sent to the adrenal gland to secrete adrenaline to increase the pulse rate and help bring the blood pressure back up to normal levels.

One characteristic of WS sufferers is that they commonly have low blood pressure and "relaxed" blood vessels. Because of the decreased vascular tone, these patients have a more difficult time maintaining normal blood pressure. They frequently can get lightheaded when they stand up too fast because of their body's inability to maintain adequate blood supply to the brain. It seems then, that the blood pressure of such patients bounces around just above the threshold, below which a compensatory burst of adrenaline would be secreted by the adrenal gland to prevent fainting. So in essence, these patients may normally be on the verge of a compensatory burst of adrenaline. I feel this helps explain why the slightest provocation can trigger a burst of adrenaline that can bring on palpitations, sweating, fear, and panic. At any rate, panic attacks can frequently be easily eliminated with proper thyroid hormone treatment.

Arthritis and Muscular/Joint Aches

These symptoms seem to be related to the fluid retention, either obvious or microscopic and could be related to Wilson's Syndrome. These symptoms seem to come and go in a pattern that is similar, with regard to body temperature patterns and body temperature fluctuations to that of WS symptoms related to fluid retention. Fluid retention or swelling plays a role in inflammation. It is well known that inflammation can be painful and that it can impair wound healing and recovery from injuries. For this reason, anti-inflammatory medicines are frequently prescribed to decrease inflammation in order to decrease the pain and to aid in healing. Worsened inflammation can be a disturbing manifestation of a low body temperature pattern. For example, perhaps a person accidentally injuries his back at work and the stress of the back injury, being laid up in the hospital, and being out of work causes a drop in body temperature patterns resulting in the development of the symptoms of Wilson's Syndrome. The patient's back problems, consequently, may not resolve or respond as well as those of other patients. His convalescence and recuperation compared to other patients might be prolonged and disappointing.

WS sufferers commonly have muscular and joint aches that respond well to proper thyroid hormone treatment. The arthritis associated with Wilson's Syndrome frequently follows patterns of presentation, persistence, and resolution of other symptoms of Wilson's Syndrome. For example, the arthritis and muscular aches might be more severe in the morning upon awakening, better during the day, and worse again in the evening, and correspond with improvement and worsening of other symptoms of Wilson's Syndrome with temperature changes.

Asthma

As mentioned previously, asthma may be due to changes in histamine physiology. Regardless of the mechanism, asthma has been seen to follow the pattern of presentation of Wilson's Syndrome symptoms and frequently responds well to proper liothyronine treatment. Many patients that I have seen who have been less than adequately controlled on even several asthma medicines at a time, have been able to wean off their asthma medicine, while enjoying resolution of their asthma symptoms with normalization of their body temperature patterns If the asthma symptoms, come on later in life (as opposed to childhood asthma) especially after a major physical, mental, or emotional stress, together with other classic symptoms of Wilson's Syndrome and low body temperature patterns, then it is quite possible that the patient's asthma will respond to proper T3 therapy.

Bad Breath

Some patients and their spouses have noticed changes in the smell of the patient's breath with onset of Wilson's Syndrome. The change in breath odor was noticeable since the patients had not previously had problems with their breath. Halitosis or bad breath is well known to be exacerbated by bacterial growth in the mouth and because of other internal changes. It may be that MED secondary to WS may impair the body's ability to retard the growth of bacteria or development of plaque in the mouth or to prevent other internal changes that can result in breath problems. There have been some patients who have even noticed significantly increased tooth decay with the noticeable change occurring with the onset of WS symptoms.

Bruising, Increased

When the tone of the vessels becomes more relaxed, blood vessels can be more easily ruptured. Bruises are areas in the skin where blood vessels have been ruptured with the blood seeping into the surrounding tissue. This can result in soreness and discoloration of the skin that are familiar to all of us. Bruises are cleared by special "clean-up" cells of the body. The function of these cells, like the function of virtually all cells, is dependent upon the proper functioning of enzymes. Multiple Enzyme Dysfunction can, therefore, explain a phenomenon that is sometimes seen in Wilson's Syndrome patients.

I remember one patient who pointed to bruises on her leg and said that "I have had this bruise for six months, this bruise for one year, and this bruise for two years." I was astonished and could barely believe that she could have a bruise that could last for two years. However, it seemed to be a difficult thing to invent and she seemed quite sincere about it. And it didn't sound too hard to imagine since there are some people who have difficulty healing scratches that many remain open for as long as six months, or may take even longer to heal. At any rate, as you may have guessed, her bruises resolved within one month of her body temperature patterns being normalized with proper thyroid supplementation. Thus, Wilson's Syndrome sufferers bruise more easily, more frequently, and those bruises can last longer than is appropriate.

Canker Sores

Canker sores are certainly not the most common symptom of WS. However, it has been seen that canker sores can be influenced by Wilson's Syndrome. One patient noticed that she began having canker sores develop inside her mouth just prior to her menstrual cycle ever since she began developing other symptoms of WS, following a major stress in her life. With normalization of body temperature patterns, her symptoms of PMS, her symptoms of WS, and even her tendency to develop canker sores premenstrually all resolved.

Carpal Tunnel Syndrome

Carpal Tunnel Syndrome is the numbness and tingling experienced in the hands, fingers, occasionally with shooting pains up the arm that result from the impingement of nerves that pass through a narrow tunnel at the base of the hand. The numbness and tingling frequently follow the distribution of the nerves that pass through the tunnel. It can involve the pinky and ring finger as well as the pinky side of the hand; or it can affect the thumb, index and middle finger.

Carpal Tunnel Syndrome (CTS) is frequently seen in people who have a job that requires constant repetition of certain hand movements, but CTS has also been long associated with DTSF. As mentioned previously, the tissue swelling that results from fluid retention caused by DTSF can cause pinched nerve syndromes, especially in areas where the swelling occurs at a site where there is only a limited amount of space. When tissue swelling occurs within the closed spaced of the Carpal Tunnel, then the nerves that pass through the tunnel can become pinched resulting in Carpal Tunnel Syndrome.

Cholesterol Levels, Elevated

Cholesterol has long been associated with decreased thyroid system function. In fact, prior to thyroid hormone blood testing, cholesterol was sometimes used as a test for decreased thyroid system function. Some doctors used to say, "Well, you have high cholesterol, therefore, you have a slow metabolism." Doctors don't often make that same conclusion now, but it is often still true. In fact, in the literature that accompanies many of the medicines used in lowering blood cholesterol levels, it is pointed out that the medicine should not be prescribed until hypothyroidism (one cause of DTSF) is ruled out. It is well known that thyroid system function should be one of the first things evaluated in a patient with persistently elevated blood cholesterol levels, especially those that do not respond well to dietary changes. Unfortunately, it is again assumed that DTSF can be satisfactorily ruled out based solely on thyroid hormone blood tests, even in the face of classic signs, symptoms, and presentation of DTSF.

I remember a classic WS sufferer who had cholesterol levels in the low 300's (normal is below 200) in spite of being treated with several different cholesterol lowering drugs and in spite of strict dietary changes. With normalization of his body temperature pattern with proper T3 therapy, his symptoms of Wilson's Syndrome resolved and within 1 1/2 months, his blood cholesterol levels had dropped below 200 for the first time in years, in spite of having not taken his cholesterol lowering drug during that I 1/2 month period.

Most Americans are aware of the importance of blood cholesterol levels, thanks to the media. In the last sixty years there is evidence that the average blood cholesterol levels and heart disease in Americans are increasing. These increases have baffled scientists who have been unable to attribute the increases to any observable changes in dietary, environmental, or health trends. However, these increases are easy to understand when one realizes that due to our improved medical technology more and more people who would be susceptible to developing Wilson's Syndrome are living into adulthood. And, of course, our world is continually becoming more and more stressful. It is easy to imagine then, that more and more people are developing decreased thyroid system function as a result of developing Wilson's Syndrome. This could easily account for the increases in average blood cholesterol levels and increased heart disease. Of course, not every person who has elevated blood cholesterol levels is suffering from Wilson's Syndrome. But obviously, body temperature patterns and other characteristics of Wilson's Syndrome deserve special consideration in patients who have stubbornly elevated blood cholesterol levels.

It seems that substances such as T3 and T4, which are found in every person's body, would be preferable to cholesterol lowering agents which are "not found in nature," especially if they better address the underlying problem, are more effective, and especially if they can be used to bring about a persistent correction of the underlying imbalance that would eliminate the need for a person to remain on medicine for the rest of his life. Wilson's Syndrome explains what many people already know, and that is that their elevated blood cholesterol levels depend on more than just what they eat since their diet contains as little cholesterol as is possible, while their cholesterol levels remain elevated.

Cold hands and feet and Raynaud's Phenomenon

WS patients often experience cold hands and feet. At first glance this does not seem to be a very disturbing complaint. However, it can be quite troublesome at times. It can be the cause of a great deal of self-consciousness or embarrassment. Several patients that I have seen have stated that they are actually embarrassed and self-conscious to shake people's hands because of how frequently people will exclaim about the coldness of their hands. People will sometimes tease them and make comments about them having a cold heart, being an ice cube or glacier, or being dead. These comments, and others can be a great source of embarrassment and self-consciousness. Cold feet seem to be most often disturbing in relation to sleeping with one's mate. Patient's spouses will often complain about the coldness of the patient's feet in spite of many blankets and covers. The coldness sometimes literally jolts the patient's spouse. Patients themselves often find it very disturbing that their feet feel extremely cold in spite of being dressed warmly, wearing socks, and doing whatever they can to keep their feet warm.

One of the most severe incidents of this type of complaint that I have seen was in patient who had been diagnosed as having Raynaud's Phenomenon. Raynaud's Phenomenon is a condition characterized by vasoconstriction or vessel tightening in response to exposure to cold. It can cause impaired circulation for a period of time resulting in skin color changes. The patient that I had seen, upon exposure to cold, would experience her hands turning blue. The discoloration would sometimes extend thorough her forearms and even halfway up her upper arm. There often would be quite a line of distinction between the color of her normal skin and the bluish discoloration of the affected skin, looking almost as if she was wearing a long blue stocking glove extending up past her elbow. This cold sensation, of course, was quite uncomfortable and disconcerting. It was recommended that she change her occupation, which was that of a surgical assistant. Because she was an operating room assistant, the cold conditions of the operating rooms aggravated her condition. However, with proper thyroid treatment, her tendency to develop cold hands and to experience the blue discoloration of her arms resolved and it was not necessary for her to change her occupation. In fact, the patient was a scuba diver, and whenever she entered significantly cold water, she would experience this disturbing complaint, but now when she puts her hands in cold water, she no longer develops the symptoms that had been previously associated with Raynaud's Phenomenon.

Constipation/Irritable Bowel Syndrome

Constipation is an extremely common associated symptom. Multiple Enzyme Dysfunction caused by low body temperature patterns can result in the slowing down of the gastrointestinal tract. This may lead to less frequent bowel movements, constipation, bloating, gas, abdominal cramping, irritable bowel syndrome/spastic colon, and indeed diarrhea. So decreased bowel motility can lead to constipation or maldigestion of food, and gaseous bloating leading to spastic contraction of the colon and diarrhea. As mentioned previously, these symptoms can respond remarkably well to proper liothyronine treatment, even when many other approaches have failed.

Coordination, Lack Of

Occasionally, patients notice with the onset of Wilson's Syndrome becoming more "clumsy or klutzy." They sometimes notice that they have begun to drop things more easily, run into things more easily or temporarily lose their balance while walking. These abnormalities have been seen to resolve with the symptoms of Wilson's Syndrome (just as they came on with the symptoms of WS) with proper T3 therapy.

Depression

The depression associated with WS will frequently respond to antidepressants, sometimes for only two or three months, sometimes longer, and, at times, not at all. Interestingly, there have been many studies about T3 being used to enhance the effects of antidepressants - sometimes converting non-responders to a particular antidepressant into responders. It is my feeling that many of these patients' depression would have responded to T3 therapy alone. The correction was probably due to the T3 itself and not necessarily because of the enhancement of the antidepressants' effects. Thus, the correlation between thyroid hormone (T4 and T3) and depression has been long known. I have seen many patients with intractable (difficult to treat) depression, having unsatisfactory results to years of antidepressant therapy, who have responded within weeks to proper liothyronine therapy.

One such patient that I have treated developed significant depression approximately 25 years ago. Since then it has plagued, shaped, and colored her entire life. It contributed to her getting a divorce and it became so severe and debilitating at one point almost 20 years ago, that it caused her to feel constrained to give up custody of her children, thinking that they might be better cared for by someone else. The various antidepressants with which she has been treated over the years did help some, but did not provide her with satisfactory improvement. The complete resolution that came within two weeks of weaning her antidepressant medication and beginning proper T3 therapy, was bittersweet. Of course, she was extremely pleased to feel normal again and to be able to see clearly that the symptom had a large physical component that predictably correlated with body temperature patterns. But at the same time, she came to the realization that 25 years of her life had been spent suffering from a debilitating, unrecognized, and easily treated condition. It was poignant to see her realize that once 25 years have been spent, they are spent. It's great that she feels better now, yet it is sad that it has taken 25 years. Such cases also make one wonder: Do hard times cause depression and a drop in body temperature patterns? Or, do hard times cause low temperature patterns which can result in depression?

The depressions that come on **premenstrually** and after the birth of a child (post-partum) deserve special mention. Although the depression associated with PMS can be transient, it can also be quite severe. Several days or more per month taken over many years of a person's life, can add up to a lot of serious depression. Learning to cope with this periodic depression can sometimes be more difficult, since patients may tend to "drop their guard."

It is easy to understand a period of depression that occurs **post-partum** (frequently called baby blues), because the stress of childbirth is the number one cause of Wilson's Syndrome. It is normal for the body to leave the conservation mode and enter into the productivity mode once again. Commonly, this process may take approximately three months which is usually the amount of time it takes for post-partum depression to resolve. Unfortunately, it sometimes doesn't resolve. After the birth of a baby, the patient's body temperature can drop, causing severe depression immediately after the birth of the child. With proper liothyronine treatment, this troublesome symptom can often be easily remedied.

Dry Eyes/Blurred Vision

WS sufferers sometimes notice drying of their eyes, with their tears becoming more "gummy," which can result in blurred vision. The blurred vision may be associated with drying of the outer layers of the cornea. In some cases, the blurred vision seems to come and go with the patient's level of fluid retention. This suggests that the blurred vision may be caused by a degree of fluid retention within the eyeball causing temporary changes in the shape of the eye. The blurred vision associated with Wilson's Syndrome sometimes comes and goes, and is not always persistent. A patient's vision strength can also change and may come and go as well.

One patient that I can remember in particular, developed Wilson's Syndrome quite a few years previously after a severe stress. Over the ensuing years, not only did the other symptoms of Wilson's Syndrome worsen but she noticed that the prescriptions for her glasses needed to be made stronger and stronger because her eyes were weakening more quickly than they had in previous years. With normalization of body temperature patterns, not only did the other symptoms of Wilson's Syndrome improve, but she found that she was able to return to the previous prescriptions for her eyesight.

Quite frequently, patients find that they can't read the fine print on some days while they can on others. They may need glasses or someone else to read the fine print, whereas on other days they might be able to read the print easily. Interestingly, these vision changes do not seem to be improved even after rubbing of the eyes to clear it. So it is probably not related to the tears.

Dry Hair, Hair Loss

Dry hair is a common complaint and can include the hair shafts breaking off at the ends. As mentioned in a previous chapter, hair manageability and luster can begin to return within two weeks of beginning proper thyroid hormone therapy, suggesting that the condition of the hair is greatly dependent on the oils secreted by the scalp and not just the composition of the hair shafts themselves. These patients frequently experience hair loss to some degree, especially from the head, but they can lose hair from sites all over the body. Thinning of the lateral one-third of the eye brows is a classic sign of decreased thyroid system function. Patients may also lose their eye lashes, leg hair, and even pubic hair. Most patients with Wilson's Syndrome that experience hair loss notice generalized hair loss, especially from the top of their head, near their hair line, and on the sides of the head also (at the temples). Their hair may become so thin that one can often see their scalp. It is usually first noticed as hair on the pillow in the morning or clogging the shower drain. Everyone knows that losing some hair from day to day is normal. But they often notice a significant increase in the amount of hair being lost each day, especially when it comes out seemingly by the handfuls as one passes one's fingers through one's hair. One such patient had noticed a 50% decrease in the amount of hair present on her head. This thinning of her hair had been persistent for several years. With proper liothyronine treatment, the 50% loss of hair was restored, giving her back her full head of hair.

Patients also notice that with the onset of Wilson's Syndrome, their hair may not hold a perm as well as it used to. They may find that the perm will only hold for a couple of weeks, when previously it would hold for several months. Sometimes their hair will not take a perm at all. Interestingly, most hair dressers are already quite aware of the correlation between decreased thyroid system function and the patient's ability to maintain a hair permanent.

Dry Skin

Dry skin is a classic symptom of DTSF in general, and Wilson's Syndrome in specific. Skin may become dry, coarse, and scaly. The skin may become so dry that a patient may be able to write one's name by gently scraping one's fingernail across the skin. Interestingly, the skin on either side of the nose and underlying the eyebrows (overlying the sinuses) is quite susceptible to being dry. Of course, the sinuses are where air passes through the head on the way to the interior of the body. And the areas over the sinuses can, therefore, be slightly cooler than other sites of the body. The skin over the sinuses frequently can become dry because its enzymes might then not function as well, leaving the maintenance level of the skin less than ideal. Similarly, the areas over the elbows, knees, backs of the hands, knuckles, fingers, feet, heels, soles of the feet are frequent areas where dry skin will be found. These areas also tend to be cooler in relation to the rest of the body because of their position in the extremities away from the core of the body, and also because they overlie bone (there is a decreased volume of blood flow to these areas). The dry skin can be widespread, however.

I recently saw a man in his late 50's who developed a skin rash over his entire body. His skin was essentially flaking off from his head to his toes. The skin was so dry on his face that it caused his mouth to be drawn tight and his eye lids to curl, appearing to make it difficult for him to close his eyes. The skin on his head, arms, legs, and all over his body was so dry and flaky that he would "snow" wherever he walked or sat. His skin flaking was so severe that when he would stand up and leave, part of him would stay. He had been to dermatologists who could find no good explanation for his condition, but upon careful history, it was apparent that his condition began after he began having a lot of financial difficulty in his business six to eight months previously. His skin became so irritated and scaly that some of his tissue fluids would actually seep to the surface of his body. The fluid would evaporate quickly, causing him to lose a great deal of body fluids and causing him to feel extremely cold. Within a few months of treatment, the skin on his mouth and face had completely returned to normal, and there was tremendous improvement on his arms, legs, and chest. He literally looked like a different person. The patient feels his skin is actually better now than previous to his stress, and he feels that his skin has not looked as healthy and youthful for the last fifteen years. He no longer leaves his skin at the places he visits, when before his skin seemed to be literally falling apart. We sometimes take for granted how important the skin is, its vital importance can best be seen when it does not function properly. Needless to say, the patient is quite happy, and for me it has been one of the most amazing cases with which I have ever been involved.

Fatigue

Wilson's Syndrome (WS) sufferers will frequently be tired all day and paradoxically have trouble sleeping at night. Their energy levels can, however, fluctuate with body temperature changes. For example, some patients relate that they are more tired in the morning, but once they get started moving around, their fatigue sometimes subsides. However, their fatigue sometimes returns in the late afternoon when their body temperatures normally decrease again (remember the symptoms may also correlate with body temperature patterns that are too high or too unsteady). Characteristically, patients with Wilson's Syndrome can usually muster their resources for a period of time (sometimes they can't), but find that their resources are easily exhausted. This can be compared to other sources of fatigue that sometimes cannot be overcome for a time, even if the patient wants to.

Sometimes WS sufferers are able to function all day at work but will collapse as soon as they get home, being worthless (as the patients say) for the rest of the day. They may be able to gather themselves up enough to work all day and evening three days in a row only to "crash and burn" for the following several days (sometimes not even getting out of bed). I remember one patient who would go to bed some Friday nights, sleep through Saturday and wake up Sunday evening for a few hours, with her husband watching the kids during such weekends.

These situations are consistent with the notion that these patients are stuck in conservation mode wherein their bodies are attempting to conserve resources for fear that their available resources may be insufficient to meet the presenting

171

challenges. So resources are available to meet some of the presenting challenges, but seem to be easily depleted. Their fatigue isn't always constant and might seem to subside in the midst of accomplishing an important task, but once the task is done, frequently they will become significantly more fatigued. In the most severe situations, they may have a hard time working at all, or even making it to work.

Many times, WS sufferers will sleep ten or twelve hours during the night, and still will wake up not feeling rested. It's the kind of fatigue wherein they feel they do not have sufficient resources to deal with their current life situation. They simply feel overwhelmed by ordinary life. Sometimes the fronts they put on at work or at home no longer disguise their disability. Some WS sufferers may have good days and bad days which seem to be well correlated with body temperature pattern changes (such as just prior to the period).

To help non-sufferers imagine what the fatigue might feel like, one might compare it to the fatigue associated with having the flu. When a person gets the flu, they may also develop a fever. Elevated body temperatures can cause Multiple Enzyme Dysfunction, and can result in fatigue and a diminished level of functioning throughout the body. Just imagine how you'd feel if you'd lost almost everything. Most of us would feel quite challenged, overwhelmed, and even fatigued under such circumstances for good reason. However, these are the sorts of feelings that WS sufferers sometimes have persistently, even when there is no good reason (making them inappropriate).

Fluid Retention

Fluid retention or edema is a serious and significant problem in and of itself. But abnormalities in how the body handles tissue fluids and vascular fluids can greatly affect the body's overall function and cause a great number of other symptoms as well. The following symptoms have been seen to be related to fluid retention in that they often worsen when the fluid retention worsens and they tend to resolve when the fluid retention resolves with normalization of body temperature patterns:

migraine headaches, numbness and tingling of the hands, panic attacks, palpitations, lightheadedness/dizziness, sweating, musculoskeletal aches and pains, and others.

The fluid retention is commonly seen in the hands of patients who often find it difficult to take their rings off and who will frequently not be able to wear their rings until their fluid retention dissipates. Their feet and ankles may also swell, and may even extend above the knees. The patient may develop pitting edema. It is referred to as pitting edema because when one presses a finger against the lower part of the leg, it leaves a "pit" or dent at the spot where the finger was pressing. There are people who have several different sizes of shoes that will fit them according to the amount of swelling they have on a particular day. In some cases, I have seen the fluid retention to be so severe that such a patient might scratch a leg against a piece of furniture and although it may not bleed, they sometimes notice tissue fluid collecting along the scratch such that it may even drain down the outside of the leg. It sounds incredible, but seeing is believing.

Periorbital edema, which is fluid retention around the eyes, is a classic sign of decreased thyroid system function. DTSF patients can have thick tongues giving them difficulty in forming words.

The severity of the fluid retention correlates very well with the body temperature patterns. The fluid retention is most severe when the body temperature is too low, too high, or unsteady, which is characteristic of all the other symptoms of Wilson's Syndrome. Increased fluid retention often correlates with increased body temperature fluctuations. Likewise, as body temperature patterns become more and more steady over a period of days, the fluid retention usually improves.

I believe that abnormal body temperature patterns (especially low temperatures) cause the muscular tone of the vessels to decrease, making blood vessels more leaky, which results in tissue fluid retention. Proper thyroid hormone treatment can be used to normalize the temperature patterns, causing them to be closer to 98.6 and causing them to be more steady. When this is accomplished, it improves vascular tone of the blood vessels in the body causing them to be less leaky and enabling them to more effectively prevent too much fluid from leaking into the tissues and to more effectively carry tissue fluid back into circulation. I believe that this one aspect of Wilson's Syndrome itself, has profound physiological consequences when one considers how it can influence so many other symptoms.

Flushing

Many of us have noticed the "blotches" of flushing that sometimes appear on the neck and upper chest of someone who is in a very nervous situation (like speaking in front of a group of people). Flushing of the neck and chest is a classic symptom of DTSF, and patients with WS can be far more prone to such episodes than are others. Occasionally, the flushing can be severe with a clearly defined area of persistent discoloration as seen in one patient who said it felt as if she was "on fire". Her flushing responded very well (90%) although not completely to proper T3 therapy.

Food Cravings

Only those who have had inappropriate or unusual food cravings can appreciate fully that they do, in fact, exist. The food cravings associated with pregnancy are legendary: ice cream and pickles, and other bizarre combinations. Food cravings have also been seen to be related to WS, especially just prior to the menstrual cycle. This seems to be a symptom of PMS. But as we have mentioned previously, PMS can frequently be corrected with proper T3 therapy. It may be that rapid changes in body temperature occurring premenstrually cause Multiple Enzyme Dysfunction and blood sugar fluctuations. Unstable blood sugar levels may lead to sweet cravings and taking in of sweets may satisfy the cravings temporarily. However, the body often over compensates to the sugar ingested which can lead to a subsequent rapid drop in the blood sugar level (BSL) causing the BSL to be unstable. In the conservation mode, to better balance the ratio between the

174

body's perceived increased challenges and decreased resources, the body can decrease the amount of energy that is used and can seek to increase the amount of energy taken in. This may also lead the body to crave foods. This also explains the common observation that the body often craves more high-energy foods like chocolate which contain both sugar and caffeine. This increase in appetite and increased drive to obtain high energy foods can be quite overwhelming or dramatic. These cravings are often viewed as personal weaknesses. They seem to be personal weaknesses the way it is weak for a person under water to crave air. Of course, the body can live without sweets or chocolate, but not without air. It only sometimes seems to "think" that it will when it is inappropriately stuck in conservation mode (leading to a perception by the body of having critically low resources). It is not extremely uncommon that patients who have a history of never even liking chocolate previous to developing Wilson's Syndrome and who have never ever been sweet eaters, find themselves craving chocolate prior to their menstrual cycles and/or at other times. They may find themselves eating an entire box of cookies or an entire chocolate cake, even though they don't really like chocolate. These cravings represent a definite change from before to after developing WS.

Food Intolerances

Some patients may also notice that they develop an incompatibility with certain foods such as wheat, milk and dairy products. They may find that they can no longer eat certain foods without diarrhea, gas bloating, or indigestion. One such patient had a long-standing history of lactose intolerance that was managed fairly well with certain enzyme supplements (to digest the lactose) in her diet. With proper thyroid therapy, her intolerance to lactose and dairy products resolved in conjunction with resolution of her other Wilson's Syndrome symptoms. Apparently, the elevation in her body temperature pattern caused the return of the enzymatic function that had been impaired and was preventing her from digesting lactose. Many patients have found that with normalization of their body temperature patterns they can once again eat, without difficulty, foods that used to cause them diarrhea, gas, bloating, or indigestion. It is noteworthy that food intolerances have sometimes been thought of in terms of allergies and it has been seen that allergies can sometime be related to WS.

Headaches Including Migraines

Wilson's Syndrome can contribute to allergy, stress, and migraine headaches. The most debilitating of these are migraine headaches. I feel that the migraine headaches associated with WS are related to fluid retention. This fluid retention is probably secondary to the vessels in the body becoming leaky because of decreased vascular tone, and changes that occur in the vessel walls when the body temperature patterns are abnormal. As these vessels become more leaky, fluid escapes from the vessels causing fluid retention in various parts of the body, even the brain. When this fluid retention occurs in a closed space, it can cause problems. If it occurs in the carpal tunnels of the hands, it can cause a pinching of the nerves know as Carpal Tunnel Syndrome. When it occurs in a narrow passageway of the spine where there is only so much room for the nerves to pass, then it can also cause a pinched nerve syndrome. When a drop in body temperature patterns results in the vessels of the brain becoming more leaky, migraine and other forms of headaches may result. Characteristically migraine headaches sometimes come on after a warning know as an aura. An aura is a small group of characteristic symptoms that migraine patients will frequently have prior to the onset of their migraine headaches. Some patients will notice a peculiar odor or notice characteristic vision changes, such as wavy lines, or some other neurological manifestations, that hint that a migraine may be about to occur. After the aura, the headache pain may begin, frequently having a throbbing nature in the beginning and sometimes progressing to a more constant type of pain. In some cases of severe migraine, the headache may progress to cause nausea and vomiting, difficulty with bright lights bothering the eyes, and even temporary numbness or paralysis of various parts of the body.

176

One can easily see how these characteristics of a migraine headache can be explained by leaky vessels and fluid retention. As the dilated vessels and fluid retention begin to exert pressure on the brain tissues at the beginning of the headache, it is not hard to imagine that this pressure might be manifested to a patient through some kind of "aura." As the fluid retention continues and the swelling brain begins to reach its confines (limited by the bony skull), it is easy to see how the swollen brain's pulsations (resulting from intermittent surges of blood from the heart) could cause the brain to begin to "bang" against its confines, causing pain of a throbbing nature. If the swelling were to continue, one could see how the brain tissue could more fully occupy the available space within the skull causing it to press more steadily against its confines resulting in a pain of a more constant nature. The pressure exerted on the brain's tissues could cause malfunctioning directly or possibly by inhibiting blood supply. This could explain neurological manifestations such as numbness and tingling or temporary paralysis. So any treatment that can diminish the resulting dilated and leaky vessels can help in the treatment of these migraine headaches. This explains why ergotamines can sometimes ward off migraine headaches since they are *vasoconstrictors* and can constrict the dilated vessels possibly making them less leaky and thereby helping to ward off the migraine headaches before they have fully progressed. Interestingly, ergotamine therapy is usually ineffective once the migraine has taken hold, possibly because by that time too much fluid retention has already taken place.

Beta-blockers, a type of blood pressure medicine, are frequently used long-term to decrease the frequency and severity of migraine headaches, possibly by reducing the body's tendency towards higher blood pressures (of course, the greater the pressure, the greater the force working to push fluid out of the vessels and into the tissues). I remember one migraine patient that I treated who described herself as a "migraine headache experiment." She had suffered from migraines for over thirty years, and over that period of time, every new migraine treatment was given to her as it became available. Her migraine headaches were reduced by some of the therapies, but they were never satisfactorily controlled and they caused her a great deal of disability (having severe headaches almost on a daily basis). As is characteristic with the migraines associated with Wilson's Syndrome, they worsened during stressful periods in her life. Within only a few short weeks of proper T3 therapy, her migraine headaches had improved dramatically. In fact, they were all but eliminated. She has been able to go months without any migraines, rather than just days. Of course, she was astonished and I, myself, continue to be amazed.

It is difficult for me to remember a case where the patient's migraines did not improve tremendously, if not completely, with proper T3 therapy and normalization of body temperature patterns. Apparently, normalization of body temperature patterns restores proper muscular tone in the blood vessels of the body, and can thereby eliminate the migraine headache condition. Although thyroid hormone therapy can't correct all body temperature abnormalities, or all migraines, I certainly am of the opinion that proper thyroid hormone treatment is the most widely effective treatment for migraine headaches currently available. I am even beginning to wonder if abnormal body temperature patterns (especially low) are not the cause of migraine headaches.

Heat and/or Cold Intolerance

WS sufferers frequently have temperature sensation abnormalities. They will not tolerate temperature extremes very well and often feel extremely uncomfortable in heat, and/or under air conditioning that is a little too cold. Some patients may sweat extremely easily, while others may not sweat at all. Some patients may be convinced that their body temperature runs above normal since they feel hot all the time and sweat easily. These patients are often extremely surprised to find that their body temperature patterns run consistently **below** normal.

These temperature discomforts can lead to conflicts. I refer to these conflicts as "thermostat wars." These thermostat wars take place every day around the country, on the job and at home. I am aware of them because I am frequently told of them by patients. One employee will need sweaters to stand the temperatures that are maintained in the office by coworkers, or a person may need to have a fan to keep cool in an office that is seemingly too hot. Frequently, a husband will turn the thermostat down with the wife turning the thermostat up and vice versa. These wars often carry over into the bedding department also, where spouses may fight over what covers are to be used, with one complaining of freezing while the other is complaining of sweating.

I remember a story of one husband who would complain of being practically scalded each time he went in to use the shower after his wife (who was a WS sufferer). These body temperature sensation abnormalities and intolerance to temperature extremes and sweating abnormalities frequently resolve with normalization of body temperature patterns with proper thyroid hormone treatment.

Hemorrhoids

MED secondary to low body temperature pattern, secondary to DTSF, secondary to Wilson's Syndrome, can result in decreased bowel motility. This can result in constipation and increased "straining at the stool." Straining at the stool, in turn, can lead to increased pressure in the veins surrounding the rectum and anus leading to a bulging of those veins known as hemorrhoids. Hemorrhoids can be extremely uncomfortable and bothersome to say the least. Treatment is frequently directed at the symptoms of hemorrhoidal swelling, hard stools, and straining; through the use of creams, ointments, stool softeners, and dietary changes. When Wilson's Syndrome is the underlying cause, the situation can often be far better handled with proper T3 therapy. With proper therapy, there is a normalization of body temperature patterns which eliminates the MED that is causing the decreased bowel motility resulting in more regular bowel habits, decreased straining at the stool, and thus a decreased tendency for developing hemorrhoids. The condition of these patients hemorrhoids can often be returned very close to normal, leaving them in better shape than they have been in years.

Hives

Hives have been related to Wilson's Syndrome in that they have been seen to come on and resolve together with other symptoms in a pattern characteristic of Wilson's Syndrome. The hives can be precipitated at times of stress, changes in the balance of body fluids, and after a shower. Hives characteristically result from changes in histamine physiology. To the extent that hives, allergies, asthma, itchiness have been seen to sometimes be related in the context of Wilson's Syndrome, I am led to suspect that changes in body temperature patterns can affect histamine physiology.

Hypoglycemia

Hypoglycemia is the condition of having low blood sugar. Symptoms of low blood sugar include shakiness, headaches, breaking out in a sweat, and possibly even lightheadedness or anxiousness when going too long without eating. Interestingly, these symptoms are also similar to those associated with low blood pressure. They can be resolved by eating less simple sugars and more proteins in an attempt to maintain more constant blood sugar levels. That these inappropriate symptoms are sometimes only controlled when the hypoglycemic diet is adhered to closely, supports the idea that the hypoglycemic diet often addresses the symptoms and not the problem. If the diet addressed the problem, then one would expect the inappropriate symptoms to remain improved even after more normal dietary patterns were resumed. One would expect that the patient would be able to be free of hypoglycemic symptoms similar to the way other people are free of these symptoms under similar conditions. Hypoglycemic symptoms have been seen to resolve even persistently through proper administration weaning of T3 therapy.

Infections, Recurrent

The body fights infection with the immune system. Low body temperature patterns resulting in MED can adversely affect the function of the immune system leading patients to have frequent upper respiratory tract infections as well as recurrent urinary tract infections. WS sufferers can have recurrent ear infections, wound infections, fungal infections, and even yeast infections. Antibiotics are commonly required to treat these infections. Sometimes such infections respond less than optimally to antibiotics. Such a predicament might be more worrisome in more serious infections such as severe abdominal infections and bone infections (osteomyelitis) which are more difficult to treat.

When patients' physical resources are already greatly impaired because of trauma or surgery, Multiple Enzyme Dysfunction (resulting in less immune system function) can make it more difficult to fight the infection. This can result in longer hospital stays and even less favorable outcomes.

Some Wilson's Syndrome patients have been seen to have frequent vaginal yeast infections that have cleared up with normalization of body temperature patterns with proper T3 therapy. Some patients have been diagnosed with having a systemic (throughout the body) candida yeast infection. Their candida yeast titers (levels) measured in the blood have been seen to persist even after being treated with nystatin by their doctors. Nystatin is an antifungal medicine used in the treatment of candida yeast infections. In some cases, the candida yeast titers have been seen to drop to zero upon normalization of body temperature patterns with proper T3 therapy. It seems that candida yeast grows in the body more easily in patients who have low body temperature patterns. This may be due to decreased ability of the body to fight the yeast infection because of decreased immune system function, or it might be because the yeast organism finds low body temperatures to be more hospitable for growth than normal body temperature patterns. But, in any case, patients are quite happy when their recurrent yeast infections and urinary tract infections resolve, and they are quite happy when they are able

181

to go through the winter months without having colds and sore throats.

Infertility

Thyroid **gland** function is well known to be one of the first things checked in a patient with a history of infertility. Unfortunately, normal thyroid **gland** function does not always correlate with normal thyroid **system** function. If DTSF can be present even when thyroid blood tests are normal (and it can), then it is easy to understand how infertility can be aggravated by Wilson's Syndrome. One unfortunate patient had finally been able to conceive for the first time, after years of trying, when she was started on thyroid hormone supplementation. Sadly, she miscarried shortly after she switched doctors, and her new OB/GYN doctor discontinued her thyroid medication because he felt that it was not necessary based on her blood tests. Of course, her miscarriage may have had nothing to do with stopping the thyroid medication, but the patient understandably suspected such. With proper thyroid hormone supplementation her symptoms of DTSF once again resolved and she was able to conceive again. This time her thyroid hormone supplementation was maintained throughout her pregnancy and, of course, she was delighted when she gave birth to her first baby.

Insomnia and Narcolepsy

As mentioned previously, patients with Wilson's Syndrome commonly have trouble sleeping at night even though they can be very tired and sleepy during the day. The fatigue noted during the day makes the insomnia related to WS all the more disturbing.

Narcolepsy is the tendency some people have for falling asleep at inappropriate times, whether they like it or not. Several patients that I have seen have gotten into fender-benders because of falling asleep at the wheel. One patient burned her hand when she awakened to find the food she was cooking on the stove had started a fire. In one interesting case, the patient actually fell asleep while she was walking for exercise. As odd as it sounds, she had actually awakened to find herself having taken a couple of steps and veering off her path. She sat down, resting her chest on her legs, and slept for ten or twelve minutes before completing her walk. Such complaints can respond quickly and dramatically to proper thyroid hormone treatment, restoring normal sleep-wake cycles, helping people to sleep at night soundly and to awaken rested so they can face the day without fatigue.

Irregular Periods And Menstrual Cramps

Abnormalities of the menstrual cycle have long been associated with DTSF. In fact, thyroid function is recommended as one of the first things to be checked in a patient with irregular menses. Unfortunately, DTSF is often incorrectly ruled out merely on the basis of thyroid hormone blood tests being within the "normal range," even in the face of classic signs, symptoms, and presentation of DTSF. Low body temperature patterns often result in frequent and heavy periods, but may result in light or skipped periods, as well as other abnormalities. Heavy menstrual cramping is also commonly associated with low body temperature patterns. Again, irregular periods can be seen to follow a pattern of onset, persistence, and resolution characteristic of Wilson's Syndrome symptoms and can respond very well to proper T3 therapy.

Irritability

We discussed previously how Wilson's Syndrome can result in a patient being inappropriately left in "conservation mode." The body may be left in a mode which leads it to feel that it does not have enough resources to address presenting challenges. This explains why WS sufferers often feel as if they are "at the end of their rope". This sensation of being overwhelmed can lead WS sufferers to be profoundly irritable, which is recognized as being clearly inappropriate to themselves and to those around them. Many feel that the symptom of irritability is one of the most devastating aspects of Wilson's Syndrome.

WS sufferers may suffer from mood swings. Mood swings can cause a night and day change in a person's temperament in a period of a day, hours, or even minutes. One minute a person might be having a very good day and then all of a sudden, out of the blue, without any particularly good reason, the patient might plunge into a significantly bad, irritable, or depressed mood. Later, these bad moods may resolve as quickly as they appeared. Patients frequently describe it as an "emotional roller coaster." This phenomenon often disappears completely when body temperature patterns have been normalized with proper T3 therapy.

Itchiness

The itching associated with Wilson's Syndrome can be quite severe, annoying, and even maddening. It may be worse after a shower, associated with dry skin, worse in the evening or in the morning (when body temperatures are usually lower), and associated with the other patterns and characteristics of Wilson's Syndrome. Sometimes the itchiness is so severe that it leads people to scratch enough to break the skin with their nails, thereby developing sores. The scratching can also prevent wounds from healing.

Lightheadedness

The lightheadedness that is sometimes associated with Wilson's Syndrome, and sometimes resolves with normalization of body temperature patterns with proper T3 therapy, seems to be related to body fluid balance and blood pressure and/or blood sugar changes associated with Wilson's Syndrome.

Low Blood Pressure

Low blood pressure can cause lightheadedness, clamminess, anxiety, and others. Low blood pressure symptoms can frequently be made worse when a patient stands very rapidly. Normally, changes take place in the vascular system that enable a person to maintain their blood pressure when

184

changing from a lying or sitting position to a standing position. When these vascular changes are not as responsive as they should be, or when the body has difficulty maintaining normal blood pressure because of low body temperature patterns, or because of decreased blood volumes (due to blood loss, shock, or dehydration), then one might have difficulty in maintaining a normal blood pressure. Proper T3 therapy has been seen to alleviate these symptoms of intermittently low blood pressure. It is my feeling that MED leads to decreased vascular tone and decreased vascular responsiveness leading to more difficulty in maintaining adequate blood pressure. It's a little like using a pair of vice-grips or adjustable pliers that are set at the wrong setting to exert pressure on a particular pipe. If the pliers are set too "loose" even though one may be able to squeeze the handles all the way together, the "jaws" may still be positioned so far apart that they cannot exert the proper pressure upon the pipe to accomplish what is necessary.

Memory and Concentration, Decreased

Many times patients state that they feel as if they are in a mental fog. They describe having short-term memory problems of the sort where they will walk from one room to another and forget why they are there. During their conversations they may begin a sentence and forget their point halfway through. They may hear an interesting news story and wait anxiously for the opportunity to relate the exciting news break to their spouse, only to find that they are able to remember so few of the details that they may not even be able to communicate the gist of the story. They may have short term memory problems at work and may even forget temporarily the last names of people with whom they have worked closely for years. They frequently have difficulty studying for exams, finding themselves reading the same page over and over and over again six or seven times, still not being able to remember what they have read. Some patients will pick up old novels they have read before and will realize they have already read it only after reading three quarters of the way through the book. They frequently have difficulty concentrating on tasks at work and find that their minds wander easily. With proper T3 therapy, the mental fog can be lifted enabling people to remember what they are saying, what they are doing, and what they are reading. Proper therapy can even help WS sufferers in their studies.

When a patient has difficulty remembering things or paying attention as an adult, it may be said they have a short term memory problem or decreased concentration. When such symptoms are found in children, especially when coupled with other symptoms of Wilson's Syndrome such as irritability, such patients are sometimes said to have attention deficient disorder (ADD), be "hyperactive", or be learning disabled.

Learning that the tendency for developing Wilson's Syndrome can be hereditary, a patient who had been responding very well to T3 therapy, brought her son in to be evaluated as well. It was found that he was frequently quite tired and had trouble concentrating at school and was having difficulty with his studies. Multiple body temperature readings demonstrated that his average body temperature ran consistently below normal, around 97.8 degrees. In many ways he was similar to the way his mother was prior to treatment. Somewhere along the line he had been diagnosed as having attention deficit disorder (he was approximately 12 years old). With normalization of his body temperature pattern with proper T3 therapy, his fatigue resolved and he found his classes more interesting. In fact, shortly after he had started therapy, he brought home a decidedly uncharacteristic A+ on one of his assignments. Both mother and son could see an unequivocal improvement in his school performance.

Motivation/Ambition, Decreased

As discussed in previous chapters, there can be a good physiological reason WS sufferers frequently feel as if they do not have enough resources to adequately address the challenges that face them. Molehills often seem to be mountains. We all know what it feels like to have days when we just don't feel like doing much, whether because of illness or discouragement or other reasons. These same feelings often are very exaggerated in patients with WS. Their

186

overwhelmed feelings, and lack of ambition or motivation are often quite inappropriate in relation to their current living situation (with there being no apparent reason or explanation).

This one symptom accounts for a scenario repeated time and time again every day throughout this country to which most of are completely oblivious. There are seemingly able-bodied people, who for no apparent reason (and not because they want to), will spend hours during the day, days on end, for even weeks and months virtually doing nothing more than sleeping or sitting in a chair. It is hard to imagine the impact this one symptom can have in the quality of life and productivity in the lives of these individuals and, therefore, in our society. I have seen, first hand, working with some of these patients the toll it takes in terms of their careers, days off from work, lost business opportunities, failed businesses, and the costs to employers.

Musculoskeletal Strains

Sprains and strains of tendons, ligaments, and muscles might persist inappropriately in WS sufferers. For example, shoulder strains may take too long to heal in weight lifters. Calf muscle strains may recur too frequently, too easily, and last too long in an aerobics instructor. When the fluid retention is in the joints of the chest around the breast bone or in the tissues of the chest, it can cause significant chest pains. These chest pains can mimic myocardial infarction or heart attack. A few patients with Wilson's Syndrome develop severe crushing chest pains for which they are rushed to the hospital. EKG and all other tests show no significant cardiac abnormalities. These patients' chest pains may continue intermittently. After cardiac stress tests and other of the most reliable predictive tests available rule out cardiac abnormalities, the patients are left to find some other explanation for their chest pains. Occasionally, these chest pains can follow patterns of onset and resolution consistent with other symptoms of Wilson's Syndrome.

WS sufferers who have inappropriately nagging musculoskeletal problems, frequently find their musculoskeletal systems return to more appropriate levels of functioning with correction of their Wilson's Syndrome.

Nails, Unhealthy

Patients with WS often notice that their nails are brittle, peeling, splitting, pitting, ridged, soft, or not growing as well as compared to prior to the onset of WS. They can also be more susceptible to fungal infections of the nails and skin infections around the nails.

Pigmentation, Skin And Hair, Changes In

Chloasma is a mask-like area of pigmentation of the skin on the face that can frequently be associated with pregnancy (sometimes referred to as a "pregnancy mask") and birth control pills. Chloasma is known to be related to hormonal changes. Chloasma is a darkening of the pigmentation of the skin sometimes resembling "blotches," a collection of freckles, or can even resemble someone who has gotten a suntan that has partly peeled. The discoloration is commonly seen on the forehead, above the upper lip (like a "mustache"), and over the cheeks.

When chloasma persists after the birth of a child or after birth control pills have been discontinued or after other such events, it can frequently be difficult to correct and is not generally considered to be "curable." Amazingly, the chloasma of some patients has been seen to fade considerably (even up to 90 - 95%) upon normalization of body temperature patterns with proper T3 therapy. This is especially true in cases where the patient's chloasma followed typical pattern of presentation of a Wilson's Syndrome symptom.

In the beginning of this book, we discussed how body temperature can affect the color of a Siamese cat's fur. I remember one patient who found that her hair began changing in color from brown to white with the onset of her Wilson's Syndrome symptoms. She, her hairdresser, and I, myself, were able to observe her hair color returning more to its original color as her symptoms of Wilson's Syndrome resolved with proper liothyronine treatment. This may give credence to stories that are sometimes told about people's hair turning white after being terrified, or after a severe physical stress such as a heart attack. There are fables about people's hair turning white after "seeing a ghost." There may be some basis for this popular saying about terror causing a person's hair to turn white.

Poliosis is the medical term for premature graying of the hair. Poliosis has been seen in the past to be a possible effect of severe hypothyroidism. (*Emergency Medicine Reports*, Volume II, Number 23, 11/5/90). Since WS is a cause of DTSF, one can see some basis for the common comment that stressful ˙times can give people "a few gray hairs." Some people notice that their hair can become more gray at stressful times and less gray when the stress has passed. Their hair can sometimes be observed to go back and forth between more and less gray several times in their lives.

Another interesting phenomenon that has been observed to follow the pattern of presentation and resolution of Wilson's Syndrome symptoms, is that of the skin under a person's rings becoming black. Some patients may find the skin under their wedding band becomes black in spite of wearing 18 or 24 karat gold. Some patients find that white gold will not cause the phenomenon, while yellow gold will. The interesting thing is that the blackening of the skin sometimes comes and goes with other symptoms of Premenstrual Syndrome, occurring only for a period of time prior to the monthly menstrual cycle and then disappearing again after the menstrual cycle. In one memorable case the patient's symptom of "black finger" resolved and did not occur premenstrually, or at any time, once her body temperature patterns were normalized with proper thyroid therapy. Her "black finger" resolved together with her other symptoms of PMS and Wilson's Syndrome.

Post-prandial Response, Increased

We all are familiar with the increased fatigue and sleepiness that sometimes settle in after a large meal. Post-prandial means after a meal. With a meal, the body "changes gears" in order to digest the food. It accomplishes this by changes that take place in the nervous system. The body decreases what is called the sympathetic nervous system tone and increases the parasympathetic tone, which results in the shunting of more blood away from the skeletal muscles and towards the digestive tract. The sympathetic nervous system is sometimes thought of as the "fight or flight" side of the nervous system that is involved in more active pursuits. The para-sympathetic nervous system is sometimes remembered as the sleep/feed/breed side of the nervous system and is useful in more relaxed pursuits. It is normal to feel more relaxed or drowsy after a meal because of the increased para-sympathetic tone of the nervous system. However, in Wilson's Syndrome sufferers, the post-prandial response can be very inappropriately exaggerated. This may lead WS sufferers to practically "collapse," "pass out," or be "useless" after a meal such as lunch. This exaggerated response has been seen to resolve in many cases with normalization of body temperature patterns with proper T3 therapy.

Premenstrual Syndrome

Premenstrual Syndrome is an extremely fascinating aspect of Wilson's Syndrome. In may ways, the symptoms of Premenstrual Syndrome (PMS), are remarkably similar to the symptoms of DTSF and may include lightheadedness, dizziness, gas bloating, weight gain, fluid retention, headache, depression, irritability, fatigue, constipation, increased bruising, muscular aches, and others. It is also well known that PMS symptoms follow a menstrual pattern, typically being more severe right before a woman's menstrual cycle begins. However, I have seen some cases where the patients' symptoms are aggravated just after their period with their symptoms being exactly like the symptoms of PMS except happening "post"-menstrual. So there are some people who have PMS **after** their period or—"Postmenstrual Syndrome." This can easily be explained within the framework of Wilson's Syndrome. It is well known that a woman's body temperature will change during her menstrual cycle, commonly spiking (rising sharply and then decreasing sharply) at ovulation and then usually increasing again more gradually, and averaging highest prior to or at the beginning of a woman's period. The temperature typically will decrease gradually during the menses and may even reach a low point after the period is over.

As discussed previously, the symptoms of Wilson's Syndrome are preeminently symptoms of Multiple Enzyme Dysfunction that are caused by aberrations in enzyme temperature. Temperature changes that can affect enzyme function can include temperatures that are too low, too high, or too unsteady. Rapidly changing body temperatures can cause enzyme dysfunction because of a too rapid change of enzyme shape/configuration that does not allow proper enzyme function. Premenstrual symptoms can easily be explained by enzyme dysfunction brought on by abnormal body temperature patterns (too low, too high, or especially unsteady/changing rapidly). This can also explain why some women have similar symptoms at the time of ovulation (there are still those who do not believe that some women who can tell fairly well when they ovulate), and **post** menstrually. Women trying to get pregnant will frequently take advantage of these well known menstrual cycle related body temperature changes by taking daily temperatures, in an attempt to identify the time of ovulation by the mid-cycle body temperature "spike".

Incidentally, this can explain what one might call "reverse PMS." There are patients who will feel the symptoms of MED, being tired, depressed, bloated, irritable, etc. for most of the month, but notice that just prior to their menstrual cycle, they may enjoy two days out of the month when they feel much improved before feeling worse again. It may be that the patients' MED symptoms are resulting from persistently low body temperature patterns that improve briefly just prior to the period as the female hormone system raises the body temperature. This causes the patients' body temperature patterns to more closely approach normal for a brief period of time, helping them to enjoy improvement in their symptoms of MED. When patient's symptoms of MED come and go giving them good days and bad days, patients can frequently see that their body temperature patterns are closer to normal on their good days as compared to their bad days.

Of course, menstrual cycles are female hormone related. And certainly, body temperature patterns change in a predictable and reproducible way during the menstrual cycle. It stands to reason, therefore, that female hormones may have an influence on body temperature patterns. Thyroid hormones also affect body temperature patterns, and body temperature patterns correlate well with symptoms of MED. **So it follows that body temperature patterns depend, to a degree, on the relative influences of the female thyroid system (a**

cyclic influence) and the thyroid system (a more constant influence). It seems that the more steady thyroid hormone influence on body temperature pattern, normally dilutes the more cyclic influence of the female hormone system, preventing the body temperature pattern from being so aberrant that it result in the symptoms of MED. However, when the thyroid system influence decreases because of Wilson's Syndrome, more of the cyclic influence of the female hormone system can be "unmarked" leading to symptoms of MED that can worsen and improve in a pattern that correlates with the menstrual cycle (Premenstrual Syndrome).

When PMS is caused by Wilson's Syndrome, the MED symptoms that seem to follow a female hormone influence can often be completely resolved with proper T3 therapy. By restoring the more stabilizing influence of the thyroid system to normal levels, one may dilute the cyclic influence of the female hormone system once again ("masking" it), thereby, eliminating the symptoms of PMS. (See Diagram 9-1) This explains why female hormone therapy can sometimes be used to improve the symptoms of PMS (by altering the female hormone influence). It is difficult, however, to diminish the cyclic influence of the female hormone influence using female hormones because it is difficult to predict when that influence is on the way up and when it is on the way down. If the female hormones are added at the wrong time, the additional influence may add on to a "peak" rather than filling in a "valley" which can make the situation worse.

DIAGRAM 9-1

HOW THE INFLUENCES OF THYROID HORMONES AND
FEMALE HORMONES CAN RESULT IN CYCLIC PATTERNS OF
MED (PMS) IN WILSON'S SYNDROME PATIENTS

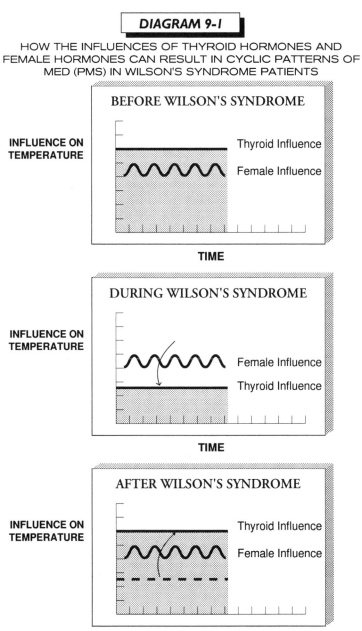

BEFORE WILSON'S SYNDROME

INFLUENCE ON TEMPERATURE — Thyroid Influence / Female Influence

TIME

DURING WILSON'S SYNDROME

INFLUENCE ON TEMPERATURE — Female Influence / Thyroid Influence

TIME

AFTER WILSON'S SYNDROME

INFLUENCE ON TEMPERATURE — Thyroid Influence / Female Influence

TIME

193

For this reason, female hormones frequently fail to eliminate the symptoms of PMS completely. And the PMS symptoms do not commonly remain persistently improved after female hormone therapy has been discontinued. This suggests that the female hormone therapy may not be addressing the underlying problem.

I sometimes use the following analogy to explain the use of female hormones and thyroid hormones in addressing the problem of PMS: If you needed something that was on a shelf that was too high to reach, you could either lower the shelf or get a stepladder (two solutions to the same problem). In that same way, both thyroid and female hormones can be used to affect the symptoms of Premenstrual Syndrome. The most appropriate treatment depends on the underlying cause of the symptoms. If the symptoms of PMS appear in combination with other symptoms of WS and they appear in a group, especially worsening after a major stress, then it is more likely that all the symptoms are related, and it is more likely that they are related to an impairment in the conversion of T4 to T3 resulting in aberrant body temperature patterns. Patients with Premenstrual Syndrome related to Wilson's Syndrome often find that when they are properly treated with liothyronine, that their symptoms can be alleviated greatly and often completely. Again, when careful history is taken, one may find that a patients' PMS symptoms appeared initially or became especially worse after a major stress such as childbirth or divorce. I have treated many patients who have continued to be troubled by severe and even disabling PMS in spite of having received other treatments for years. Many times with proper T3 treatment normalizing their body temperature pattern, the patients will find that for the first time in years their period can sneak up on them (and their clothes) without the first PMS symptom or warning. Needless to say, these patients and their families are quite happy when the PMS resolves.

Psoriasis

Psoriasis is characterized by silvery, scaly patches of skin found commonly on the elbows, knees, and knuckles of the hands. The cause of psoriasis, as yet, is not known and it is frequently difficult to treat. It is interesting that the pattern of distribution of psoriasis is similar to the pattern of distribution of dry skin that can be associated with Wilson's Syndrome. These areas of the body are characterized by having lower temperatures than other areas of the body. I have seen in some cases, that the psoriasis can improve considerably with normalization of body temperature patterns with proper T3 therapy. However, this symptom does not respond as predictably and reproducibly as many of the other symptoms of Wilson's Syndrome.

Self-esteem, Decreased

Another corresponding or accompanying complaint is a feeling of overall low self-esteem, and the feeling of being out of control which can lead to, among other things, anorexia and bulimia. Patients sometimes find themselves functioning at obviously inadequate levels. They often feel as if they cannot control their emotions, their reactions, or their thoughts. They find it difficult to find the motivation to accomplish even simple tasks. Yet, when they notice these shortcomings and they cannot, by looking at themselves in the mirror, see anything wrong, they can begin to have diminished self-esteem. They sometimes have an overwhelming feeling of not being in control of their lives. All these feelings are very understandable when one considers the physiological process underlying Wilson's Syndrome and the consequent decrease in available resources to cope with the normal tasks of daily living. Occasionally, these feelings can be coupled with an increased tendency toward inappropriate weight gain. This can lead to feelings of guilt and self-disgust. Such a situation may lead a person to resort to eating-disorder behavior such as anorexia and/or bulimia.

One such patient I recall was a 26-year-old woman complaining of classic signs and symptoms of Wilson's Syndrome. She admitted to a four-year history of bulimia that had ended one year prior to seeing me. With treatment her symptoms quickly resolved. Only after her symptoms of WS had resolved was she able to admit that she had not quit her bulimic behavior a year previously, but was still actively bulimic with episodes of vomiting even up to nine times a day up until the time that I began treating her. As her level of resources, and balance of variables affecting her weight were normalized, she noticed that her inappropriate feelings of being overwhelmed and having a lack of resources lifted. Her improvement has persisted even though proper T3 therapy has since been weaned. She stated that since the thyroid treatment had restored her to feeling "normal" again, she has found that she no longer has the tendency for bulimic behavior. Interestingly, the patient's weight was not significantly different after treatment as compared to before.

Another patient I had treated had a long standing history of anorexia. With treatment and resolution of her other symptoms of Wilson's Syndrome, her feelings about herself and her priorities changed over a period of months. Her anorexia tendencies have resolved. She is now so appreciative of feeling happy, healthy, strong, and functional, that she is not preoccupied about her weight. Prior to treatment, she was eating virtually nothing and it was only after treatment that she began eating three meals a day in a more normal meal pattern. To the astonishment of her children, she would even share meals with them at the table, which is something the children had not seen in years. They weren't accustomed to their mother sitting down for dinner in front of a plate of food and eating dinner with them. They were extremely excited at this development.

With such dramatic responses, in some cases, to proper recognition and treatment of WS and DTSF, one can see that some of the psychological, social, and mental disorders that people many times assume are in people's minds, frequently have an extremely significant physiological component.

Sex drive, Decreased; And Anhedonia

These patients frequently suffer from a diminished interest in sex, or decreased enjoyment of sex. As far as survival goes, it is certainly a luxury function. It is necessary for propagation and continuation of the species, but is not critical for the day to day survival in the way that food and water are. Being a luxury or expendable function, it is one of the first things to go when one goes into conservation mode. In other words, with the onset of Wilson's Syndrome, decreased libido is a very common finding. It can also be one of the last things to return in the course of proper thyroid therapy. Nevertheless, sometimes the change in sex drive or returning of the sex drive with treatment can be dramatic. Some patients comment that they have forgotten over the years what it felt like to have a normal sex drive and helps them to remember what it was like to be young, and it helps them to have more empathy for the younger generation and the issues and circumstances which they face.

I remember one patient who had such a dramatic increase in her sex drive with normalization of her body temperature patterns, that she was, as she says, literally "beside herself," especially since her lover was to be out of town for another week. Of course, this is an extreme but many patients relate that their husbands (and husbands relate personally) are quite happy about being "attacked" by their wives for the first time in a long time.

Another patient had been having uncomfortable, if not painful intercourse for months. She was only 26 years old, but after the death of a pet for which she cared deeply (her dog), she developed a constellation of symptoms consistent with WS together with sexual intercourse becoming more and more uncomfortable, even painful. This disturbing complaint did not respond well to treatment by her gynecologist. When the patient was referred to me from her gynecologist, it was suspected that she might have been suffering from Wilson's Syndrome. Two weeks after therapy was initiated, all of her symptoms had resolved completely, without exception, and she and her husband were both very pleased about her first sexual encounter without pain in many months (possibly years).

Anhedonia is a decreased or complete lack of the capacity to enjoy life, causing people to be unable to even find enjoyment in the things they used to find interesting.

For example, a once avid golfer who may go through a surgery or the death of a loved one or some other significant stress, may develop a constellation of symptoms characteristic of Wilson's Syndrome. He might be so fatigued, depressed, and tired that he may no longer have any desire or interest in golf, even though he once found it extremely enjoyable. This lack of interest in a formerly favorite pastime might persist even after the emotional trauma or physical trauma has passed. All other things in his life remain the same. He may have a great family life, a great marriage, great children, great job, and satisfaction in the other aspects of his life. However, his huge lack of interest in his favorite pastime may persist, even though he is physically capable. When the body temperature patterns were normalized in one such patient, his interest returned together with the resolution of other of his typical symptoms of Wilson's Syndrome.

Sexual Development, Inhibited

It is well known that the function of the thyroid system is very critical in the normal growth and development of people. When babies are first born, one of the first things checked is thyroid function. This is to prevent complications that would arise with deficient thyroid system function, primarily mental and growth retardation. We have already discussed the interaction between the thyroid hormone and female hormone systems. One of the first things checked in patients with PMS, infertility, or irregular periods is thyroid system status. How a person's body develops sexually certainly has a lot to do with the influence of available sex hormones. It is easy to understand how the thyroid system might be an important consideration in patients who are experiencing delayed growth and/or delayed secondary sexual characteristic development such as the growth of pubic and axillary hair, facial hair in men, genital development, and breast development. One memorable patient I was treating had come from a family with a hereditary predisposition for Wilson's Syndrome (her mother's WS also responded well to T3 therapy). This 18-year-old young woman had one menstrual cycle when she was in the 8th grade and had not had another on her own since. She had difficulty gaining weight, was extremely fatigued, had significant hair loss, and several other symptoms of Wilson's Syndrome. At the age of 14, because of very little sexual differentiation or development, she was started on female hormones and did enjoy gaining a little bit more weight in the hips and upper legs. She was able to have periods with the regulation of these female hormones, but still was not developing physical sexual characteristics in a way that she and others would consider normal. At the age of 18 years old, she was started on T3 therapy. Her WS symptoms improved over a period of 6 to 8 months or more. Finally, when her symptoms of fatigue, hair loss, and other WS symptoms were 80 to 90% resolved, she was able to wean off the female hormones. Later with further adjustment of her T3 therapy, she was able to have a period on her own again for the first time in 10 years. It had been the only other time in her life that she had a menstrual cycle on her own without the aid of female hormones. She was also quite pleased to notice, that at the age of 18, she began to enjoy the development of physical sexual changes. Her skin became less pale with a thickening of subcutaneous (under the skin) tissue, which resulted in a softening of her features causing them to appear more feminine and womanly. Also at the age of 18 her breasts began developing. Her menstrual cycles were irregular at first, then were coming every 2 weeks, then every 3 weeks, and now she enjoys a normal monthly menstrual cycle. These improvements have persisted, even though her T3 therapy has been weaned to extremely minimal levels.

Hers is a good case to demonstrate how some people's growth and development can be greatly affected by thyroid system function and that impairment in this function can be commonly overlooked. It can be easily treated and have an untold influence on the lives of these patients. Her case is among the most notable because of the enormous impact that I feel that proper thyroid treatment has had on her life.

Skin infections/Acne, Increased

The body fights infection through the immune system. The immune system relies heavily on the action of enzymes for its function. Because of MED, the function of the immune system can decrease leading to more frequent, more severe, and longer lasting skin infections. Of course, acne is a well known symptom of DTSF. Acne is frequently a disease of adolescence and early teen years and is usually outgrown. When a person develops acne later in life after a major stress together with other symptoms of Wilson's Syndrome, presenting in a way that is characteristic of other WS symptoms, and when it resolves with proper T3 therapy, it is easy to see how acne can be related to WS. WS patients frequently say with regard to their acne problems: "I'm too old for this." Of course, WS can occur at any age, and body temperature patterns should be considered in any patient who is complaining of acne. Acne is frequently treated with antibiotics such as tetracycline, long term. One WS sufferer had been less than perfectly controlled on four years of daily tetracycline therapy for her acne. With proper T3 therapy her acne resolved and she was able to wean off the tetracycline enjoying a persistent improvement in her acne even without tetracycline therapy.

Susceptibility to Substance Abuse, Increased

With Wilson's Syndrome there is a very good physiological reason for feelings of being overwhelmed and of not having the levels of resources, energy, or enjoyment of life that many of us take for granted. Many times these patients turn to caffeine consumption for energy and an increased feeling of well-being. They will often pick up cigarettes as a habit because the nicotine seems to provide them with just a little more energy. Chocolate is a commonly used substance especially prior to

200

the menstrual cycle. These patients also sometimes turn to alcohol and drug use. Inappropriate weight gain is common after one quits smoking, as many smokers are well aware. Many times patients will return to cigarette smoking, even after having successfully quit the habit, because of their weight gain. With proper thyroid treatment, some WS sufferers have noticed being less susceptible to substance abuse such as smoking, caffeine, chocolate and alcohol.

Swallowing and Throat Sensations, Abnormal

Some of the more fascinating complaints associated with WS are a variety of complaints involving the throat and swallowing. Upon careful questioning, patients will often admit to abnormal throat sensations. Their complaints are variously described but are consistent with the other symptoms of WS in that they follow patterns of onset and resolution consistent with WS symptoms. Sometimes they complain of the sensation of there being a "lump in their throat" or feeling as if somebody is pushing in on their throat with a pointed finger. Many times they cannot stand to have anything resting snugly around their neck. They are often bothered by tight collars, turtle necks, snugly-fitting jewelry, another person's hand, or even the thought of anything resting against their neck. I call this "collar intolerance." It is a very interesting complaint, considering it can be present even without any visible or palpable ("feelable") abnormality of the patient's neck. And, the complaint can resolve with proper thyroid treatment even without any discernible change of the patient's neck being detected by the patient or doctor. It is difficult to explain why this symptom occurs, but I suspect it may be due to changes in pharyngeal (throat and swallowing) muscle tone resulting from MED. I feel that the decreased muscle tone leaves the patient's neck feeling more vulnerable.

Patients do also occasionally complain of difficulty swallowing that follows typical presentation and resolution patterns of Wilson's Syndrome symptoms. One such patient had so much difficulty swallowing that she had the misfortune one day of having a lump of mashed potatoes get stuck in her throat.

Since she could not swallow it, it was necessary for her to poke a hole through the center of the mashed potatoes with her pinky finger in order to have a passage through which to breathe. This difficulty swallowing was present despite of the lack of any obvious swelling or inflammation of her thyroid gland (which, of course, is a small butterfly shaped gland at the base of the neck below the "Adam's apple"). Yet her swallowing difficulties responded well to T3 therapy.

Many times such patients will undergo intensive ear, nose, and throat evaluations in search of some explanation for their complaints, with all test appearing to be within the normal range. Patients are frequently concerned about having a "tumor", or some kind of cancer growing in their neck to explain the sensation of having a "lump" in their throat. Of course, these examinations, evaluations, and tests to rule out cancer are always advisable. However, it is interesting that no tumor growth, lump or any other anatomical abnormality can be seen with even the most sophisticated scanners, and yet, the odd sensation will frequently resolve with normalization of body temperature patterns with proper T3 therapy. Occasionally, patients will also complain of pains radiating or shooting up their neck towards their ears and may sometimes have ear pain as well.

Sweating Abnormalities

Interestingly, WS sufferers sometimes notice that they no longer sweat - at all. Other patients describe having the onset of excessive sweating, to the point of pouring like a faucet. In some cases, where the patient has essentially suffered form Wilson's Syndrome since birth, treatment can resolve the symptoms of Wilson's Syndrome while helping the patient to sweat, even if they have never (according to them) sweat before. Most of the patients welcome this change. Frequently, excessive sweating resolves as well, especially if it follows the typical pattern and presentation of Wilson's Syndrome symptoms. I believe that the excessive sweating may be due to increased amounts of adrenaline secondary to the body's compensation to persistently low blood pressure, resulting from low body temperature patterns. Patients often describe their sweating to be continual, but frequently it will be made worse upon standing rapidly, which is consistent with low blood pressure problems. They may experience profuse sweating which they will frequently be able to correlate with a sensation of lightheadedness or dizziness when the sweating is at its worst. The body compensates for low blood pressure by gearing up the nervous system (and thereby the sweat glands) to prevent the body from fainting. This process can result in not only sweating, but also increased heart rate, lightheadedness, and even palpitations.

One common manifestation consistent with WS is night sweats. WS sufferers will frequently notice that they might be awakened out of a sleep dripping wet. Often, they will also notice their heart to be pounding at the same time. These patients may also notice dizziness when they stand up to get out of bed while they are having a night sweat. It is felt these night sweats, heart poundings, and dizziness are probably due to low blood pressure, low blood sugar (because they improve sometimes with a nighttime snack), or both. If patients suffer from low blood pressure secondary to MED, secondary to low body temperature patterns, it would be understandable how the symptoms might be worse at night, since the body temperature patterns are usually lowest while a person is sleeping.

Tinnitus (Ringing In The Ears)

Many patients suffering from WS notice a disturbing ringing in their ears that often correlates closely with the pattern of onset and resolution of the symptom of fluid retention. Many times they will go to several doctors and get many sophisticated tests on their hearing and inner ear with the tests showing no apparent abnormality. They are left without any predictive diagnosis or any effective treatment. This symptom can be very disabling at times and very annoying. Some patients complain that the ringing in their ears is essentially driving them nuts. This ringing of the ears is sometimes, but not always, associated with dizziness as well. But tinnitus has been seen to come on with other symptoms of WS after a stress and resolve with the other symptoms upon normalization of body temperature patterns with proper thyroid treatment.

Weight Gain, Inappropriate

The issue of weight is an important one. Doctors are continually advising patients of the importance of maintaining a normal weight. And, in our society, all manner of praise, reward, criticism, and disrespect are ascribed to people according to their weight. How people are seen by themselves and others can sometimes be greatly influenced by the issue of weight. Health and life insurance premium tables are often determined in part upon height and weight charts. Apparently, it is felt that abnormal weight can increase the chances of one having adverse medical conditions and can decrease life expectancy. Excessive weight has been seen to aggravate certain breathing and heart problems, and can contribute to the onset and interfere with the treatment of diabetes.

It is well known that decreased thyroid system function can lead to inappropriate weight gain. With decreased levels of active thyroid hormone at the site of the cells, the resulting decrease in the body's metabolism can lead to an increase in one's weight, even if there is no change in a person's diet, exercise, or life style patterns.

This inappropriate weight gain is easy to understand in light of DTSF. No doctor is surprised by a patient's inappropriate weight gain when it is accompanied by fluid retention, fatigue, depression, migraines, dry skin, dry hair, hair loss, decreased memory, constipation, cold intolerance, and thyroid hormone blood tests that are outside the "normal range." In such cases, physicians might feel a great urgency in correcting the patient's thyroid hormone deficiency and tell the patient, "No wonder you gained so much weight so quickly and so easily."

It is very odd that many of the same doctors react much differently when the thyroid blood tests are found to be in the "normal range." Even when the patient is suffering from even **more** dramatic inappropriate weight gain coupled with even **more** severe fluid retention, fatigue, depression, dry skin, dry

204

hair, hair loss, constipation, heat and cold intolerance, and decreased memory. The doctor might completely dismiss the possibility of DTSF based solely upon the "normal" results of some currently available thyroid hormone blood tests. It seems very odd in situations such as these that physicians seem to reach such definite conclusions based on a few currently available thyroid hormone blood tests. Many physicians seem to act as tests directly measure or directly reflect (predictably and reproducibly) the interaction of the thyroid hormone at the thyroid hormone receptor in every cell of the body, which, of course, is not necessarily the case. Currently, the thyroid hormone blood tests available can be useful in showing that there probably is a problem that could cause DTSF. They are not, however, useful in determining that there definitely is **not** a problem present that could result in DTSF. This distinction is made when one considers the percentage of false negatives, false positives, true negatives, and true positives of a given test as discussed in chapter 4.

To illustrate the point, one may easily conclude as one approaches a pay telephone with a severed receiver cord that the phone is probably out of order. However, just because the receiver cord is intact does not necessarily mean that the phone is **not** out of order. Likewise, just because a patient has no problem that is immediately obvious with currently available tests does not necessarily mean that the patient **has no** problem. Hence the old medical adage: "Treat the patient not the blood tests." This adage discourages doctors from being too closed-minded and discourages us from being lead to faulty conclusions by blowing the significance of tests out of proportion to their obvious limitations.

For the sake of discussion, let us say that almost all physicians are familiar with the signs and symptoms characteristic of DTSF. Let us also say that they are familiar with some of the causes of DTSF (such as hypopituitarism and hypothyroidism). Many physicians, however, seem to have overlooked the most common cause of DTSF (Wilson's Syndrome) and aren't yet well familiar with it.

Of course, not everyone who feels that they are gaining too much weight in relation to their diet and exercise level is suffering from DTSF. But DTSF is more than enough to explain why someone may have difficulty with their weight. Easy weight gain has long been associated with DTSF, but the most common cause of DTSF (Wilson's Syndrome) is often overlooked. It is easy for most doctors to understand how a patient could gain weight on 800 calories when the patient is suffering from DTSF. It seems odd then how some physicians can boldly declare that it is impossible for a particular patient to be able to gain weight on 500 to 800 calories based solely on the results of a few far-less-than conclusive blood tests.

It is well known that different people have different caloric requirements to maintain their health and body weight. Some sources suggest the average woman needs approximately 1700 calories per day and the average man approximately 2300 calories per day. Of course, a person's caloric requirements can change under various conditions. Under starvation conditions or during fasting, the amount of calories utilized can decrease because of the body's compensation to the conditions. To some extent, this is accomplished through the compensatory decrease in T4 to T3 thyroid hormone conversion. This was well demonstrated by a study done by A.G. Vagenakis (University of Massachusetts Medical School, *Journal of Clinical Endocrinology and Metabolism*; 41, 191) who showed that under fasting conditions the level of T3 in certain patients dropped by 50% as their levels of RT3 increased by 50%. Also, a decrease in the amount of calories burned per day during fasting conditions, and persistently even after fasting conditions ended, has been documented. (*Adaptation of Energy Metabolism of Overweight Women to Low-energy Intake, Studied with Whole Body Calorimeters*, American Journal Clinical Nutrition 1986; 44:585-595.)

The amount of calories burned per day can vary tremendously. How this is possible can be understood by considering the difference in energy required to make a car, as compared to the energy required to drive a car. To make a car one needs to dig up ore that can be refined into metal, one needs to drill oil wells to have the oil necessary to lubricate the cars, one

206

would need to get the vinyl and other materials to make the car's upholstery. One would have to design and make molds to fabricate certain parts, hire the necessary labor to put the parts together, build the factories necessary to make the car, obtain the rubber for the tires, and assemble the parts into the proper order so that the car functions. All these activities take a huge amount of energy to accomplish. The energy required to drive and operate the car is far less. Once there is sufficient gasoline in the gas tank, one must sit behind the wheel, turn the ignition key, put the car in gear, press the gas pedal, and use the steering wheel to direct the car. So one can operate a car, traveling all over the country, on a similar amount of energy required to make, for example, just the transmission. In the same way the vast majority of the energy used in the affairs of the human body are used in producing and maintaining the molecules, cells, and tissues of the body. In other words, the energy to make hair, skin, and teeth is a great deal more than the energy necessary to brush hair, brush teeth, and wash the skin. To make heart muscle, skeletal muscle, and bones takes a great deal more energy than is necessary to walk around the house or through the mall. To make and maintain babies, ear drums, eye balls, throats, etc. takes a great deal more energy than does exercising in a spa for two hours every other day or week. A great deal of energy is also necessary to make memories, good moods, ideas and emotion. The body can greatly adjust or change the amount of energy that it uses by affecting how much energy is used at any given time in the production and maintenance of tissues.

Under periods of stress, the body can decrease the maintenance of tissues to conserve energy that instead may be necessary for operation of the body. It can do this by impairing the conversion of T4 to T3, thereby dropping the body temperature. When the body temperature drops, the function of the enzymes that are most susceptible to temperature changes can be impaired. It is interesting that the body chooses the most expendable tissues to sacrifice under periods of stress to ensure the survival of the organism. For this reason these patients will first complain of dry skin, decreased hair growth, brittle hair, hair loss, peeling and splitting fingernails, thin eyebrows, decreased sex drive, etc., as opposed to functions more vital for survival, such as vision, hearing, heart and muscle function, etc. Under severe conditions (fasting for days, weeks, and even months at a time), the body's maintenance of tissues can decrease to a very low level, enabling a person to survive even on 300 to 500 calories per day. When times are better and when the stress is relieved, the body's metabolism returns to normal leading to regeneration and renewed maintenance of the tissues that have been neglected.

Some tissues can maintain their function quite well for long periods of time, even after their maintenance has been drastically reduced (for example much of the protection afforded by the skin can be attributed to layers upon layers of cells that have actually already died, which makes those layers less dependent on maintenance of living cells for considerable lengths of time, even weeks, while still providing function). The unfortunate thing is that sometimes after the stress has passed, the metabolism does not come back up and does not regenerate the tissues as well as it should, resulting in a persistence of the classic symptoms of DTSF. This can explain the phenomenon that has been observed many times in many places all over the country. Many times I have seen patients who have tried to convince others that their weight problem was not caused by them eating too much. To get to the bottom of the matter, many of these patients have been hospitalized, with their doctors giving the nursing and hospital staff strict instructions to observe the patient and to monitor everything that enters the room and every bite that enters the patient's mouth. Under strict conditions of observation, some of these patients have been observed to take in less than 500 calories per day, and have actually gained weight. This scenario has left many a doctor scratching his head, yet none of these doctors would have difficulty understanding this phenomenon if it was associated with a cause of DTSF that could be detected with available blood tests.

As strange as it may seem, the overlooking of one small point (which is no great leap in reasoning) has caused this phenomenon to remain such a mystery: **Thyroid hormone**

208

blood tests are not adequate to detect every cause of DTSF or to fully assess the functioning of the thyroid system. It is difficult to understand how this point has been overlooked by so many for so long, especially since the presentation of decreased thyroid system function is so reproducible and recognizable. It is hard to understand how it can be concluded that a patient with a very typical and classic presentation of DTSF, necessarily has normal thyroid system function based only on the far less than predictive and reproducible information afforded by thyroid blood tests. It's like concluding that "even though this bird looks like a duck, has webbed feet like a duck, floats like a duck, paddles like a duck has a bill like a duck, waddles like a duck, and quacks like a duck, it cannot be a duck, because I have taken one of its feathers and it looks to me like some of the feathers that I have removed from these turkeys." "I can't accept the possibility of this bird being a duck just because it has all the characteristics of a duck, but I can accept the impossibility of this bird being a duck solely because it has one similarity to a turkey."

Contrary to popular belief, it is possible to gain weight on less than 500 calories a day. It is also possible, as many people can attest and as more and more people are coming to realize, that one can actually sometimes **gain** weight by decreasing one's caloric intake. As discussed previously, when a person diets, their body can respond with a compensatory lowering of the metabolic rate. For example, if a person is eating 1400 calories per day and maintaining his or her weight, it stands to reason that the amount of calories burned is equal to the amount of calories taken in so that there is no change in the person's weight. However, if that person chooses to try to lose some weight by cutting his caloric intake to 1100 calories, he or she is likely to lose weight. But, in some cases the body can respond to that decrease in caloric intake by slowing down the metabolic rate and can sometimes even over compensate. So the body might cut the caloric expenditure down to say 900 calories per day by decreasing the amount of energy devoted to tissue (hair, skin, etc.) maintenance, in order to cope with the condition of fasting. In this way, a 200 calorie per day excess can be realized enabling a person to actually gain weight under dieting conditions.

Persistent impairment in the conversion of T4 to T3 can also explain the common phenomenon observed in patients who lose weight by dieting, only to gain it back and then some. Because the caloric deprivation might incite the body to further compensate and enter further into the conservation mode, causing further impairment in the conversion of T4 to T3, setting the metabolic rate at an even lower level than previously. This can also explain why many patients who undergo a diet notice a worsening of their symptoms of Wilson's Syndrome, with these symptoms frequently remaining persistently worse even after the diet is over. For example, they may find their skin becomes more dry during the diet and remains dryer even after the diet is over. Their dry skin problem may persist together with a rebounding of their weight. The well observed phenomenon of gaining back weight lost during a diet after the diet has been discontinued is sometimes referred to as "Yo-Yo Syndrome."

Wilson's syndrome can also explain the frustration that some people experience when they are doing everything that is accepted as being correct while the weight still doesn't come off, and their symptoms still do not improve. They have read every book, they have tried every exercise program, they have read every diet, they have tried every diet—following them to the letter strictly without variance - and still have not been able to achieve a normal weight. If they have been able to get to a normal weight, they are frequently unable to maintain it, and frequently suffer continually from the symptoms of MED. Indeed, some of their symptoms may worsen in spite of their best efforts. This can all be explained by T4 to T3 conversion impairment.

Patients are sometimes accused of "cheating" on their diets by their doctors (apparently because their doctors are unaware that it is possible for **some** patients to *gain* weight on 500 to 800 calories per day. It is often concluded that there is no possible way that patients could be adhering strictly enough to their diet, because if they were, they would be losing weight.

However, patients with DTSF and low body temperature patterns can sometimes gain weight on less than 500 calories per day, and will sometimes respond poorly to protein sparing modified fasting liquid diets and even to stomach stapling. One patient I treated had undergone a stomach stapling procedure and her stomach was so small that she was unable to hold down more than three or four ounces at a time and she had the misfortune of vomiting up to eleven times a day. Through the course of a day it was physically impossible for her to retain in her stomach more than 400 calories/day, yet she was gaining weight in spite of it. Many patients with Wilson's Syndrome that are treated with protein sparing modifying fasting diets have found that they are able to lose weight with the liquid diet. However, their symptoms of MED often worsen while the diet is in progress. And, once the diet is over, their symptoms of MED often remain persistently worse and they have a tendency to gain all their weight back and then some. This is understandable since it may prompt the patient to enter more deeply into conservation mode and the more deeply one is in conservation mode, the more likely one is to get stuck in that position, causing an aggravation of one's Wilson's Syndrome.

I'm not saying that every person who has trouble losing weight is suffering from Wilson's Syndrome. I am merely pointing out that DTSF has long been known to be more than enough explanation for a person's inappropriate weight gain. Wilson's Syndrome and its treatment is not the answer underlying all people's weight problems, just as dieting, exercise, liquid diets, stomach stapling, or other approaches aren't the solution to all people's weight problems. The issue of weight is a multifaceted one since people's weight can be affected by many different variables. It can be affected by female hormones, adrenal hormones, thyroid hormones, dieting (including caloric intake and composition of food ingested), exercise, stress levels, psychological attitudes, surface area to volume ratio, and other variables. For this reason, no one approach can be used to help all people, in all circumstances, maintain an appropriate weight. There never will be one approach that works for everyone. The approach that works best will depend on the underlying problem.

Certainly, a change in diet helps some people to maintain a normal weight. However, there are others who may make the exact same change and **gain** weight. Some people are able to use exercise to get in shape, and maintain a normal weight. However, there are those who can exercise several hours a day, seven days a week and still be unable to control their weight. The resolving of one's psychological issues surrounding food may help a person to overcome his weight problem, whereas the resolving of such issues in another may be inadequate to address the problem. It is well known that the weight problems of many have been eliminated once their underlying hormonal imbalance was corrected. DTSF does not, in and of itself, account for the weight problems of all people; but it does represent one more obstacle that can hinder the maintaining of a normal weight, thus, a person's weight problem can be an extremely complicated one. In addressing the problem, the best that one can do is to favorably influence each variable that can affect the person's weight as maximally as possible (do the best you can with what you have). Of course, the best approach will depend most on the underlying problem. Unfortunately, the underlying problem is sometimes difficult to determine (because many of the processes that influence a person's weight involve some of the most fundamental levels of organization of the body - as discussed previously).

I would like to point out more fully the importance of a certain variable discussed previously, especially as it pertains to the issue of weight: surface area/volume ratio. Of course, the body's weight depends on the amount of calories taken up by the body and how many calories go out of the body. Calories "go in" by the body absorbing and processing nutrients from the digestive tract, and calories "go out" by being used in maintaining body tissues, providing for body functions, providing for body movement and activity, and by the amount of heat that passes from the body to the atmosphere. We have discussed previously the importance of the surface area to volume ratio. We have pointed out that the shape that holds heat the best is a ball because it has the smallest surface area to volume ratio. So the less one looks like a ball and the more one looks like a stick, the easier it is to dissipate calories. And if it didn't make a significant difference, then people wouldn't tend to ball up or curl up in cold weather.

The body maintains its temperature within a very narrow range. It must be that the body has some special means or system to accomplish this exceedingly non-random event. This system can be thought of as a "thermostat" for the body. When body temperature tends to drop too low, then energy absorbed by the body through food stuffs are utilized to bring it back up. When the temperature goes too high, less "fuel is added to the fire" and certain other mechanisms are implemented to increase the amount of heat that passes out of the body. As everyone knows, in the winter time a better insulated home maintains heat better and requires less fuel to maintain a comfortable temperature then do poorly insulated home. Since a ball is the shape that holds its heat the best, the more a person is shaped like a ball, the better they retain body heat (all other factors being equal). If a person retains their body heat better than another (being well insulated in a sense) then less energy or calories will be required to maintain a given body temperature. Although people's sizes and shapes vary tremendously, as do their abilities to retain and dissipate calories, their body temperatures don't. There is an extremely small amount of variation in body temperature from one person to the next, with most people running very close to 23 1/2 degrees above room temperature, and with a 1.4 degree elevation (giving a fever of 100 degrees F) being recognized as such a significant indicator of illness that one would be excused from work.

With houses, conserving fuel is usually the goal, but some people and their doctors feel that they are storing too much fuel (fat). And, in some cases, it is apparent that they are storing it inappropriately under conditions that would ordinarily provide for the maintenance of normal weight. The thermostat of a house keeps it at a certain temperature. When the temperature begins to drop, it turns on the heater to maintain the certain temperature. If it begins to go too high, the thermostat decreases the amount of heat produced, to again maintain the temperature. The "thermostat" system of the body works in a similar way to maintain a precise temperature range. How well a body can get rid of excess stored fuel depends, in part, on how well that body can get rid of the heat (calories) generated by its consumption. To the extent the heat is retained in the body, the body temperature tends to rise. But as the temperature tends to rise, the body responds by decreasing fuel consumption and heat production to maintain the precise temperature range. Thus, since the more ball-shaped people retain heat better (are better insulated) than the more stick-shaped people, they tend to dissipate fewer calories before their temperatures rise to the point that their thermostats decrease fuel consumption. More stick-shaped people, like more poorly insulated homes, do not retain heat as well and require more fuel consumption and heat production to maintain the same temperature as the better insulated. So just being more ball-shaped can be viewed as a considerable disadvantage in being able to dissipate calories in order to maintain a normal weight.

Theoretically, a person might also be able to increase their surface area to volume ratio, to an extent, by sitting with their arms outstretched over the back of the couch more often than sitting with their arms and legs folded. So, too, it would be advisable to dress with lighter clothing that exposes more of the body's surface area.

The principle of surface area to volume ratio explains some unusual situations. For example, a given person might weigh 145 pounds and have no difficulty maintaining 145 pounds at his current level of dieting, exercising, and life style activities. This person may for a time change his eating habits, exercise levels, or lifestyle to the extent that he gains 40 pounds to weigh 185 pounds. Then, that person may resume his previous regimen of diet, exercise, and lifestyle fully expecting to be able to return to 145 pounds, and be dismayed to find that he or she finds it close to impossible to lose even 5 pounds.

For many people this frustrating reality seemingly defies reason. However, more has changed in the meantime than just the person's diet, exercise, and lifestyle habits. The person has gained 40 pounds and has become less stick-shaped and more ball-shaped which can sometimes, in and of itself, change the balance of variables. Proper T3 therapy can bring a person's body out of the inappropriate conservation mode in certain cases. Under these circumstances, one can observe an interesting phenomenon which can be explained by the influence of the surface area to volume ratio. A patient with classic WS who also happens to be overweight, might respond completely to proper T3 therapy **except** that he may still not lose a pound of weight without a change in diet or exercise (even though the excess weight *came on* with the onset of Wilson's Syndrome without a change in diet or exercise). However, the patient might begin an aggressive diet and exercise regimen and manage to lose 10 or 20 pounds, grow wearisome of the regimen, and go back to his or her old (prior to developing Wilson's Syndrome) habits. The patient may find that the weight **continues** to gradually come off until s/he is once again at their pre-Wilson's Syndrome weight. I am convinced that the explanation for this phenomenon rests in the fact that once the patient's Wilson's Syndrome was resolved, the patient might not have automatically returned to a normal weight because of the surface area to volume ratio changes that had changed the balance of variables that were dictating the patient's weight. However, once the patient was able to get the ball rolling by losing 10 or 20 pounds, and thereby returning the surface area to volume ratio back to more normal levels (I call this "breaking the surface area/volume barrier"), the balance of variables was able to be restored to the extent that the patient could then return to the original weight with the original diet and exercise habits.

It is interesting that even pioneer settlers noticed that during the wintertime they seemed to be able to maintain more body warmth by eating more meat. This may help explain why some patients with Wilson's Syndrome (in conservation mode) seem to be able to return to a normal weight more easily through the use of hypoglycemic diets (which include more meats/protein and less carbohydrates). The increased protein may help them to, among other things, more easily maintain more normal body temperature patterns to help prevent the body from fighting itself so much every step of the way.

In summary, the principle of the body's surface area to volume ratio is an **extremely** important factor that can have a huge impact on a person's ability to gain, lose, or maintain one's weight. The surface area/volume ratio should always be kept in mind when addressing or attempting to understand a person's weight problems.

We know that the body can be encouraged to enter or remain in the productivity mode through diet and exercise. However, sometimes diet and exercise alone are not sufficient to normalize body temperature patterns and to eliminate the symptoms of MED. To say that the symptoms of MED can be caused by low body temperature patterns, does not mean that everyone who has a low body temperature pattern has DTSF or MED. Nor does it mean that everybody who had any or all of the symptoms of MED, may not be having those symptoms from some other cause. To say that exercising can increase a person's metabolism doesn't mean that exercising is able to increase **everybody's** metabolism. To say that certain dietary changes can improve a person's metabolism doesn't mean that any particular diet can increase **everybody's** metabolism. **All that is meant, is that a low body temperature and Wilson's Syndrome and DTSF are more than enough to explain symptoms of MED which may respond to proper liothyronine treatment.**

Possibly the saddest twist of fate that I see in some patients is when a spouse will begin to criticize a Wilson's Syndrome sufferer for even small excesses of weight. As these criticisms become sharper, the patient may make every effort to diet and exercise. Under the conditions of stress and fasting, the patient's body may enter more deeply into the conservation mode, contributing to disappointing weight normalization. When the diet is over, such patients may frequently gain their weight back and then some, leading to more criticism (even ultimatums), more dieting, more frustration, and more weight gain.

Of course, if a person's DTSF is being caused by Wilson's Syndrome, the last thing that such a person needs is significantly increased emotional stress or pressure. Through harsh criticism, the spouse can prevent the outcome that he or she is demanding should be achieved. Sometimes when a couple does divorce, the additional stress can further aggravate the patient's Wilson's Syndrome, contributing to further weight problems. By the end of the process, an inappropriately critical spouse can cause almost irreversible damage to the patient's metabolism, making it sometimes impossible to normalize body temperature patterns and to be able to return to normal weight, with proper diet and exercise, without proper thyroid hormone treatment of the patient's underlying cause of DTSF (Wilson's Syndrome).

In severe cases, correction of the problem can prove to be difficult (especially due to surface area to volume ratio considerations), even with proper thyroid hormone treatment. It is sad that the inappropriate and demeaning criticisms, projections, and predictions of others can sometimes come true in the lives of good people. It is amazing, also, to see the literal physical damage that people can cause one another through verbal, emotional, mental, and social interaction.

Wound Healing, Decreased

Since low body temperature patterns can result in Multiple Enzyme Dysfunction and enzymes are quite important in the process of maintaining and repairing bodily tissues, it is not hard to imagine how patients with Wilson's Syndrome find that they do not heal as well after surgery as others. In fact, in some cases, patients have found their wounds heal so poorly that they have required opening up and surgical revision. WS sufferers frequently notice that scratches and sores frequently take a long time to heal.

In the case of serious or life-threatening wounds, the patient's survival may depend on his body's ability to heal. In cases of severe physical stress, such as severe trauma and life-threatening wounds, a person's body might be encouraged to enter into the conservation mode, which might result in lower body temperature patterns causing Multiple Enzyme Dysfunction and a decrease in a patient's wound healing ability.

An interesting study, done by Dr. Silberman at the University of California (*Surg. Gynecol. Obste.* 166:223-28,1988), was performed on 73 patients in the surgical and medical intensive care units at L.A. County-USC Medical Center. The levels of all the different thyroid hormones were measured to see if any pattern could be seen in the outcomes of the patients. When all of the values were stratified and indexed, it was found that the patients with lower T3 levels and elevated RT3 levels, were significantly more likely to die, as were those with low T4 and high T3 uptake tests. Impaired T4 to T3 conversion typically results in less T4 being shunted towards T3 and more T4 being shunted towards RT3. This could explain the study's findings. The researchers were quoted in *Family Practice News Magazine* (Nov. 1988), as saying that alterations in peripheral conversion of T4 appear to be responsible for the abnormal thyroid (results) that have been observed in patients with a wide variety of non-thyroid illnesses.

Another interesting study done by a Japanese doctor (Shigematsu, H.) published in October 1988 (*Nippon Geka Gakkai Zashi*, 89 (10): 1587-93) involved dogs in cardiogenic shock. Needless to say, these dogs were facing a great physical stress. Some of the dogs were administered T3, some RT3, and some no thyroid medicine. Many more of the dogs that were administered T3 survived as compared with the large number of dogs administered RT3 that died. This study suggests that RT3 can further impair the function of the body's metabolism and that proper T3 therapy can mean the difference between life and death. Interestingly, critically ill patients often **look** like they are suffering from DTSF. They often have bloating, fatigue, and decreased concentration and mentation, among other things.

Believe it or not, the preceding list of symptoms and findings associated with Wilson's Syndrome is not exhaustive. It does, however, represent some of the most common manifestations of Wilson's Syndrome seen in the normal course of practice. Considering that the function of the thyroid system can affect virtually every cell, every process, and every function of the body, it is easy to understand how DTSF resulting from Wilson's Syndrome can have such far reaching effects on the human body. There are many more details and considerations involving Wilson's Syndrome (for example, how it interfaces with many other health problems and many other aspects of life) which cannot be fully addressed in this one book. Rather, it is the purpose and scope of this book to provide enough information to help one imagine, to help one consider, to help one look for, and to help one understand the significance, impact, and importance of Wilson's Syndrome. It is the purpose of this book to help us to no longer overlook this condition, and to help us look for and try to track down all of its almost infinite implications and ramifications. This information opens up a whole new field. The information in this book opens many new avenues shedding new light on how we might approach and manage many of the health problems addressed by medicine today. The ramifications are innumerable as we look at each facet of the field of medicine from a new perspective, rethinking our attitudes towards, assumptions about, and approaches to many of today's medical problems in the context of Wilson's Syndrome. It is hoped that there is enough information in this book to persuade one to realize that it is possible that such a condition can exist, does exist, and should be considered and treated. Especially when one considers how common, how debilitating, how costly (in terms of quality of life and productivity both individually and as a society), how easily recognized, how far-reaching (with many implications and ramifications), and how easily treated it is.

Chapter Ten

10. WHAT CAN BE DONE?

People usually go to the doctor when they are being bothered by a medical problem which they cannot easily solve on their own. When addressing such a problem, the doctor may consider the possible causes of the problem and the alternative approaches in addressing it. Pros and cons, risks and benefits of each alternative are weighed in deciding how to proceed. In patients suspected of suffering from Wilson's Syndrome, because there is no explanation with blood tests or otherwise to account for the patient's classic presentation and complaints, there are several alternative approaches.

1. **Non-treatment**
2. **Alternative treatment** including behavioral and dietary changes
3. **Definitive treatment**, when necessary, with proper T3 therapy.

Non-treatment

Some people may wonder why Wilson's Syndrome is so common. They may be surprised that so many people could suffer from such a condition. Yet these same people may not be surprised that people bleed when they are cut with a knife. It is not at all unexpected that if a person is cut with a knife that he might bleed. It's a normal response, but it may not be very desirable. Great measures have been taken to counter this "normal" response such as bandages, sutures, blood banks, surgeries, etc.

In like manner, some may say that it is normal for people to become depressed, tired, irritable, headachy, forgetful, and have trouble sleeping during periods of significant physical, mental, or emotional stress. Yet again, there is a difference between normal and desirable, especially when the response persists inappropriately even after the stress has passed. Even in the midst of the stress, the response is not necessarily favorable or adaptive but may be deleterious. If a person gets cut with a knife, they bleed, and if a person is sufficiently pulverized from stress, they can likewise be "injured," leaving

221

them with a persistently impaired system. If one is bleeding from a knife wound, the wound might stop bleeding on its own, heal up eventually and leave a scar. On the other hand, if the wound is sutured, treated with antibiotics and dressed with bandages, it may be less likely to develop an infection, it may heal more quickly, and it may leave less scarring. If the wound is severe and left untreated, it may not heal by itself, and the patient could bleed to death.

So the choice of treatment approach can certainly affect the outcome. Likewise, with Wilson's Syndrome, how the problem is addressed can certainly affect the outcome. It can be left untreated, and if it is not too severe, it may resolve spontaneously without treatment returning to normal after the stress is over, leaving very little persistent impairment ("scarring"), if any. If the condition is more severe and is left untreated, more persistent impairment may result and the body's system may not return to normal on its own without definitive intervention. In severe cases, definitive intervention may be disappointing, just as it is sometimes not possible to fully restore the function of a person who has been injured in a severe auto accident. However, definitive T3 therapy can sometimes prevent a WS sufferer from losing decades of productivity and quality of life.

It is "normal" for women to go through menopause later in life and develop hot flashes, vaginal dryness, and increased bone loss, but that doesn't prevent intervention from often being desirable and appropriate. Female hormones are often given routinely to post-menopausal woman because it is felt that intervention frequently favorably affects outcome. Wilson's Syndrome is not usually life-threatening, just as menopause is usually not life-threatening. However, proper intervention can make all the difference in a person's life; and getting it treated, perhaps more than any other medical problem, may make all the difference in our society as a whole. Getting it treated can have everything to do with eventual outcome.

The symptoms may be seemingly unrelated until they get better simultaneously with proper T3 therapy. Many times patients state that they didn't fully realize how badly they were feeling until their symptoms were alleviated. They frequently state that, "Now I remember what it feels like to be normal again."

Occasionally patients will state that the resolution of a secondary symptom has proven to be more beneficial than the resolution of their primary complaint. For example, a patient with fatigue, migraines, PMS, depression, dry skin, dry hair, constipation, fluid retention, insomnia, inappropriate weight gain, and others might state prior to treatment that the primary complaint is fatigue. But when **all** of the symptoms resolve, the patient might later report that the resolution of the migraine headaches has actually had a larger impact on his life. This is frequently because the patients themselves can sometimes not fathom that the symptoms could get better together. They may not be able to picture that a particular symptom, such as migraines, might resolve. However, seeing is believing. Many patients state that one really can't appreciate one's good health and normal functioning until its gone, and sometimes they don't realize how bad off they were until their normal health and functioning is restored with proper T3 therapy.

Considering the information presented thus far in this book it is hard to understate the tremendous impact that WS can have on a person's life. Once developed, Wilson's Syndrome can, after a period of time, resolve on its own; but in other instances, it can persist for 20,30,40 years or more.

Alternative Treatment Including Behavioral And Dietary Changes

Considering the origins of Wilson's Syndrome, it stands to reason that there may be non-medical alternatives in its management. If emotional, mental, or physical stress can lead to the development of Wilson's Syndrome or can aggravate it, then the elimination of stress from one's life might be a good place to start. Of course, eliminating destructive stress is one of the great secrets of life. A certain amount of stress is unavoidable, and in some cases it may actually help us grow stronger and more adept at overcoming obstacles. But when the stress is overwhelming, then "injury" can result.

Considering the reduction and/or elimination of stress from one's life as an alternative treatment of Wilson's Syndrome calls to mind a fascinating case history. It is very interesting because prior to seeing this patient I was in the habit of suggesting to people to eliminate stress when they asked me about what they could do to correct Wilson's Syndrome without medical treatment. As I would review the alternative measures that one might implement, I would include that one could "completely eliminate stress out of his life." With that they would frequently look at me with a look on their face as if to say, "Yeah, right, who is ever going to be able to completely eliminate stress out of their life?" Sometimes I would jokingly say, "Yes, if you didn't have any job concerns or family concerns, and you lived in the Bahamas and you walked, ran, swam at the beach or exercised all day, and you ate pineapple, fruit and practiced good nutrition all day long and relaxed, then you would probably be much better."

Coincidentally, much later, the patient with the following case history came to my office. She had many complaints including fatigue, depression, fluid retention, PMS, irritability, itchiness, dry skin, dry hair, and inappropriate weight gain. One of the things that troubled her, however, was something that she could never understand. There was a brief period of time in her life that lasted approximately two years in which she did not suffer from these complaints. Prior to these two years, she had developed Wilson's Syndrome and, among other things, had quite a bit of difficulty with maintaining her weight. But then she went through that two year period of time losing 60 to 80 pounds, no longer having a tendency to gain weight inappropriately. Then after that two year period was over, she suddenly began gaining weight inexplicably (with no increase in dietary intake or decrease in activity) and gained all of her weight back. She couldn't understand how she could possibly feel badly and have a weight problem, then feel well with the weight problem resolving on its own, and then all of a sudden feel poorly **again** and have a weight problem **again** out of the blue. After a careful history and questioning, a very interesting

224

pattern became apparent. The patient had undergone a stressful living situation which started her Wilson's Syndrome. At the beginning of the two year period she also underwent a life-style change. What had happened, believe it or not, was that her husband who was in the military, had been transferred to the **Bahamas**. He was stationed on a military base, and while they were there, the utilities were paid, their food was paid, their rent was paid, as were all their other necessities of life, including clothing and other needs. She had spent a great deal of time on the beach laying out in the sun. Notably, she did not get an excessive amount of exercise, but she did rest a lot. And she remembers eating more at that time than she had previously or afterwards. When the two years ended, she and her husband moved back to the states and once again needed to concern themselves with living expenses and other problems associated with daily living. Without an increase in her appetite or dietary intake and without a decrease in her physical activity, her symptoms returned as did her weight problem. This patient's case clearly illustrates how Wilson's Syndrome can sometimes come and go under periods of stress and relaxation respectively.

The body can also be prompted to leave the conservation mode and return to the productivity mode by leading it to think that certain important things need to get done. The conservation mode is not productive and not favorable when it prevents the human body from protecting himself from predators; and when it prevents him from hunting, obtaining food, and building a shelter for his family and for himself. So if a patient can mimic the physical activity that would be required for a human to protect himself from a predator (to flee or to fight), and the level of physical activity that would be required in hunting game and building shelters, it may be possible to coax his body to return back to the productivity mode. The body may pull out of the conservation mode and return to the productivity mode if it is persuaded to realize that it is necessary for survival. In other words, a good moderate exercise program, even 12 to 15 minutes at a time, 2, 3, or 4 times a day, especially after meals, may be enough to encourage the body's metabolism to come up out of, and stay out of the conservation mode. This can be accomplished by walking, swimming, treadmill, exercise bike, or similar activities.

Since Wilson's Syndrome is, among other things, a coping mechanism for starvation gone amuck, it is easily understandable why patients often do better on hypoglycemic-type diets. Hypoglycemic dieters are characterized by small frequent meals, usually six small meals a day rather than the usual three. These diets are usually higher in protein and lower in carbohydrates than other diets; that is, they are higher in meats such as chicken and turkey as well as others and include eggs, tuna fish, and other sources of protein. They have less carbohydrates such as potatoes, bread, fruits, vegetables, and refined sugars such as cookies, candy, cakes, etc.

I sometimes describe a very simple diet for people to follow that involves eating from these different groups. The protein group includes tuna fish, yogurt, cottage cheese, chicken, turkey, fish, and even beef and pork. The carbohydrate group includes bread, cereal, potatoes, pasta, crackers, rice, and preferably should be of the less refined variety. The fruit and vegetable group includes, of all things, fruits and vegetables. To make it easy, I suggest that the patient trace a silver dollar and two nickels. I recommend that patients eat foods from the three groups in those **proportions**. A "dollar" size of protein, a "nickel" size of carbohydrates and a nickels size of fruits and vegetables six times a day. Some patients may do better with a little less protein than this, and it can be adjusted. One patient with a classic story for Wilson's Syndrome was able to correct her symptoms and return back to normal merely by changing her eating habits and using a hypoglycemic type diet. She was able to have her symptoms of Wilson's Syndrome disappear with her metabolism returning back to the productivity mode.

The benefit of hypoglycemic diets are interesting from several different perspectives. First, it can be pointed out that foods that are higher in protein have higher "biological" value than carbohydrates. To illustrate the principle of biological food value, let us consider a typical food chain. If one considers a field of grain, that grain might be harvested and consumed directly in the form of carbohydrates by people; or the grain may be first be consumed by pigs, cattle, and chickens, and in turn the chickens, cows, and pigs might then be consumed by the humans. Because the cows and pigs feed on the grain, they are higher up in the food chain than grain, with humans being at the very top. Because the pigs and cows are higher in the food chain, they are considered to have a higher biological value than does grain. One reason is that since the cows and pigs feed on the grain and burn up the calories of that grain in their daily activities and in the development of their bodies, quite a bit of grain can be consumed in the raising of those domestic animals.

For argument's sake, let us suppose that a human can survive on the grain harvested from a two-acre field for a period of one year, subsisting only on that grain. Let us suppose that a pig would require 1 1/2 acres and a cow 3 acres. Let us suppose that one cow and two pigs would be necessary to sustain that same person for the period of one year if that person subsisted only on the meat of the 2 pigs, and the cow. Then, if he subsisted on grain alone, he would account for only two acres of grain in a year's time. However, if that same person were to subsist on one cow and two pigs, he would account for six acres of grain. So more acreage of grain would be necessary for the sustenance of one person, the higher up in the food chain he eats.

So it can be said that the cow and two pigs have a greater biological value because as sustenance for a person they represent **six** acres of grain, as compared to the two acres of grain a person would consume if he ate the grain directly. It is an interesting consideration to me because it seems to me that if conditions became severe (famine), then less grain might be "wasted" on domestic animals and more grain would be consumed directly by people, in order that the available harvest and food would go farther in feeding them and there would be enough food to go around. It would seem that under such conditions the people would live less "high on the hog." They would probably eat more beans and rice and grains rather than the biologically "costly" meats and proteins.

This causes me to wonder if diets high in carbohydrates and low in protein do not send a signal to the body that times might be hard, encouraging the body to enter into the conservation mode. I wonder too if diets higher in protein and lower in carbohydrates signal the body that times are plentiful, and by keeping a little bit of food on the stomach all day (with six meals a day) the body might have less incentive (won't think it's starving) to enter into the conservation mode, and indeed might be more prompted to enter into the productivity mode. This may partly explain why hypoglycemic diets are very helpful for WS sufferers. Second, some of the symptoms of Wilson's Syndrome are consistent with symptoms of low blood sugar, for example, night sweats that wake a person in the middle of the night, clamminess, lightheadedness, shakiness, headaches, and even anxiety.

Patients have noted that these symptoms are sometimes improved in the short run by drinking a glass of orange juice or having something to eat. **It is interesting that many diabetics have noticed that when their blood sugars are low, their body temperatures are low and when their blood sugars are higher, their body temperatures are higher.** Hypoglycemic diets may be helpful in these patients to the extent that they help prevent low blood sugar levels and, therefore, help prevent lower body temperature patterns.

Patients suffering with Wilson's Syndrome occasionally suffer from intense and previously unfamiliar cravings for sweets. The low body temperature patterns might affect the function of enzymes involved in glucose metabolism which may result in lower blood sugar levels which might contribute to sweet cravings.

Another observation is that WS sufferers frequently do most poorly on a diet regimen that might put more of a strain on blood sugar levels namely; not eating anything all day and just eating dinner at night right before going to bed. Interestingly, many patients with WS, especially those who work have fallen into this very eating pattern - which is not preferable.

As an aside, many times a patient's predisposition towards having these symptoms of hypoglycemia has been resolved with normalization of body temperature patterns with proper T3 therapy. Proper T3 therapy may help eliminate hypoglycemic tendencies by limiting blood sugar fluctuations by limiting temperature fluctuations.

Definitive Treatment With T3 Therapy

Proper T3 therapy for Multiple Enzyme Dysfunction due to low body temperature patterns is directed towards normalization of body temperature patterns in order to relieve the symptoms of MED. In many cases the symptoms of MED have been seen to be almost inseparably related to body temperature patterns. To date, proper T3 therapy is the best tool to effectively, predictably, reproducibly, and comfortably influence body temperature patterns. The symptoms of MED and body temperature patterns have frequently been seen to remain persistently improved even after T3 Therapy has been discontinued. So T3 therapy can be useful as a symptomatic (addressing the symptoms) and/or a therapeutic (correcting the underlying problem) intervention for the symptoms of MED due to low body temperature patterns especially when due to Wilson's Syndrome. This book contains a good description of the treatment for Wilson's Syndrome but any doctors, or patients for that matter, that are actually pursuing the treatment of Wilson's Syndrome are referred to the Doctor's Manual for Wilson's Syndrome (currently in its 2nd Edition). Over a year was spent carefully revising it. It contains the treatment protocol in full detail, including the answers to all the questions that come up with the T3 therapy. There's an illustration on almost every page, 8 case studies, 12 pages of management flow-charts, and lists of the important points and questions, and their answers. When this book and the first edition of the manual first came out, the response was overwhelming. There are over a thousand doctors treating this now. It became immediately obvious that I would not be able to personally assist every doctor or patient with the protocol. But perhaps only WS sufferers themselves, felt any more acutely than I, the need for me to make my experience available to other doctors. So I poured it into the Doctor's Manual. The protocol is finite, and it's in there.

Rationale For Treatment

The proper treatment for decreased thyroid system function in any given patient certainly depends on the underlying cause. As discussed previously, there are several causes of DTSF, low body temperature patterns, and the symptoms of MED, and more than one cause can be present at the same time. DTSF can be caused by a hypothalamic problem, hypopituitarism, hypothyroidism, and Wilson's Syndrome.

Hypopituitarism and hypothyroidism both result in deficient production of T4, which is the raw material the body uses to produce the active thyroid hormone T3. In such cases the treatment of choice is T4 because of its long half-life (which helps provide steady T3 levels), once-a-day administration, and usefulness in the treatment of such cases. Patients with hypopituitarism and hypothyroidism may, however, suffer with Wilson's Syndrome at the same time. In such cases, T4 therapy may not be adequate because impaired conversion of the T4 supplementation to the active compound T3 may prevent sufficient normalization of body temperature patterns, and, in some cases, can even feed the vicious cycle of Wilson's Syndrome.

T4 Or T3?

Let us consider the case of a perfectly healthy (no symptoms of any kind), 35-year-old woman who suddenly develops classic signs and symptoms of DTSF due to hypothyroidism (low thyroid **gland** function), demonstrated with blood tests showing T4 levels below the lower limits of normal and TSH levels being above the upper limits of normal. The patient is started on T4 therapy (the treatment of choice for decreased **gland** function) with many of her symptoms improving and many of the symptoms resolving completely. The T4 therapy is used to return the blood test levels to their normal ranges in the hopes of eliminating all of her symptoms completely. Unfortunately, even upon normalization of the blood test levels, and even after months and years of T4 therapy, the symptoms of DTSF, which first appeared with the development of her hypothyroidism, are still not resolved completely and the patient's function still remains quite unsatisfactory. The symptoms persist, even after T4 therapy has been used to correct the T4 and TSH blood test levels to within normal limits. So the T4 therapy might replace the T4 that the body is not producing in sufficient levels to bring the T4 level on the blood test back up within the normal range, and satisfy the pituitary gland resulting in normalization of TSH test levels, but the patient may still have symptoms of DTSF. So blood tests aren't always extremely predictive in how well a patient is going to feel with treatment and how well the thyroid **system** will be returned back to normal. The reason for this is obvious, because, again, where the "rubber meets the road" in the thyroid system, is not in the pituitary **gland**, nor the thyroid **gland**, nor the blood stream, but at the level of the thyroid hormone/ thyroid hormone receptor interaction at the level of the nuclear membrane of the body's cells.

Therefore, just because circulating raw material (T4) levels have been changed through the use of T4 supplementation to the satisfying of the pituitary and thyroid hormone blood tests does not necessarily mean that adequate levels of T3 are being provided to the active site of the thyroid system. To think so is a little like thinking that one can tell how fast a car is traveling based on how far down the gas pedal is pressed. The pedal may be pressed down, but whether a car is traveling 55 MPH depends also on how well the engine is combusting the fuel, what gear the car is in, and whether it is going up or down hill. Some cars cannot travel 55 MPH no matter how far down the gas pedal is pushed. So a patient can have normal blood tests all day long and still have classic signs and symptoms of Wilson's Syndrome or DTSF.

This explains some blood test abnormalities and responses to treatment which many people apparently think are not possible.

For example, it is commonly thought that elevated T4 levels and low TSH levels necessarily indicate excessive thyroid system function. Most people think that such blood test findings should correlate well with symptoms of hyperthyroidism (excessive thyroid gland function). However, I have seen patients with elevated T4 levels and low TSH levels who showed the classic signs, symptoms, and presentation of Wilson's Syndrome, and whose symptoms of WS or DTSF resolved quickly and easily with proper T3 therapy. This situation can be seen in both patients who are on no thyroid medication and, especially in patients who are being treated with T4 therapy prior to presentation. In fact, many times patients will come to my office being treated with T4 medicine with T4 levels being above normal in the 15 to 18 range, when the normal range is between 4 to 12. They also sometimes have exceptionally low TSH levels (thyroid stimulating hormone) indicating almost complete suppression of their pituitary gland and, therefore, their own thyroid gland function by the T4 medication they are being given by mouth. Such blood test findings would usually lead a doctor to conclude that if the patient is having any complaints that they necessarily would be due to hyperthyroidism. But sometimes these patients have classic signs and symptoms of **decreased** thyroid system function and respond very well to weaning the patient's excessively high T4 supplementation and to the administration of proper T3 therapy. So even though the patients have more than enough T4 floating around in their blood stream according to their blood test levels, they may still lack sufficient levels of the active thyroid hormone at the level of the nuclear membrane of the cells due to impaired T4 to T3 conversion.

Actually, impaired T4 to T3 conversion can be made worse with T4 therapy. If a patient cannot convert the T4 produced by their own **body** very well, then it is likely that they will not be able to convert effectively T4 given by **mouth**. In such cases, T4 can actually **feed** the vicious cycle which leads to Wilson's Syndrome. That is, if more T4 is given to the body and that T4 cannot be properly converted to T3 either, then more T4 will be shunted towards RT3 which may result in further competitive inhibition of the enzyme 5'-deiodinase, leading to further T4 to T3 conversion impairment.   In fact, some of the most severe derangements of the thyroid system that I have seen are in patients who seem to have been pushed too far in the wrong direction with the wrong thyroid hormone medicine, namely T4. The RT3 levels are frequently more elevated in these cases than in other cases of Wilson's Syndrome.   Frequently, these patients will also have the highest RT3/T3 ratio.   So non-judicious use of thyroid hormone supplementation may feed the vicious cycle of Wilson's Syndrome rather than reverse it.

I'm not saying that T4 medication is not sometimes a preferable and excellent method of treatment.   I'm just saying that it is not **always** the treatment of choice.   And, in every case the choice of thyroid hormone medication, how it is started, how it is adjusted, how it is monitored, and whether or not it should be changed, depends on the underlying cause of the patient's DTSF.

"Resetting" The System

Of course, one approach to alleviating Wilson's Syndrome is to address and eliminate possible contributing causes or factors. If Wilson's Syndrome is made worse under conditions of severe stress, one may seek to eliminate such conditions.   If periods of starvation, excessive dieting, or certain kinds of diets send signals to the body that times are "tough" and that the body should enter into the conservation mode, then one may also seek to change those conditions when possible.   If elevated levels of RT3 serve to perpetuate the vicious cycle of Wilson's Syndrome, then one may seek to decrease the levels of RT3 in a person's body.   RT3 is produced by the body from T4, so one way of reducing the levels of RT3 is by reducing the levels of T4.   Of course, lowering T4 levels results in a decreased supply of raw material with which the body may make T3.   However, the body's T3 levels can be supplemented with T3 taken by mouth.

One may decrease T4 levels by decreasing the levels of thyroid stimulating hormone which regulates the body's production of T4.   The body's thermostat (pituitary gland) decreases TSH production when there is a certain amount of T4 and/or T3 already present in the system. So TSH production can be decreased when the body **itself** produces a certain level of T4, when it produces a certain level of T3, or when it produces certain levels of T4 and T3.

Likewise, the body's production of thyroid stimulating hormone can be decreased when a certain amount of T4 is added to the system **by mouth**, when a certain level of T3 is added to the system by mouth, and when certain levels of T4 and T3 are added to the system by mouth. Interestingly, when **T4** is added to the system by mouth, decreased TSH levels and increased T4 levels may result. However, when **T3** is added to the system by mouth, there may result decreased levels of TSH and **decreased** levels of T4. In either case, the body still has a source for the critical thyroid hormone T3. How adequately those sources are being utilized, however, depends on how adequately the body is converting the T4 to the critical T3, and how sufficiently and steadily the T3 is being supplied by mouth and absorbed by the system.

T3 therapy by mouth can kill two birds with one stone. It can provide sufficient levels of T3 at the active site to generate adequate body temperature patterns _while_ reducing TSH production, thereby reducing T4 production, thereby reducing Reverse T3 production, thereby decreasing the impairment of T4 to T3 conversion by decreasing competitive inhibition for the converting enzyme. This is important because it can provide for a "resetting" of the system, thereby improving the body's chances of being able to once again properly convert T4 to T3.

As an analogy, we can consider the function of a seat belt. If a person's seat belt "catches" before it can be fastened when it is only half-way across the person's lap, then, try as he might, he will not be able to pull the seat belt any further in order to fasten it until he first lets it go backwards. The seat belt mechanism is reset by disengaging the component that is preventing further advancement. This is accomplished by letting the seat belt be retracted to its starting position.

234

Likening the thyroid system to this analogy, one component that can hinder the return of a temporarily impaired conversion of T4 to T3 back to normal is the transient elevation of RT3 levels that can result from the impaired conversion. This may lead to a vicious cycle which causes the system to be "stuck" in a position in which there is insufficient conversion of T4 to T3 (this cannot be easily be detected with blood tests). But in order for this conversion to be increased, it must first be decreased in order to "reset" the system by decreasing T4 levels and thereby, decreasing RT3 levels in order to disengage the component that is preventing further advancement. Then when the treatment is weaned, the T4 to T3 conversion can return to more normal levels. The only difference between the analogy of the seat belt and the thyroid system is that the T3 therapy is not only useful in "resetting" the system, but also in providing necessary levels of T3 for adequate, if not ideal, functioning in the meantime.

Another example that can be considered in understanding the rationale for proper T3 therapy, is the example of the use of birth control pills in patients with irregular periods. There are times when women begin having irregular periods. Their periods can be out of synchronicity, excessively heavy, too light, or skipped completely. In such cases female hormone blood tests and other tests are often found to be completely normal. The only indication that there is a problem is that the woman notices a change in the pattern of her menstrual cycles which she feels is inappropriate and undesirable. Upon careful history and examination, her physician may agree that the symptoms she describes are inappropriate and undesirable. Without any tests available to determine the underlying problem the doctor often suspects a female hormone imbalance. Based on that suspicion, every day, many such patients across the country are given a therapeutic trail of birth control pills by their doctors in an attempt to "regulate" their menstrual irregularities. These patients can sometimes be "cycled" on birth control pills for several months causing their female hormone system and menstrual cycle to fall into a normal pattern again. After the system has been placed into a normal pattern again, the patient may be weaned off the birth control pills and enjoy a persistent improvement and normalization of her menstrual cycles.

This is the same goal of therapy for DTSF due to Wilson's Syndrome. If a patient's thyroid system is inappropriately stuck in the conservation mode, then the patient may be cycled on proper thyroid hormone treatment to again establish the proper pattern and balance for a period to time. Then when a patient gradually weans off the medicine, the responsibility of normal thyroid system function is returned to the body gradually, and the patient is frequently able to enjoy persistent improvement and normalization of the system even after thyroid medication is weaned.

When birth control pills are given to women with irregular periods, their own female hormone system function decreases to a great extent, if not completely, while the birth control pills are taking control of the system. Once the proper pattern has been set or the female hormone system has been "regulated", the birth control pills can be weaned in the hopes that the patient's body can maintain the newly reset proper pattern on its own once again. In that same way T3 therapy can be used to take control of the thyroid system for a time, and set it into a proper pattern. When the body temperature patterns have been normalized, then the T3 therapy can be weaned in the hopes that the body can maintain the newly set proper balance once again on its own by gradually returning the responsibility of proper thyroid system balance back to the body.

So no matter where the problem is located in the thyroid hormone system, whether it is in the hypothalamus, pituitary gland, thyroid gland, conversion of T4 to T3, or even in the thyroid hormone receptors, the bottom line of therapy is always to adjust the medication in the thyroid hormone system in such a way as to provide a sufficient and desirable pattern of interaction between the thyroid hormones (primarily T3) and the thyroid hormone receptors at the nuclear membrane of the cells of the body.

If the problem is in the hypothalamus, pituitary gland, or thyroid gland, resulting in insufficient production of T4, then T4 supplementation can be given to provide sufficient raw material for the body to make the active thyroid hormone T3. In this way T4 supplementation can indirectly produce sufficient T3 stimulation of the receptor sites, to generate normal body temperature patterns (providing the body can adequately convert the raw material T4 to the active thyroid hormone T3). But if the problem is in the conversion of T4 to T3 and the body is already having difficulty converting its own T4 to T3, then it often has difficulty converting T4 given by mouth (which again can actually worsen the thyroid hormone imbalance responsible for Wilson's Syndrome). So, many times T3 supplementation is preferable in treating patients with Wilson's Syndrome, since not only can it provide the T3 necessary for thyroid hormone receptor interaction, but it can also reverse the imbalance of the thyroid hormone system that may have caused the impairment to begin with.

T3 Therapy Helpful For Many

It is really hard for anyone to understand how debilitating Wilson's Syndrome can be until they have experienced it personally or have been closely associated with someone that has suffered from it. It is so common that there are a whole lot of people who could benefit from proper T3 therapy just as there are a whole lot of people who benefit from taking aspirin, birth control pills, female hormone replacement therapy, blood pressure medicine, and others.

Some wonder, "How could so many people benefit from the same medicine? Shouldn't different people need different medicines?" Giving T3 therapy to a Wilson's Syndrome sufferer can be similar to giving insulin to a diabetic. If one is treating diabetes, then one frequently prescribes insulin; and when one treats Wilson's Syndrome, one frequently prescribes liothyronine (T3). Diabetics are frequently deficient in insulin and therefore, are supplemented with insulin. Wilson's Syndrome patients are frequently deficient in T3 and are frequently best supplemented with T3. And, if it is very common, a significant portion of the population may benefit from T3 therapy at one time or another in their life. Just as many of us have sustained injuries that "needed stitches" to better treat the wound and promote healing, many of us have and will sustain "injuries" that may "need T3" to reverse the impairment and promote the return of normal functioning.

T3 therapy is a tool that can be commonly used to make all the difference in a person's life. It is not candy and should not be taken for the fun of it, nor is it completely without risk. But when used properly, it can produce benefits that many patients have considered to be in the "miracle" category. **The treatment is not intended to elevate anyone's level of metabolism or thyroid system function <u>above</u> normal, but to bring it back up <u>to</u> normal**. The T3 therapy is not intended to "burn the candle at both ends" and make someone able to perform at above normal levels. Thyroid hormone medication is not "speed" and excessive levels do not cause a person to feel well, high, or above normal, but actually results in side effects and decreased benefit. Thyroid hormones don't have their action specifically on the nervous system but on the **cells** of the body, in general.

Patient Evaluation

The treatment in this section is not the treatment of choice for <u>all</u> causes of decreased thyroid system function, just Wilson's Syndrome (due to an impairment in the conversion of T4 to T3). Proper treatment of DTSF depends, in every case, on the underlying cause and this chapter describes only the preferred treatment for Wilson's Syndrome.

As described more fully in Chapters 4 and 6, the following are useful in the workup for WS.
1. **Past Medical History** including previous surgeries, reproductive history, current medical problems, and the like.
2. **Family History** in terms of thyroid, cardiovascular and other problems is also important.
3. **Current Medicines** considered in terms of how they may interact with thyroid medicine, and in terms of whether or not they might be contributing to the symptoms, if not the problem.

4. **Patient's Complaints**, when they started, and under what circumstances they improved or worsened are also important. When the symptoms come on together, it is more likely that they are related.
5. **Body Temperature Patterns** are extremely useful in helping to predict whether or not a patient's symptoms may respond to proper T3 therapy.
6. **Nationality** or heritage can be like the icing on the cake.

If no other apparent cause of the symptoms can be found, then one might consider proper T3 therapy. **Useful tests for this purpose include multichemistry tests, complete blood count, EKG, and even ANA, SED rates and possibly others when indicated. Thyroid hormone blood tests (including T4, TSH, Total T3 Radiolmmuno Assay (RIA), Total RT3 RIA) are recommended to rule out other obvious causes of DTSF, and as a baseline to which later tests can be compared.**

Temperature Patterns

Because of the daily cycles (and monthly in women) in body temperature, I recommend that it be taken three times a day, three hours apart, beginning three hours after awakening three days in a row, at times other than ovulation or immediately premenstrually. Once treatment has been initiated, however, I recommend that the body temperature patterns should be monitored every day even at ovulation and premenstrually. It should be remembered that although these are typical patterns, there are people whose body temperatures do not follow these patterns. Special attention should be made to the patient's body temperature patterns in relation to the pattern of their presenting complaint. For example, if the patient feels worse in the morning, what happens to their temperature pattern at that time? And if they feel worse at 3 o'clock, what happens to their temperature pattern at that time? And if they feel worse two days before their period what happens to their temperature during those two days?

Dr. Barnes' basal temperature test involves taking the body temperature under the arm prior to getting out of bed each morning. It is often suggested that it be taken especially on the third day of the period when body temperatures are supposed, by some, to be most normal.

Since I am mainly concerned with the symptoms that these patients complain about, I am more concerned about the body temperature patterns at the time their symptoms are most disturbing. If the patient's complaints affect their productivity primarily during the bulk of the day, preventing them from functioning normally at home or at work, then I am more concerned about their body temperature patterns during the bulk of the day. If their complaints are more severe in the morning or evening, then I may be more interested in the body temperature pattern at those times. However, there are two more reasons that I usually recommend that patients take their body temperatures more during the bulk of their day, or what should be their most productive hours. **One** is that most Wilson's Syndrome sufferers' symptoms take their toll in terms of productivity, especially during the "productive" hours during the bulk of the day (even though the symptoms may be worse in the morning until the body temperature rises as the patient "warms up"). The **second** reason is that if the patient's body temperature runs low when measured several times a day, several hours apart, during the bulk of the day when the body temperatures are usually at their highest (as compared to low body temperature readings taken in the morning when body temperatures are **usually** lower), then it is even more likely that the patient's body temperature patterns are abnormally low. By taking several temperatures during the bulk of the day when the temperature is usually at its highest, it is felt that the results may be more meaningful, with few false positives.

It should be remembered that one temperature by itself doesn't mean a thing, since body temperatures normally fluctuate at different times under different conditions. However, body temperature **patterns** can be quite useful. I like to look at body temperature readings the way one looks out over an ocean to determine whether it is choppy or calm or whether it is high tide or low tide. Certainly the level of the body temperature is important with both "low tide" and "high tide" being capable of causing symptoms. When the body temperature patterns are "choppy" or unsteady, symptoms may also result. Preferably, the body temperature pattern should be normal and steady to provide maximal enzyme function and efficiency. One cannot determine by looking at the crest of one wave whether it is high tide, low tide, choppy, or calm. One must look out over the whole ocean to get a feel for the marine conditions. Likewise, one cannot tell by one body temperature reading the nature of a person's body temperature patterns, but one may get a feel for them by looking over all the body temperature readings.

Patients' body temperatures are usually higher in the doctor's office (like pulse and blood pressure readings presumably because of nervousness). Because they are frequently higher, and because one body temperature by itself does not tell very much, body temperature readings taken in the doctor's office are not very useful. Patients are often already aware that their body temperatures run consistently below normal. They have been told by nurses in hospitals or doctor's offices that their temperatures run unusually low, that the "thermometer must be broken", or asked by the nurses, "are you alive?"

Many times WS sufferers will come down with a cold or flu, feel feverish, and measure their body temperatures expecting high temperatures, only to find that their temperatures are not very high and may actually be **below** normal. WS sufferers frequently indicate that temperatures that might not be considered significant in most people indicate severe illness for them. They equate a temperature of 99.4 for them to be like a fever of a 102 or 103 for other people who are just as sick. They often say, "I have to get sick to run a normal temperature," or, "If I run a temperature of 99.6 then I've got to be **really** sick." Patients are often surprised when they follow their body temperature patterns to see how low, and sometimes how erratic their body temperatures do run. Some patients who feel hot all the time and sweat easily are astounded to find that their body temperatures never get above 97.8 (8/10th's of a degree below normal).

I prefer glass thermometers since I feel that their readings are more consistent. Readings taken by digital thermometers can vary from one minute to the next especially when the battery is low. There are less things that can go wrong with glass and mercury. However, digital readings are faster than glass readings and if pressed for time at work, a digital reading is better than no reading. Temperatures should be taken at least 15 minutes after eating or drinking and should be taken for a least 4 to 5 minutes when using a glass thermometer. Fortunately, body temperature patterns end up being of great predictive value in the monitoring of T3 therapy. I consider daily temperature ranges of 2 to 3/10th's of a degree to be consistent with a relatively steady body temperature pattern. Some patients, however, are surprised to find that their body temperature patterns can fluctuate from 1 to 2, or even 3 whole degrees. Most patients that I treat typically present with body temperature patterns averaging about 97.8 degrees, although symptoms can be caused by temperatures closer to 98.6 degrees. Some patients have temperatures between 96 and 97.8 degrees. A few have body temperatures less than 96 degrees, and I have seen some patients with body temperatures that can go as low as 93 degrees at times.

The best indicator that a patient's symptoms are related to their temperature pattern is that when the patient takes the right kind of thyroid medication, in the right way, to get their body temperature pattern up to 98.6 degrees, and if the patient's complaints resolve within two days to two weeks, then that is a pretty good indicator that one is on the right track. If the patient's symptoms remain gone and his body temperature remains in the 98.6 degree range even after T3 therapy has been discontinued, then that is a pretty good indicator that some persistent correction has been effected. This is what is known as a therapeutic trial.

In a sense, everything in medicine, as discussed previously, is a therapeutic trial. One never knows how a patient will respond to high blood pressure medicine, asthma medicine, ulcer medicine, or antibiotics until they are administered and the patient's response evaluated. In many ways, medicine is far less of an exact science than some people make it out to be. The patient's response to treatment helps to more firmly establish the diagnosis of the patient's presenting problems and complaints. So, just like everything in life, physicians can

242

only do the best they can with what they have, going about their business with the best tools available, working on correcting problems.

In spite of the fact that there are few medical problems that respond to treatment as predictably as Wilson's Syndrome, the particulars of the patients' response to treatment vary tremendously. The clinical patterns and presentation of the classic signs and symptoms of Wilson's Syndrome, and the body temperature pattern, can be extremely predictive and can predict favorable response to therapy in 95% of cases. There are few problems in medicine that can respond as predictably and reproducibly as Wilson's Syndrome can to proper T3 therapy. In this sense, the clinical pattern of presentation or clinical picture and body temperature patterns are extremely accurate and valuable tests. Nevertheless, as in all medical therapies, the treatment itself may be the test that best helps determine whether the diagnosis was correct. If the patient responds well to a specific therapy directed at the cause, then it is more likely that the suspected cause was indeed the cause of the patient's complaints, and it is more likely that the therapy resolved their complaints by successfully addressing this cause, particularly if the symptoms remain resolved even after the therapy has been discontinued.

Potential Risks And Benefits

Before starting T3 therapy as with any other medical therapy, one must first consider the potential risks and benefits. **One can increase the chance of benefit and decrease the risk by ruling out other obvious causes of the patient's presenting complaints.** Some of the more important things to rule out are Addison's Disease (adrenal insufficiency), Cushing's Disease (excessive glucocorticoid), congestive heart failure, anemia, leukemia, atrial fibrillation, irregular heart rhythms, lupus, Sjogren's Syndrome, and others. It is important to rule these conditions out as well as possible and to think of these things when considering treatment for Wilson's Syndrome because some of these conditions can get worse with thyroid hormone treatment. This is especially true of Addison's Disease, for example, which is sometimes characterized by severe abdominal pain. These conditions are really quite rare, but are, nevertheless, important to consider.

Let us now consider more specifically the risks of T3 therapy. Thyroid hormones have been continually present in every person's body since birth. Adequate thyroid hormone levels are necessary for survival. If someone is living, they necessarily have T3 in their blood stream and if they are not on any medication, then they have T4 in their blood stream as well. **Unlike most other medications, thyroid hormones are found in nature and in every person's body.** This helps explain why there has not been a reported incident of anyone having an allergic reaction to thyroid hormone medication. Most other medicines, however, are designed by men in laboratories, are foreign, and are different from the molecules that are produced by the body naturally. For this reason, it is unlikely that thyroid hormones have many long term side effects. It is unlikely that thyroid hormones can directly damage tissues such as the brain, lungs, heart, or other tissues, since these tissues have been exposed to the very same hormone since birth. Thyroid hormones have been on the market for over 40 years and have not been shown to increase the chance of a person developing cancers or other unusual reactions in patients who have been treated with thyroid hormones for several decades. In fact, patients are frequently told, once they have been diagnosed as having DTSF, that they will need to take thyroid hormone medication "for the rest of their lives." Thyroid hormone medication has been seen to be tolerated well enough and to be sometimes necessary to take daily for the rest of one's life.

There have been some studies recently to show that patients in their later years who are being replaced with T4 supplementation levels that are so high that the TSH level is below the lower limits of normal over a period of years (even ten years), may have a higher degree of bone loss or osteoporosis as compared to patients who are not on thyroid hormone medication. However, that these patients TSH levels were suppressed significantly, indicates that they might have been taking excessive levels of T4 supplementation. We have

244

already discussed how some patients' thyroid systems can be pushed too far in the wrong direction with too much T4 supplementation. The cause of bone loss in these patients has not yet been determined and body temperature patterns have not been taken into account, and it may be that these patient's thyroid systems were not being properly monitored and regulated.

Thyroid hormone supplementation cannot be properly monitored if body temperature patterns are not taken into consideration. Just because the patients' T4 levels were excessive does not necessarily mean that they were getting sufficient levels of the active hormone T3. T4 is the thyroid hormone preparation most often prescribed for long-term maintenance therapy and is generally considered to be quite benign (not harmful). Of course, T4 is not the physiologically active thyroid hormone, T3 is. T4 has to be converted to T3 before it has its action. So essentially, T4 is "T3 waiting to happen." Therefore, in a sense, when one takes T4, one is taking T3, thus T3 therapy does not expose the body to any substances that T4 therapy doesn't. The effects of T4 and T3 therapy on the body differ mainly in the extent to and the steadiness with which they provide the body with the physiologically active thyroid hormone T3. These effects can be maximized through the use of correct pharmacological principles. Also T3 and T4 therapy can be judiciously combined in certain cases to take advantage of the effects of each.

One interesting study showed that when some people are born with out thyroid function, they can sometimes be supplemented with T3 instead of T4. One such person was raised entirely on T3 medication and never had any T4 in his body during his entire life. By the age of 26, he had grown and developed normally.

The more substantive risks of thyroid hormone therapy are more short term rather than long term. They are more due to the <u>indirect</u> effects of the medicine (on blood pressure and pulse), than they are due to <u>direct</u> tissue damage. If every medicine has a risk and I were to assign one for T3 therapy, then I would say that if a person was on the verge of having a heart attack or stroke anyway, changes in his or her blood pressure or pulse could aggravate the situation like the straw that broke the camel's back. Other factors that fall into the same category include: getting into arguments, driving in heavy traffic on the interstate, and many other types of medicine (such as caffeine, alcohol, decongestants, blood pressure medications, and others). If a person already has a tendency towards having an irregular heart rhythm (of which he or she is already aware, or that can be seen on an EKG), then T3 therapy might increase that patient's chances of having irregular heart rhythms. If a patient is not on the verge of a heart attack or stroke, then it would be hard to see how T3 therapy can bring them there, since it is a hormone that has been well tolerated in his/her body since birth.

Proper T3 therapy is generally extremely well tolerated, and when used with proper care and consideration, it is usually quite easily managed. When properly managed, one does not expect any drastic problems because one makes no drastic changes. The medication is started at extremely low levels and increased in very small increments, so that if the patient does develop any complaints, they usually come on gradually, not all at once. **It is important to take the medication on time and as directed.**

Another important thing to remember is that not every doctor currently understands proper T3 therapy or Wilson's Syndrome. It is important not to stop thyroid hormone medicines (especially T3) abruptly.

There is quite a bit of **mythology** about the thyroid system and thyroid hormone supplementation. This is easy to understand considering the difficulty available tests have had in predictably and reproducibly measuring the **function** of the thyroid system (in relation to signs and symptoms of DTSF). Some say that once on thyroid therapy, always on thyroid therapy, but this is not necessarily true. Some say that taking thyroid hormone medication will cause a person's gland to atrophy and that the gland will be ruined so that he will always need thyroid therapy. That some patients will need to take thyroid hormone medication for life is true, especially those patients who no longer have a thyroid gland. However, not all patients on thyroid medication will have to take it forever. And temporarily suppressing the gland does not mean that the gland will be ruined. I have seen many patients who have been treated with T4 therapy for years (even 20 and 30 years), with their TSH levels all the while being at or below the lower limits of normal (which indicates that their pituitary gland's secretion of TSH had been suppressed by the T4 medication resulting in almost complete suppression of the patient's thyroid gland). These patients sometimes present, nevertheless, with classic signs and symptoms of DTSF in spite of being on years of T4 therapy. With careful weaning of T4 therapy and administration of proper T3 therapy, the patients' cause of DTSF (concurrent Wilson's Syndrome) can often be reversed with resolution of their symptoms of MED with normalization of body temperature patterns. Upon gradually weaning the T3 therapy, these patient's thyroid gland production of T4 can often resume again on its own for the first time in 20 to 30 years (especially in cases in which the patients' original diagnosis was based on less than solid evidence - which is often the case). These patients are sometimes able to wean off the T3 therapy and maintain normal body temperature patterns and resolution of the symptoms of MED on their own. If a thyroid gland can function normally after being suppressed for 20 or 30 years, it is hard to imagine a normal thyroid gland's function not resuming after being suppressed for two weeks, two months, or even two years. There is no medical literature that demonstrates that suppression of the thyroid gland with thyroid hormone supplementation can result in permanent damage to the thyroid gland. In the approximately 5, 000 cases that I have treated, I have never seen it happen. Of course, I suppose in medicine anything that **can** happen **does** happen, and therefore, thyroid hormone supplementation should not be taken casually and should only be taken if it is decided by the patient and the doctor that the potential benefits outweigh the potential risks. Then one might consider a therapeutic trial of proper T3 therapy.

It is understandable how the body and thyroid gland tolerate thyroid hormone supplementation so well when one considers that the thyroid system is not a static system but a dynamic one. The thyroid hormone levels are constantly being adjusted by the body to accommodate different circumstances. So if the thyroid system can adjust to drastically different physical and environmental changes, and then can adjust back to normal once those changes have passed, it is easy to see how the thyroid system can adjust back to normal after "artificial" adjustments have been exerted on the thyroid system for a time with thyroid hormone supplementation.

The potential side effects of thyroid hormone treatment are very similar to the symptoms of DTSF. This is because the symptoms are "thyroid" symptoms. If the symptoms are treated properly, then they will improve. If they are improving with treatment for a time and for some reason the treatment is not done properly or other problems occur, then the symptoms that have improved might begin to get worse again. So in that sense, they might be considered side effects from the treatment. In other words, if the system is affected properly, the symptoms get better and if the system is being affected improperly, the symptoms can get worse again and in that sense be considered "side effects." That is why many patients can have many of the "side effects" **prior** to treatment that are correlated **with** treatment such as shakiness, lightheadedness, hot flashes, fever blisters, weakness of the legs, panicky feelings, fatigue especially after a meal, jitteriness, diarrhea, constipation, sweating, dizziness, leg cramps, etc. **If a patient should develop any symptoms or side effects from the treatment, it is an indication that the thyroid hormones are not adjusted properly and that the medication needs to be adjusted.**

Thyroid hormone therapy should not be considered a "no pain, no gain" treatment. There is no point in "toughing out" any sensations that might remotely be considered side effects of therapy, because ideally, the symptoms are supposed to only improve with absolutely no complaints. Again, **any** complaint that is in any way suspected to be related to the medicine should be considered an indicator that the thyroid hormone treatment might be less than ideally adjusted. The side effects, like the symptoms, can be caused by body temperature patterns that are too low, too high, or unsteady.

The medication should not be stopped abruptly. One might wonder what effects such an action would have. If patients stop their T3 therapy abruptly, nine times out of ten, they will not be able to tell the difference. Five times out of one hundred, the patient may notice being more tired and achy; about one time out of a hundred, the patient may become significantly more tired, lightheaded upon standing, clammy, aware of low blood pressure, and have other such symptoms for several days and even a few weeks. So it is not advisable to stop the medicine abruptly.

Most of the patients that I treat have normal thyroid hormone blood tests (which is typical of Wilson's Syndrome), and, by far, the majority of them get better with treatment. In previous chapters the limitations of the thyroid hormone blood tests have been thoroughly discussed. Suffice it to say that thyroid hormone blood tests can be misleading, having a large number of false negatives in the evaluation of DTSF and the symptoms of MED. Most of the patients that I treat have normal blood tests much the way patients with migraines, premenstrual syndrome, depression, irregular periods, and infertility frequently have normal blood tests. Of course, patients are treated for migraines, depression, and PMS every day because many doctors understand that our medical technology is not exhaustive. They understand that there are still more things that are unknown than are known.

How does the doctor **know** when a patient is suffering from the symptoms they are describing, which happen to be consistent, for example, with the clinical picture of migraine headaches? The only way he has of knowing that a patient is suffering from such complaints is because the patient says so and because the doctor believes the patient. Since there is no "migraine-o-meter," **the doctor is left to make a provisional diagnosis and begin therapeutic trials in an effort to alleviate the patient's condition.** The same situation holds true for depression and the administration of antidepressants which are among the most widely prescribed medicines in the world. Doctors are doing the best they can with what they have, and by approaching the problems of migraines, depression, and PMS analytically, doctors have been able to relieve untold anguish and misery. It seems very strange then, that the limitations of blood tests and medical technology are so well recognized in certain areas of medicine, while the results of tests seem to be unduly considered cut-and-dry, conclusive, exhaustive, and infallible in others. Perhaps it is because thyroid hormone blood tests **can** be useful in identifying **some** of the causes of DTSF. But we must not jump to the conclusion that necessarily means that they can identify **all** causes of DTSF.

With all of our knowledge, advancements, technology, and sophisticated tests, we sometimes lose sight of the fact that tests are only as valuable as they are useful in predicting the outcome of therapy and directing treatment to make patients' problems better (which is the real goal of medicine). The value of a test isn't always best measured by how difficult the test is to perform, how much it costs to make or develop the machine used, or how expensive the test is to obtain. Just because a test is extremely complicated, sophisticated, and expensive, doesn't necessarily mean that it is extremely useful, predictive, or valuable in addressing certain problems. Wilson's Syndrome signs and symptoms, their clinical presentation, and body temperature patterns aren't expensive, complicated, or technologically highly sophisticated, nevertheless, they are extremely valuable in helping to predict who will and who will not respond to proper T3 therapy, and in helping to direct that therapy. Often objective (from tests) information has more predictive value than subjective (from the patient) information in the diagnosis and treatment of medical problems. However, in the diagnosis and treatment of Wilson's Syndrome, information obtained from the patient ends up being extremely predictive.

For example, if a patient has a classic presentation of Wilson's Syndrome, it is easy to predict that a patient has a low body temperature pattern and is likely to respond to proper T3 therapy. In fact, if I see 200 patients with a classic presentation of Wilson's Syndrome, less than one would have a normal body temperature pattern (running 98.6 degrees on average). In fact when a patient relates to me a classic presentation of Wilson's Syndrome, I will often tell them, "I know your body temperature runs low, have you ever noticed that?" In many cases the patients are already aware that they have consistently low body temperature patterns, but in some they are not. A few patients having classic presentations for Wilson's Syndrome have gone home and measured their body temperatures and found that their body temperatures were averaging normal or above. To such patients, after making sure that they were not taking their temperatures at the time of ovulation or just prior to their menstrual cycles, I have made the comment: "That means your thermometer is broken and you should check your temperature with another thermometer." These patients are often astounded when they go home and find that sure enough, their body temperature patterns do run consistently below normal when measured with another thermometer. I have been so bold as to make such statements because **in a patient with a classic presentation of Wilson's Syndrome, there is more chance that the patient's thermometer is broken than there is that the patient has a body temperature pattern that runs consistently normal or above.** Patients with classic signs, symptoms, and presentations of Wilson's Syndrome will notice an unequivocal improvement in their symptoms with proper T3 therapy in 95% of cases. There are very few medical problems that respond as reproducibly and predictably to treatment (with or without technologically sophisticated testing) as does Wilson's Syndrome respond to proper T3 therapy. DTSF symptoms that come on after a major stress associated with low body temperature patterns and normal thyroid blood tests are almost pathognomonic for Wilson's Syndrome. Pathognomonic is a medical term that means that it is specifically distinctive or characteristic of a disease or pathologic condition; denoting a sign or symptom on which a diagnosis can be made.

Goal Of T3 Therapy

If blood tests and physical examination reveal no other good explanation for the patient's classic signs and symptoms of DTSF, then one may suspect an impairment in the conversion of T4 to T3 thyroid hormones and one may consider a therapeutic trial with T3 therapy. The goal of T3 therapy is really made up of two subgoals.
1. Feel well while on T3 therapy.
2. Remain well after T3 therapy has been discontinued.

These subgoals can be achieved separately or concurrently. During the course of treatment, the symptoms may resolve, but that doesn't necessarily mean that they will stay resolved after therapy is weaned. Sometimes several cycles of treatment are necessary in order to have the symptoms resolve and remain resolved even after T3 therapy has been discontinued. Sometimes the symptoms resolve only **after** T3 therapy is discontinued. This is because the accomplishing of each subgoal is predicated upon a different factor. The first subgoal is predicated upon providing sufficiently normal and steady T3 levels to provide sufficiently normal and steady body temperature patterns to maintain normal enzyme activity, to eliminate and prevent the symptoms of MED characteristic of DTSF due to Wilson's Syndrome. The second subgoal is predicated upon reversing the imbalance leading to impaired T4 to T3 conversion well enough that the body can maintain, on its own, proper thyroid system function once the T3 therapy has been discontinued. T3 therapy accomplishes this goal by reducing competitive inhibition at the level of 5'-deiodinase by systematically reducing RT3 levels, and possibly by establishing a new pattern or new balance in the body's overall system by indirectly effecting changes in other systems such as the female hormone system, adrenal hormone system, glucose metabolism system, and others (rope and ring analogy, see chapter 2).

Sometimes RT3 levels can be lowered to reduce their inhibition of T4 to T3 conversion, even though the artificial levels of T3 have not been stabilized sufficiently to completely eliminate the symptoms of MED. Yet, in such cases, with the underlying impairment corrected and the body's own thyroid system function being restored as T3 therapy is gradually discontinued, the symptoms of MED may resolve more going **off** T3 therapy than they ever did while **on** T3 therapy. This demonstrates that the body's own system can be "reset" to function properly on its own, even if artificial T3 therapy could not be stabilized well enough (during a treatment cycle) to eliminate or prevent the symptoms of MED in the meantime. Usually both subgoals can be accomplished concurrently, but it should be remembered that they are not inseparable. It is fortunate that, in almost all cases, the two subgoals can be accomplished at the same time.

Thyroid Medicines

Let us take a moment to discuss different types of thyroid medications available. Some medicines contain only **levothyroxine (T4)**, while others contain only **liothyronine (T3)**, while still others contain a combination of **T4** and **T3**. A distinction can also be made between thyroid medicines that originate from animal sources, and those that are made synthetically. In thyroid hormone supplementation, it is important that each dose of the same strength of medication given contain extremely similar amounts of the medication to help provide normal and steady levels. Medications prepared from animal sources are not considered to have as much consistency as compared to synthetic preparations. Consistency is particularly important in T3 therapy. T3 medication is prepared synthetically. There is quite a controversy over the consistency of generic medications as compared to brand-name medications. In many instances, with many different medications, the distinction may not be very important. **But with T3 therapy, steadiness and consistency are everything and I believe the brand-name product is superior to the generic product. Brand-name T3, however is an "instant release" preparation, and I almost always use a special T3 preparation that incorporates a sustained-release agent or vehicle used in many sustained-release medicines on the market. It is to be taken every 12 hours.**

To review, T3, T4, and RT3 look exactly the same, the way 3 keys look exactly the same except having one notch that's different (see diagram 2-3). The interesting thing is that RT3 has no activity at all, T4 has a little activity, and T3 has four times more activity than T4 at the active site. Interestingly, T4 is converted to T3.

It takes 7 1/2 days for 50% of a certain amount of T4 to be degraded by the body, giving it a "half-life" of 7 1/2 days. The half-life of T3 is shorter than that of T4 being only 2 1/2 days. Since T3 is four times more active and is a third as long acting, and since the whole goal of T3 therapy is to provide normal and **steady** T3 levels to the active site in order to provide normal and **steady** body temperature patterns, it becomes apparent that T3 therapy is most effective when done in a precise manner. T4 medication having such a long half-life needs to be taken only once a day and can provide steady levels of T4 and T3. Unfortunately, as pointed out previously, Wilson's Syndrome sufferers who have a hard time converting their own T4 to T3 often cannot convert T4 medication sufficiently to provide **sufficient** levels of T3 at the active site in a sustained manner, nor in a manner that could help reverse the vicious cycle that contributes to persistent T4 to T3 conversion impairment. T4 is usually not helpful in the treatment of Wilson's Syndrome because it is not useful in systematically reducing RT3 levels, and because improvement of WS symptoms with T4 medication is usually short-lived (usually about 3 months, if achieved at all). Increases in T4 therapy are then required to maintain the improvements, thereby, often feeding the vicious cycle rather than helping to reverse it. In fact, further increases in the T4 therapy can then even begin to make the WS symptoms worse.

T4 medicine is a very good medicine, and is the treatment of choice for the other causes of DTSF. But since it is not generally useful in accomplishing the two subgoals of treatment for Wilson's Syndrome, T3 therapy is the treatment of choice. **The whole trick to T3 therapy is to keep the levels of T3 steady.** This requires some care, consideration, and effort considering the short half-life of T3. Most doctors seem to think of thyroid hormone medication in terms of weeks and months, possibly because it takes weeks for T4 medication to provide a "steady state" or prescribed level of T3. However, T3 can be thought of in terms of minutes, days, and weeks since it can start being absorbed into the body within 35 to 45 minutes after the dose and can begin having an effect at the nuclear membrane receptors soon thereafter. This is especially true with T3 therapy since it is already "active" and does not need to wait around to be activated by the body.

Available medical resources suggest that T3 levels are more steady when patients are given T4 than when T3 is given directly, and that side effects are more likely when T3 levels are unsteady; yet they also suggest that T4 medication and T3 medication both be given once a day. This does not even make pharmacological sense. Normally, T4 is converted to T3 a little at a time, **thousands** of times around the clock 24 hours a day. Is it any wonder that this steady supply of T3 can't be closely approximated with T3 given only **once** a day, or even several times a day? Is it any surprise that T3 levels may be more unsteady when T3 is supplied only once a day as compared to thousand of times around the clock? Perhaps this is one reason why the usefulness of T3 has been overlooked for so long and it may be why T3 therapy is sometimes considered to be somewhat prone to causing side effects. Of course, all medicines are prone to being less useful and more likely to cause side effects when taken in ways that do not make pharmacological sense.

There is nothing inadequate about T3 as a medicine or as a molecule, apparently only our understanding and application of it has been inadequate. In fact, it is one of the most important and useful of all medicines, and is a molecule the body can't live without. There are some studies and people that have "concluded" this and "determined" that about T3, the way one can look through the wrong end of a pair of binoculars and "conclude" that they are not useful for seeing long distances. It is amazing how using something correctly can make all the difference in the world.

Some patients can tolerate T3 therapy given in single daily doses, some tolerate doses taken twice a day, some three time a day. However, in my experience, taking all patients as a whole, I feel that instant-release T3 therapy should be taken at least every three hours, six times a day, consistently by the clock in order to decrease the chances of side effects, and to increase the chances of benefits. **A new approach, however, involves incorporating T3 into a sustained-release vehicle used in many sustained-release medicines on the market. It is intended to be taken every twelve hours and to deliver a little T3 thousands of times over a 12-hour period to provide a more steady supply of T3. When taken twice a day, such a preparation is designed to provide a more steady supply of T3 24 hours a day.** So it is easy to understand why such a preparation is far more effective in the treatment of Wilson's Syndrome than instant-release T3 therapy. Since the possible side effects of T3 are most often related to unsteady T3 levels, it is easy to understand also, why there are far less side effects with T3 therapy incorporating a sustained-release vehicle as compared to instant-release T3 therapy, and why it is much better tolerated. The T3 incorporating a sustained-release vehicle needs to be taken only twice a day as compared to six times a day, which makes it far easier for the patients to take the medicine properly, and on time. Such a preparation incorporating a sustained-release vehicle is not being mass-produced on the market, but is being custom made or "compounded" by some pharmacists with a special interest in compounding.

There are a few (approximately five percent of patients) who do respond better to instant-release T3 than the T3 in sustained-release vehicle. However, by far most patients respond far more quickly, far more completely, and with far less side effects to a T3 preparation incorporating a sustained release vehicle. In fact, the incidence and severity of side effects of T3 therapy can be reduced approximately 20-fold through the use of such a T3 preparation, as compared to instant release T3.

Many medications such as antihistamines, asthma medicines, blood pressure medicines, and many others have proven to be much more efficacious and better tolerated when administered in slow-release or time-release preparations that maintain more constant delivery and blood levels. Considering the importance of steady T3 levels, it is understandable why T3 in a sustained-release vehicle would prove to be much more efficacious and better tolerated than instant release T3. For this reason, I use, almost exclusively, such a preparation taken by mouth every 12 hours in the patients that I treat for Wilson's Syndrome. It is important that the such a preparation be taken by mouth every 12 hours, 30 days a month, at the same time every day. If a patient misses a dose by an hour, he or she will probably notice no side effects and might conclude, therefore, that the timing of the dose doesn't really matter. However, I always recommend to my patients that if they want the medicine to work exceptionally well, then they should take the doses right to the minute, not even three minutes late. It is also best that the preparation be compounded with great care and precision. I even recommend using a timer that automatically goes off every 12 hours. Because being off 20 minutes here, and 30 minutes there can add up over a period of a couple of weeks decreasing the potential benefits. Restoring the potential once decreased can take two weeks or more and may require cycling.

Purpose Of T3

The purpose of T3 therapy is to raise the body temperature patterns to average closer to normal (98.6 degrees). As soon as the starting dose of T3 is administered to the patient, the body begins to be relieved of the responsibility (for a time) of producing so much T4 and T3 on its own. Like a thermostat, the body detects the T3 medication being given by mouth, and a signal is sent to the thyroid gland to let it know that it does not need to produce as much T4, and consequently, T3. As discussed previously, the two subgoals of treatment are to reset the system and to administer T3 therapy in the meantime in such a way as to bring the body temperature patterns closer to normal. Bringing the body temperature patterns closer to normal involves supplying enough T3 to stimulate the cells to generate normal body temperature patterns. So initial doses of T3 are administered to begin the effort to restore the body temperature levels to normal.

Compensation

However, as soon as the initial doses are given, the body begins to make less T3. So more T3 can be given by mouth to continue the effect to bring the body temperature up to normal, and again the body may make less. And again, then more can be given, and the body may make less. Interestingly, this process also serves the purpose of resetting the system by diminishing T4 levels and, therefore, RT3 levels. When the body temperature is brought up to a normal level, the T3 dose does not need to be increased any further. In most cases, the patient's body temperature can be brought up to average close to normal on less than 150 micrograms per day (dosing discussed later this chapter). With the initial dose of T3 adding additional T3 to the body, the body temperature may be raised closer to normal. But when the body compensates by making less T3, the body temperature may drop back down somewhat and the next incremental increase of T3 can be given.

Different people compensate at different rates. The recommended starting dose is 15 micrograms per day and the incremental increases are also recommended to be 15 micrograms per day. On average, most people will compensate to a 15 microgram incremental increase of T3 in the system within three or four days. However, some may take up to three weeks to compensate in a reproducible way to such an incremental increase. Some may compensate to a 15 microgram increment in one day, and some may even compensate within hours. The more quickly a person compensates to incremental increases of T3 therapy, the more difficult it is to maintain very steady levels of T3 and, therefore, very steady body temperature patterns. Three-week compensators, on the other hand, are usually very easy to manage.

Sometimes, the body can compensate to supplemental T3 therapy in such a way that the body temperature can actually drop instead of going up, because of **over**-compensation. This presents a situation that is similar to wanting to cross a street that has quite a bit of water in the gutters. If you do not want to get wet, then you should run fast enough and jump high

258

enough to clear the water, or not jump at all. Because if you are too tentative, go too slowly, and don't jump high enough, then you run the risk of getting wet. So it is best to either take control of the system and to get the job accomplished or to not affect the system in the first place. T3 therapy should not be undertaken for the fun of it, but only when it is determined that the person's function and quality of life is so impaired and unsatisfactory that the potential risks are outweighed by the potential benefits. T3 therapy should only be undertaken in a deliberate way to accomplish a specific objective. T3 therapy should be administered in a very precise manner and never in a casual manner.

Cycling

It might be remembered that "the deeper the water, the deeper the waves," and the higher the dose of T3 taken, then greater the tendency for T3 levels to be unsteady. But since steadiness is everything, then it is easy to understand why the people that always do the best are the ones that are lucky enough to get their body temperature patterns up to normal on the smallest amount of medicine. People who have been "out of bounds" further and longer may require larger doses to reset their systems. If a person has only had Wilson's Syndrome for six months, it is generally easier to restore them back to a normal pattern more quickly with less medicine than those who have suffered for twenty years. Interestingly, age, sex, and weight do not seem to be very predictive in determining who will and will not require larger doses. The dose required does vary tremendously, but is usually large in patients whose condition is more severe and more long standing. Lower doses are easier to keep steady which increases the chances of benefit, and decreases the chances of side effects. If a person does happen to need more T3 than is contained in the lower doses to reset the system, then one may always be gradually weaned off the medicine and restarted on the T3 therapy again. **This process is known as "cycling" and is extremely helpful. Usually with each cycle, smaller T3 doses are needed in order to maintain normal body temperature patterns, and to further reset the system; so**

that the patient can get closer and closer to normal on less and less T3 medicine until, ideally, the patient is weaned off the T3 therapy completely.

With each cycle requiring less medicine, T3 levels and body temperature patterns become progressively more steady and the patient's symptoms are frequently more improved and the treatment is better tolerated with each cycle until eventually, hopefully, the patient is able to stay normal even after T3 therapy has been discontinued. This cycling process can be repeated, as necessary, from time to time during a patient's life if the conversion impairment returns after a major stress. However, once it has been reset, the sooner the Wilson's Syndrome relapse is treated, the easier it is to correct. If caught early, it can be more easily "nipped in the bud" such that if an initial treatment lasted six months, a subsequent treatment after another significant stress, say two years later, may only take a week if the syndrome is recognized quickly and addressed early enough in the proper manner. We have talked already about how much more beneficial it is that the medicine be taken precisely on time. This is to keep the T3 levels as steady as possible. There is a principle known as steady state. When one begins to take a certain dosage of medicine, there is a period of time over which the level continues to build until it steadies out at a certain level. When the medicine reaches this certain level it is said that steady state has been reached. In most cases, it takes 5 1/2 half-lives for a medicine to reach steady state. For liothyronine, which has a half-life of 2 1/2 days, steady state is reached in approximately 14 days. So when the dosage is changed or interrupted in some manner, it may take two weeks in order for the medicine level to "steady down" again (a significant consideration primarily in this and other medicines that work best when levels are very steady). In practice, I have seen evidence that the level sometimes continues to become more and more steady on the same dose when taken consistently with greater and greater benefit derived not over just two weeks, but sometimes even up to six weeks. It seems to settle into a groove, so to speak, when taken precisely on time, consistently, day after day. It may be that associated changes in systems other than thyroid contribute to the settling effect. Any aberration in the dosage is usually tolerated without complaints, however, it may send "ripples" through the body's T3 levels the way ripples are sent through a water bed when one taps the edge. Considering these things, and considering the fact **that steadiness is so important in T3 therapy, it cannot be over-emphasized how much more effective T3 therapy is when administered and taken precisely.** The more carefully it is done the better it works. Preciseness is important because the loss of potential will come on without warning since one can lose a whole lot of potential before one's T3 levels are unsteady enough to cause any side effects.

T3 Dosing, Steadiness Is Everything

1. Since the less T3 one takes, the easier it is to keep T3 levels steady and the less chance there is of side effects, it is best to begin with a small dose in the neighborhood of 15 micrograms per day (7.5 mcg by mouth ever 12 hours).

2. Since the half-life of T3 is short (2 1/2 days), and since side effects may result from T3 levels that are too low, too high, or unsteady, it is critically important that the medication be administered in the right dose and in a steady fashion.

3. Since the goal of T3 therapy is to normalize body temperature patterns and to resolve the symptoms, if the goal is reached by using the starting does of 15 micrograms per day, then the starting dose can be continued as maintenance, or may be discontinued in the hope that a persistent correction has been effected. These two alternatives can be considered at any time during treatment once the goals of treatment seem to have been reached. This is true even if the average body temperature is less than 98.6 degrees, but persistent resolution is more likely with body temperature patterns averaging closer to 98.6 degrees.

One may wonder how soon T3 therapy can begin to be weaned once the goals seem to have been reached. If a person's body is going to compensate to a certain dose it will probably compensate within one day to three weeks. So there is probably no benefit in waiting longer than three weeks, and, the T3 therapy may sometimes be weaned successfully much earlier than three weeks. In fact, the shortest period of time that I have seen it take to pull a patient with a classic presentation of Wilson's Syndrome from the conservation mode back into the productivity mode is ten days start to finish. The patient was able to raise her body temperature patterns up to normal within days of initiating the T3 therapy, was able to quickly resolve her symptoms of Wilson's Syndrome, and was able to wean off the medication by the tenth day, enjoying a persistent correction in her symptoms and body temperature patterns. She has been fine ever since (approximately two years).

Sometimes the smallest starting dose is not enough to accomplish the goals of treatment, namely to normalize body temperature patterns and to bring the patient out of the conservation mode and return the patient to the productivity mode. So progressively larger doses can be given to accomplish the resetting of the thyroid system. However, the only reason to use higher doses is so that one can be cycled onto lower doses. By gradually weaning off the T3 therapy, the responsibility for supplying the body with T3 is gradually given back to the body. With the levels of RT3 having been decreased, as well as other possible changes in the body having taken place, it is hoped that with decreased inhibition at the site of 5'-deiodinase, that the body will be able to better convert the T4 produced in its thyroid gland to the active thyroid hormone T3. Fortunately, this is often the case and when the body can produce sufficient levels of T3 through conversion of its own T4, it can generally do it quite steadily (often more steadily than can be accomplished with medication taken by mouth). If and when the body "tries its wings" again at T4 to T3 conversion and enjoys a persistent benefit, but not a complete resolution of its Wilson's Syndrome symptoms, then subsequent cycles can be implemented in an attempt to systematically, step by step, return the body fully to the productivity mode. The first cycle I often refer to as the "reset cycle" since it is usually there that the bulk of the work can be accomplished. Subsequent cycles remind me of "fine tuning".

4. 98.6 degrees Fahrenheit measured orally is considered to be normal body temperature under normal circumstances. Since the resolution of the symptoms correlates with normalization of body temperature patterns, and since the effects of a dosage level of T3 therapy can be evident within hours and can be maximal within days, then if the symptoms have not satisfactorily resolved with the starting dose and the body temperature is averaging below 98.6 and the patient is not having any side effects, then the daily dose may be increased by an increment of approximately 15 micrograms per day up to the next level of 30 micrograms per day. Since the risk of treatment increases with increased side effects, the dosage should not be increased if the patient is suffering from side effects (which is an indication that the medication may not be adjusted properly).

5. If at any time the patient does have any side effects, the patient may be weaned gradually off the T3 therapy. If the temperature rises significantly above 98.6 degrees, for example to 99 degrees, the patient may be reduced gradually on T3 therapy.

6. If the symptoms are not significantly improved, the temperature is averaging normal at 98.6 and there are no side effects, the patient may be weaned off the T3 medicine. In a case like this, the T3 levels often steady down as the patient weans off T3 therapy with the symptoms resolving only after the patient's therapy has been weaned. If the patient's symptoms are not sufficiently improved with the body temperature averaging around normal and the patient is without side effects, it is probably because of unsteady T3 levels.

7. If the symptoms are not sufficiently improved, if the body temperature average remains below 98.6 degrees, and if there are no significant side effects, the daily dosage may be increased every one to three days in small increments (15 micrograms per day) until: (a) the symptoms are gone; (b) the body temperature averages normal; (c) there are side effects; or (d) levels of 150 to 200 micrograms per day are reached. The higher the dose, the higher the chances of side effects and

there is usually little benefit in increasing the dose higher than 150 to 200 micrograms per day. It is usually better to wean off the medicine and then start it again (after at least a couple of days of rest), since sometimes the body temperature cannot be brought up to normal in one step no matter how much T3 is used, much the same way a car cannot be jacked up with one push on the tire iron no matter how hard that push is.

8. At this stage, T3 therapy may be weaned and restarted or cycled. By cycling, the patient usually is able to achieve more normal temperatures on lower T3 doses. The closer the body temperature pattern gets up to normal with previous cycles the more likely it is that less medicine will be needed to reach the same temperatures with subsequent cycles. This can be thought of as being like a car jack: if the weight of the car is pushed up high enough, it can catch on the next step up. However, if it is not lifted high enough, then it may slide back down to the level it is currently occupying. **The less the T3 dose, the more steady the T3 levels, the more effective the treatment, and the less the side effects. The more normal the temperature, the more effective the treatment and the less the side effects.**

To wean, the daily dosage may be decreased in small increments, for example, 15 micrograms per day at a time, at intervals necessary to prevent a drop in temperature (generally in intervals of about two to ten days). As it turns out, patients are able to increase their body temperature with T3 therapy, often enjoy their body temperatures remaining close to the new increased level even while weaning off the T3 therapy. The trick to weaning off the therapy in a way that permits correction to remain effective, is to wean slowly enough that the temperature does not drop again. For obvious reasons, this is not best attempted or easily accomplished under periods of extreme physical, emotional, or mental stress (since stress often started the problem to begin with). Patients are frequently able to wean off T3 by 15 micrograms per day, every two days on average. Some have to wean off by 15 micrograms-per-day-increments every four days and some have to go off every seven to ten days because if they go faster than that their temperatures will drop. If the patient's symptoms resolve or remain resolved completely after T3 is weaned, then the T3 therapy need not be restarted. Usually the less a patient's body temperature drops, the less medication will be needed in the next cycle to bring the body temperature up closer to normal. Sometimes with each cycle, the patient may enjoy a decrease in the necessary dosage. It is common for patients to need only a 7th, a 10th, a 20th, or a 25th of the amount of medicine in the second cycle to accomplish the same as, or more than, in the first.

9. In cases where complete resolution of symptoms have not been effected by way of the first cycle of T3 therapy, a second cycle may be implemented. This is especially called for if the symptoms are positively effected, if there was a net improvement in the symptoms from the first cycle, and if there was a net change in the body temperature pattern. Almost always the patient is able to achieve more normal body temperature patterns on less medicine than the first cycle. This represents progress and this progress can be continued until the patient is able to come closer and closer to normal (with symptoms and temperature) on less and less T3 until the symptoms resolve and remain resolved off T3 therapy.

One may wonder how much time there should be between cycles. One purpose of weaning off a cycle is to let the body's own T3 production build back up and steady down. This usually takes place within two weeks after a cycle has been discontinued and there would be little added benefit in waiting longer than two weeks. As it turns out, patients can generally tell when T3 levels are steady and when they are unsteady, a patient may have a nondescript feeling of being a little "off the mark" and the patient is often able to tell when that feeling is gone once T3 levels become steady again. So a patient does not necessarily need to stay off the T3 for two weeks between each cycle. If the patient never noticed any sensation of unsteadiness while on the T3 therapy, then the next cycle can be initiated after two or three days of the previous cycle (and after any sensations of unsteadiness have passed if they were noticed). The more time between cycles, the more time the foundation has to steady down, but one does not want the treatment to last unnecessarily long.

10. The treatment can be employed in the fashion described above anywhere along the path from the beginning of the first cycle to the ending of the last cycle. For example, if the patient is happy to feel normal again for the first time in years, is not having any complaints, and is not anxious to rock the boat, then the patient need not wean the T3 therapy. If body temperature patterns are normal and steady, and the patient is not having any complaints, they may be maintained on T3 therapy for a time. Patients have been known to take thyroid medication for decades (even T3). If the patient feels satisfactorily improved and the body temperature patterns have been normalized, the T3 therapy can be gradually weaned if the patient would like to see if a persistent correction has been effective. Or, if the patient's symptoms are quite a bit improved but not completely resolved, the patient may:

(a) continue the process of increasing and decreasing the therapy in an attempt to improve the level of correction;

(b) stay on the same dosage level in an effort to maintain the same degree of correction to not "rock to boat" by taking the chance of possibly having side effects on higher doses or by possibly losing ground by weaning off the medication (this alternative is frequently useful during periods of time when the patient is faced with severe stress such as family or business problems), or;

(c) weaning off the medicine in the hopes of being able to maintain the achieved level of correction until the treatment can be pursued again at a later time (useful, for example, when a patient needs to go out of town for many months). The problem usually gets worse in stages over time and can frequently get better in stages over time as well.

11. Not only have T3 therapy cycles been used to coax the body temperature to more normal levels, but they have also been used in cases where the average body temperatures were at a normal level but were too unsteady, for the purpose of attempting to make them more steady. Thus, T3 therapy can also be implemented as a stabilizing influence on unsteady body temperature patterns, and can thereby, sometimes

resolve symptoms of DTSF. This situation, however, is extremely rare. If the two subgoals of T3 therapy for Wilson's Syndrome include going gradually up and down on T3 therapy to: 1. Feel well while on T3 therapy, and 2. Remain well after T3 therapy has been discontinued; then one might wonder when one goes up and when one goes down on T3 therapy. Again, the only thing better than feeling well <u>on</u> medicine is feeling well <u>off</u> medicine. A rationale follows:

Time Frame Of Treatment

One can think of T3 therapy as the road that leads to a distant city. Along that road might be two or three beautiful cities. While passing through these cities on the way to one's final destination, one might appreciate them to the extent that one might prefer to stay a few days in each town, rather than driving straight through to the final city. Such decisions can be made based on available time, condition or quality of the intermediate cities, road conditions, resources (e.g., money), and priorities. Some people may prefer to drive straight through to the final destination while others may prefer to make the trip in several stages. So too are there many options in the progress of T3 therapy.

The ultimate goal or destination for most Wilson's Syndrome sufferers is normalization of body temperature patterns which are then maintained by their own body even after T3 therapy has been discontinued. Some patients might have their reason to "drive straight through" to obtain that destination (for example, they might not like taking medicine and may prefer to stop taking the medicine as soon as is humanly possible, or they may be planning to move away in the near future and may want to try to achieve their goal if possible within the time period available). Others might have greater short term needs like the tired and hungry traveler who stops for a time in a closer city to eat, recuperate, and sleep on his way to his more distant, more desirable, final destination. Some Wilson's Syndrome sufferers, having obtained a certain level of improvement in their symptoms, may prefer not to change therapy for a time, even though their improvement is less than complete. They may have felt so badly for so long and may be so glad to feel halfway normal for the first time in years, that they may not want to "rock the boat" for a time. Usually, however, after they have "rested and recuperated" for a time, they gain the confidence and desire to proceed from "city to city" a step at a time, getting closer and closer to normal on less and less medicine, enjoying more and more improvement in the symptoms with less and less chance of side effects until ideally, the process is complete with the patient being normalized and remaining so even after therapy has been discontinued.

"Road conditions" are also an important consideration. A patient may be in the midst of starting a new business, selling his house, moving, and taking care of his hospitalized mother's affairs, all at the same time. Under such conditions, it may be preferable not to add to the patient's challenges by making a lot of adjustments in his T3 therapy, especially if the preoccupying conditions are not expected to last very long. It is sometimes better to weather out the storm in one city before proceeding to the next one. The goal of T3 therapy is to use the treatment to artificially reset the system while providing sufficiently normal and steady levels of T3 therapy. The body is given the opportunity to maintain **naturally** what has been accomplished artificially. This cannot always be accomplished in one step or "cycle."

There can be setbacks in progress. Since stress and starvation are some of the things that can precipitate Wilson's Syndrome in the first place, they can also impair the body's ability to maintain naturally what has been established artificially. So again, if the patient is satisfactorily improved, then it might be preferable for him to weather out the conditions of stress and/or starvation (or perhaps significant dieting or exercise) before proceeding to his final destination.

Let's suppose a patient who has been staying in a "city" wherein her symptoms are improved, but her temperature is around 98.0, chooses to move on the next "city". Since the patient is more likely to need less medicine with the next cycle the closer her body temperature approaches 98.6, if the patient is not having any complaints, it may be preferable to increase the T3 therapy in an attempt to "punctuate" the cycle by attempting to bring her body temperature pattern up closer to 98.6 prior to weaning. Of course, the T3 therapy may be weaned if the patient develops any side effects, if the temperature goes above 98.6, or if the symptoms are not satisfactorily improved even if the temperature is averaging 98.6. Cycling and getting on less T3 therapy, is generally the "road" that leads to the final destination.

Ripples

Patients can usually manage ordinary fevers due to colds or flu's in the usual way (without changing the T3 dosage) if being maintained well on a certain level of T3 therapy. Remember that each change in the dose of T3 causes ripples the way a tap on the edge sends a ripple through an entire water bed, and these ripples can last for up to two weeks or more before settling down. These ripples may not be noticed in any side effects, and maybe not even in the body temperature patterns, but may be detected in terms of lost potential benefit.

Typical Responses To T3 Therapy

These principles may make it easier to understand typical patterns of response to T3 therapy:

1. When patients begin the first cycle of T3 therapy, they sometimes feel better in the first week of treatment than they do as the cycle proceeds. This is understandable since in the beginning, T3 therapy is building upon the steady foundation of the body's T3 with temperatures closer to normal being achieved with relatively small doses which are easier to keep steady. But as one increases the dosage in working towards the subgoals of therapy, the more one takes, the harder it is to keep it steady, and so understandably the improvement in the symptoms may not remain as great.

2. Some patients notice more improvement in their symptoms of MED as they wean **off** a cycle of T3 therapy than they ever did going **on**. This is understandable since the body sometimes maintains naturally the level of body temperature achieved artificially more **steadily** than was accomplished artificially.

3. Different levels of improvement can be achieved with subsequent cycles. For example, a patient may achieve 60% resolution of his or her symptoms with the first cycle with the symptoms remaining persistently improved to a 60% degree even after the therapy has been discontinued. Then sometime later with a second cycle, the level of improvement may be brought up to 75%, which may persist even after the cycle has been discontinued. And still another cycle may bring the results up to 90% resolution of the symptoms. However, at any time, if the patient is faced with significant stress or starvation conditions, then the level of improvement may relapse back down to, say, 40% resolution.

4. The symptoms of MED are improved by the body temperature being more <u>normal</u> **and** <u>steady</u>. The balance of these two factors determines the level of correction of the symptoms. Patterns that are less normal but more steady may result in increased benefit as compared to patterns that are more normal and less steady. But patterns that are both normal and steady are most preferable and most likely to result in a correction of the symptoms of MED.

5. It is difficult to compare the body temperature patterns of one person to another to predict the degree of improvement of MED symptoms. **The body temperature of one person compared to himself, however, can be quite useful in predicting improvement in the symptoms of MED.** For example, if a patient's body temperature patterns become more normal and more steady with T3 therapy, one can expect an improvement in the symptoms of MED even if the patient's body temperature patterns are not as normal and not as steady as the body temperature patterns that were necessary to alleviate the symptoms of some other patient.

Balancing With Other Systems

We have described the inertia of the body's systems by using the example of a ring with ropes tied to it, with each rope pulling with a different tension such that all the tensions in the ropes balance out in such a way that the ring maintains a certain position. In those simple analogies, we have imagined the balancing of only a few forces. However, we can see that there are many systems in the body and many forces at work that influence the overall balance or position of the body. So rather than just a few ropes or forces at work, there are actually many more, a few of which we have mentioned (female hormone, adrenal hormone, thyroid hormone, glucose metabolism, stress, body shape, diet, exercise, medications, etc.).

Frequently, the overall balance can be favorably normalized with proper T3 therapy. Proper T3 therapy can seemingly "pull" the thyroid system and consequently even other body systems and forces into a new balance or position. This "settling" may explain why symptoms sometimes continue to improve even after steady state has been reached (in about two weeks) or even up to six weeks or more.

Theoretically, the overall balance could possibly be manipulated through the manipulation of other systems other than the thyroid system. **T3 therapy may be so much more useful, effective, reproducible, and predictable because of the fewer number of variables involved.** Just as it is easier to turn on a light switch with one end of a ruler while holding the other end, than it is to turn on that switch using a segmented bamboo toy snake that flops or "writhes" when one holds it out by the tail against gravity. The greater the number of variables or "segments" the more difficult it is to control a tool in the accomplishing of a specific purpose. The female hormone system, for example, involves progesterones and estrogens that go up and down independently, at different times of the month. There are many different forms of estrogens and progesterones on the market, both separately, and in different combinations. Such a complicated set of variables would be, to say the least, extremely difficult to manage effectively, even if the female hormone system could be manipulated to change the overall balance of the body. 271

DIAGRAM 10-1

BALANCE OF FORCES

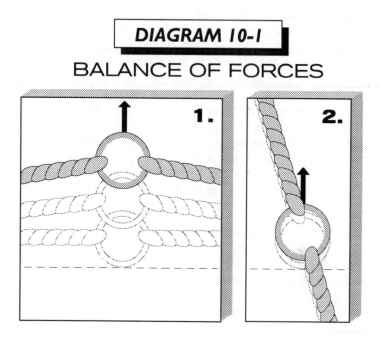

Since the overall balance of the body's system can usually be restored to a desirable position with proper T3 therapy, when progress seems to get "stuck" in terms of a lack of continued improvement in the symptoms of MED during the process of cycling, one might look for "opposing" forces that may be resisting further progress. Referring to the diagram (10-1), one may see in the first situation that if the forces are arranged in this first way then changing the tension in one rope might more easily change the position of the ring than if the ropes or forces are arranged in the second way. Since in the second situation there may be more direct opposition to progress. Thus, if progress in the resolution of the symptoms of MED is progressing predictably and then all of a sudden seems to get "stuck", then one might look for systems in which tensions can be changed to decrease resistance to improvement. For example, one might consider decreasing a woman's female hormone dosage when she is being treated with female hormones. The patient might be able to make dietary changes that can better maintain favorable blood sugar levels such as with a hypoglycemic diet. Life style changes may be effected to alter the stress levels. Likewise, exercise activity, body shape (through weight changes), and the doses of other medications can sometimes be manipulated in such a way as to permit further progress and normalization of body temperature patterns and functions. Of course, some of these measures can, and many times should be, implemented from the start of T3 therapy as part of the overall plan of action.

Remain Normal After Treatment?

Who are most likely to be able to remain normal after proper T3 therapy has been discontinued? Those who have more sturdy metabolisms, and who enter the conservation mode less easily. Those who enter into the conservation mode more easily, earlier in life, and with less provocation (especially common in certain nationalities) generally have a more difficult time maintaining more normal body temperature patterns after therapy has been discontinued. And they may relapse more easily when they are able to maintain normal temperature patterns for a time. The closer a person is able to return to a normal or ideal level of functioning and physical condition, the more likely they are to be able to maintain naturally body temperature patterns. "The further in bed you are the harder it is to fall out." And, of course, those who are under conditions of stress and/or starvation might more easily relapse and have more difficulty maintaining body temperature patterns naturally.

Important Details

The information outlined in this treatment section of the book is intended as a general overview. The specifics of treatment cannot be reviewed in complete detail because they are outside the scope of this single book. The information here is not intended to be considered exhaustive but is intended to

273

show the reader that there are definitely approaches that can be taken to alleviate and often correct Wilson's Syndrome. Of course, the proper T3 therapy outline in this book cannot and should not be attempted without the supervision of a physician. Despite the space limitation of this book it would probably be helpful to include a few more details:

1. **T3 is a temperature tool.** Taking T3 therapy does not alleviate the symptoms of MED. *Achieving more normal and steady body temperature patterns with T3 therapy frequently alleviates the symptoms of MED.* T3 is not the answer, it is a tool one may use in order to accomplish a certain purpose. T3 is not a "cure-all" but it can be very useful in correcting an imbalance in a vitally important system that can affect virtually every function of the body. One cannot begin to hope for ideal functioning of one's health unless he has adequate thyroid hormone system function.

2. Wilson' Syndrome sufferers who are being treated for **hypothyroidism** deserve special consideration. Hypothyroidism can cause DTSF through inadequate production of T4 from the thyroid gland, while Wilson's Syndrome can result in DTSF because of impaired conversion of the T4 to the active thyroid hormone T3. Some patients presenting to a physician with hypothyroidism may have their hypothyroidism or low T4 production detected with thyroid hormone blood tests which are usually very useful for this purpose. Normally, hypothyroidism is corrected with T4 supplementation to the satisfying of these thyroid hormone blood tests, causing them to return to the "normal range." In many cases, this may also resolve the patient's DTSF since the patient may be able to adequately convert the T4 supplementation given by mouth into T3.

As mentioned previously, the patients who do the best are the ones who are able to get their temperatures closer to normal on lesser amounts of T3 because, the lower the amount of T3, the easier it is to keep it steady. However, the more T4 and RT3 that may be competing with T3 at the active site, the more T3 that may be necessary in order to overcome that competition to provide more normal body temperature patterns.

If less T4 and RT3 were present, then less T3 would be needed, since less competition would be present.

One can reduce RT3 levels by reducing the levels of T4, its source. To decrease T4 levels, one may decrease T4 supplementation. T4 supplementation may be weaned from .05 - .10 milligrams per day, per week, until the T4 supplementation has been discontinued for a time. Of course, as the T4 supplementation is discontinued, levels of T3 drop as well which can result in increased symptoms of DTSF. Generally, it is preferable to withhold T3 supplementation for approximately seven to ten days after T4 supplementation has been discontinued, especially if there is not a worsening of the symptoms of DTSF. This is to allow levels of T4 and RT3 to decrease. If while the T4 therapy is being weaned, the symptoms of DTSF do worsen, then low levels of T3 supplementation may be initiated to sustain T3 levels while T4 therapy is being weaned.

It is usually best not to increase T3 therapy in an attempt to normalize body temperature patterns and to **diminish** the symptoms of DTSF until approximately the tenth day after T4 therapy has been discontinued, but only to prevent a **worsening** of the symptoms of DTSF in the meantime. In this way, one may be able to avoid inadvertently increasing the T3 therapy to higher levels than would otherwise be necessary (lower T4 and RT3 levels resulting from the weaning of T4 therapy lower the competition against T3 for the active site so that less T3 is required to overcome it and provide more normal body temperatures). By staying on lower levels of T3 therapy in the first place, one may avoid having to go through as many cycles of T3 therapy.

Cycles of T3 therapy can sometimes take from two weeks to two months each. Thus, by only increasing T3 dosage levels to prevent **increased** levels of DTSF symptoms while T4 therapy is being weaned, one can often be as far along in a few weeks as he otherwise would be in six months. Of course, in Wilson's Syndrome sufferers who also happen to be hypothyroid one must restore T4 therapy as each cycle of T3 is weaned and after the patient's Wilson's Syndrome has been corrected (since they don't produce T4 sufficiently on their own). At the beginning of each cycle of T3 therapy in such patients, T4 therapy should again be weaned before T3 therapy is used to pursue normalization of body temperature patterns. So hypothyroid patients who still suffer from the symptoms of DTSF, in spite of adequate T4 therapy because they are also suffering from Wilson's Syndrome, can often be helped. Ideally, such patients can be cycled on and off T4 and T3 therapy until eventually their Wilson's Syndrome can be corrected and they may be placed back on T4 therapy and retain resolution of their symptoms of DTSF. In fact, many times they can often feel better on less T4, after T3 therapy, than they ever did on more.

3. **T4 Test Dose.** The competition between T4 and T3 for the thyroid hormone receptor can be **used handily in the management of side effects of T3 therapy**. Side effects from 12 hour sustained-release T3 therapy (most commonly mild achiness, fluid retention, mild headaches, fatigue, and occasionally edginess) usually are related to unsteady levels of T3 resulting in unsteady body temperature patterns, leading to unsteady multiple enzyme function. Let us remember that T4 is about three times longer acting and is four times less active than T3. A small dose of the longer-acting, and, in a sense, more stable T4, can be used to **dilute** the influence of the more powerful T3 at the level of the active site, thereby, making the thyroid hormone influence at the thyroid hormone receptor more steady. A **T4 test dose** can decrease the side effects that a patient may be having from unsteady levels of T3 therapy. Interestingly, it can do it in about **45 minutes**. This is possibly because it does not take long for a dose of T4 to be absorbed from the stomach into the blood stream and to be distributed to the cells of the body, thereby, having its stabilizing effect. In this respect, T4 can almost be thought of as a wet blanket, compared to T3. Many times patients are quite astonished by how quickly and completely their side effects can resolve after a small dose of T4. This may be on the order of approximately 15% to 20% of the number of micrograms of T3 the patient is currently taking each day. For example, **12.5 micrograms (.0125 milligrams) of T4** (e.g. 1/2

of the smallest strength of Synthroid...a new pair of toenail clippers are handy for cutting them in half) may be given to a patient who is currently having some side effects on 30 to 37.5 micrograms of T3 therapy incorporating a sustained-release vehicle being taken twice a day.

Although T4 is much more stable, it should be remembered that it can sometimes feed rather than reverse the vicious cycle that leads to Wilson's Syndrome. It should also be noted that it is often not favorable to take the T4 therapy if it is not necessary for side effects, because it can sometimes block what one is trying to accomplish with the T3 therapy. The T4 dose is best taken only as needed for side effects. If the side effects resolve quickly within one or two hours of the dose, it is more likely that the patient did need the dose of T4. So the dose of T4 might only need to be taken once, possibly every three days, or only every week or so, but preferably not more often than once a day.

If the thyroid hormone influence cannot be easily and sufficiently steadied with doses of T4, then the patient should be gradually weaned off the T3 therapy and perhaps started on another cycle. Incidentally, some patients do quite well with a combination of both continuous T4 and T3 therapy, and a few respond better to instant release T3 therapy than to sustained released T3 therapy. So in every case, the choice of therapy and dosing considerations must be made based on individual patient response and laboratory findings.

4. In light of the information contained in this book, **thyroid hormone therapy that does not take into consideration body temperature patterns is not being done correctly**.

5. Likewise, considering that Wilson's Syndrome can be precipitated or made worse by starvation conditions, the use of dietary approaches such as **crash diets, low calorie diets, very low calorie diets, and protein sparing modified fasting liquid diets, without regard to body temperature patterns**, in patients already suffering from symptoms of MED, can not be considered prudent. As many people are becoming

increasingly aware, these measures can cause or worsen a patient's symptoms of MED, leaving the patient to gain all of their weight back and then some. One such measure of dieting or "starvation" may precipitate persistent DTSF due to the patient developing Wilson's Syndrome, then the patient can be left with debilitating physical and functional problems that can have a profoundly adverse impact on the person's life. Proper diet and exercise certainly are very important. And dietary systems or tools (such as certain liquid diets) do have their favorable uses. It is only inappropriate to use such tools without taking into consideration, on an ongoing basis, a patient's body temperature patterns and symptoms that may be related to MED, DTSF, and Wilson's Syndrome. These symptoms can be revealed through careful questioning of the patient as part of the monitoring of his dieting process.

6. Symptoms of low blood pressure such as lightheadedness, clamminess, increased heart rate, and shakiness may often actually be due to **low blood sugar levels**. Such symptoms can frequently be alleviated by eating a little something to bring up blood sugar levels, such as a piece of chicken, cheese and crackers, or orange juice. Refined sugars, such as candy, are usually not preferable since they may result in a rebound drop in blood sugar levels due to the body's reaction to the sugar in the candy. Patients with Wilson's Syndrome seem to have unstable blood sugar levels which can go too high when they are high and too low when they are low. This can be through a hypoglycemic diet and also through normalization of body temperature patterns.

7. Since mental and physical stress can lead to precipitation of the symptoms of MED and Wilson's Syndrome, it is recommended that one should approach diseases associated with mental stress, such as anxiety and depression, while bearing in mind the patient's body temperature patterns. Likewise, when addressing patients who are undergoing severe physical stress such as recovering from car accidents, major surgery, severe infections, or the like, one should always bear in mind the patient's body temperature patterns, since it can have a profound influence on how he will recover. This may be especially important in cases where a patient's

278

recovery could go either way, being balanced on the verge of life and death, such as in intensive care units and in critically ill patients. In such circumstances, consideration of body temperature patterns can literally mean the difference between life and death.

8. If a patient taking T3 therapy is **scheduled to undergo surgery**, then considering the short half-life of T3 and the potential for unsteady blood levels, it is usually advisable for the patient to gradually wean off T3 therapy before the surgery. The T3 therapy may be resumed once the surgery has been completed. It is important, however, to give adequate time for the weaning process so that the T3, body temperature, blood pressure, etc. are not dropped abruptly just prior to surgery.

9. **Drug interactions** - Since T3 is a substance that is normally found in every person's body, if a particular medicine does not have an adverse chemical reaction with the T3 already inside a person's body, then it will not have a direct chemical reaction with the T3 medication taken by mouth. So, any drug interactions are usually not due to direct chemical reaction between T3 and other medicines but because of indirect effects. T3 can affect a person's temperature, blood pressure, and pulse. In some instances, these effects can be additive, such as with antihistamines, decongestants, antidepressants, asthma medicines, etc. The body normally becomes accustomed to T3 therapy by making certain compensatory changes. Some medicines (such as beta blockers) may affect the body's ability to compensate or "get used to" T3 therapy. Other medication such as cortisone, progesterone, estrogens, certain anti-inflammatory medicines, and the like, can oppose the purpose of T3 therapy, thereby, making it less effective.

10. Thyroid medicine is **pregnancy category A**, which is the safest category for medicines that can be taken during pregnancy. As a matter of fact, it is usually recommended that thyroid hormone medication not be stopped during pregnancy. In some cases, the thyroid hormone supplementation is important in helping the woman to conceive the pregnancy and to maintain it to full term. However, due to the short half-life of

T3, I recommend that patients who become pregnant on T3 therapy should gradually wean off T3 therapy, mainly because if for some reason they were denied access to their medicine abruptly, they might have problems with their pregnancy. Fortunately, many women with Wilson's Syndrome do their best when they are pregnant.

11. T3 therapy can be **symptomatic** (used to treat the symptoms), **therapeutic** (used for a time to correct the underlying problem), used as a **maintenance therapy** (to maintain an effective correction through the use of continued administration of the medicine), and used as **prophylaxis** (used intermittently to prevent relapse of Wilson' Syndrome, especially during short periods of extreme stress typical of conditions that have precipitated relapses previously).

As mentioned previously, the considerations discussed in this chapter about the treatment of Wilson's Syndrome are relatively thorough, but are not nearly exhaustive. Greater details on treatment considerations in various other illnesses and situations is outside the scope of this book. The treatment protocol is explained in full detail in the **Doctor's Manual for Wilson's Syndrome.** T3 therapy should usually be monitored every two to six weeks by a physician in person, and more frequently, if necessary, by phone (and in person, if necessary). Monitoring should be more frequent initially until one can more fully predict a patient's response, and may be less frequent later in therapy. Although the information presented here is not exhaustive, an effort was made to give enough information to demonstrate that the thyroid system is far more dynamic than it is generally considered to be, and that thyroid medication can be thought of in terms of minutes and days, rather than weeks and months. Thyroid hormone therapy can be adjusted to accomplish much good, and can even make all the difference in a person's life. It should not be considered in terms of merely putting a patient on a certain dosage to see how they do, and leaving the patient on that particular regimen indefinitely regardless of whether or not their symptoms are greatly benefited. To adapt a phrase from *The Annals of Internal Medicine* article of December, 1977, entitled <u>Thyroidal and Peripheral Production of Thyroid Hormones</u>, that applies both to the information presented in the article and the information presented in this book: **This new information has forced a reassessment of long held views of the thyroid system and has profound clinical implications as well** (To say the least!).

11. IMPLICATIONS OF WILSON'S SYNDROME

The significance of a medical problem is not always measured by how complicated the problem is, how expensive it is to diagnosis, how difficult it is to treat, or how expensive it is to treat. If a swimmer swims into a cave and cannot manage to make it back to the surface to breathe, he will die. Such a problem is not complicated or difficult to understand. It is not difficult to diagnose, or prevent; but, nevertheless, the problem can certainly have a tremendous impact on a swimmer. Likewise, Wilson's Syndrome is not complicated and it can be easily and inexpensively diagnosed and treated, yet it can have tremendous impact on a person's life and on a society. The significance of Wilson's Syndrome lies in the fact that it is

1. Extremely common
2. Debilitating
3. Easily treated
4. Reversible

It is my feeling that Wilson's Syndrome takes a greater toll on our society as a whole, in terms of productivity in the work place, progress in industry, harmony in families, harmony in communities, performance in school, and overall quality of life than any other medical condition, even heart disease, cancer, and AIDS. This is primarily because of how many more people are affected by Wilson's Syndrome than there are by heart disease, cancer, and AIDS; and also because it is currently going unrecognized and untreated.

Although recognition and treatment of Wilson's Syndrome is **very** simple, it is also **very** significant. Although it may be difficult to imagine at first, there is a very good physiological reason why Wilson's Syndrome can affect so many **things** (body temperature affects all body function) and have such far-reaching effects. An effort has been made with this book to help the reader begin to see just how far-reaching those effects can be.

The ramifications of Wilson' Syndrome can be as wide-ranging and as far-reaching as those seen in any medical specialty. The problems and symptoms present in this book are most similar to the problems and symptoms seen by primary care doctors (general practitioners and family doctors). Considering that the practitioner should be continually mindful of this significant condition's many varied ramifications (directly and in relation to other medical problems and treatments), the management of this one condition and its ramifications could represent a field of practice in and of itself. Because WS is so prevalent, and because it can cause and interface with so many medical problems, a doctor could easily devote all of his time to this one area of medicine (as I do).

Considering Wilson's Syndrome derives its importance from its effect on the metabolism, this field of medicine could be called metabology (would that make us metabologists?).

TESTIMONIALS

In The Patients' Own Words

Charles C.

A rash started to break out over my entire body. It got so bad, I went from doctor to doctor looking for help. I had gone to five different doctors. They all ran tests and found nothing. They all treated me with ointments and antibiotics. I could not tolerate air conditioning at all. My skin over my entire body was continually flaking. I had to change clothes, shower, and lotion my entire body twice a day. My hair came out, and every one of my finger nails and toe nails came off. The skin on my hands and feet was thick and dry, and would burst open and bleed. I was so irritable my wife was afraid to talk to me at times. I am 61 years old, but I looked well over 100. My family and everyone else that knew me thought I was dying. I guess maybe I did too. After 7 months of this I saw another doctor, but this time it paid off. I know without a doubt that Dr. Wilson's treatment saved my life. After starting treatment and getting my temperature up, I gradually returned to normal, almost from a point of no return. After I began to improve then everyone started telling me how absolutely horrible I did look. Of course, they wouldn't say before how bad I looked. I will be eternally grateful to Dr. Wilson for giving me my life back.

Suzanne G.

In September 1989, I was referred by my own GYN to an endocrinologist for thyroid testing. I complained of debilitating fatigue, headaches, depression, and rather frightening episodes of monthly PMS. Actually these symptoms had been present for at least 3 to 4 years, and I had previously had thyroid testing (at least 3 times that I recall) and I was told that the results were in the "normal" range. The endocrinologist diagnosed me as being hypothyroid and prescribed Synthroid. In a follow up visit in January 1990, I explained that I felt no better than before I began taking the medication - I literally felt no difference and all the complaints were still present. The doctor I was seeing said that obviously these symptoms were caused by something other than the hypothyroidism. He suggested I see my "regular" doctors since there was nothing more he could do for me, and I was to continue taking the Synthroid for the rest of my life.

Needless to say, this was very disappointing, but I really had no alternative and simply did not know where to go or what to do next. My mother suggested that I had nothing to lose by seeing Dr. Wilson, since the fatigue and headaches were at a level that made daily functioning extremely difficult.

I was astounded that the profile for Wilson's Syndrome seemed to be tailored to me personally. Then when I went, I subsequently began charting my temperature and found it was always well below 97.4 and I began to hope that I had finally come to the right doctor. When I began taking the liothyronine, I literally felt better immediately and within a few days felt better than I had ever felt in my life. The fatigue was gone, the headaches were gone, and the depression was gone.

Perhaps even more phenomenal, was that days prior to my first menstrual cycle after beginning the medication, I, for the first time in as long as I could remember, experienced no discomfort **whatsoever**- no mood swings, no cravings, no depression, no irrational behavior, and no cramping. Needless to say I was ecstatic and was almost non-believing that I could feel so generally good.

The list of the additional physical changes that have taken place during my treatment would be extensive. Some specifics are as follows: Formerly brittle fingernails are now strong and growing. My skin was always blemished and dry and now is clear and more moist. I sweated excessively and now do so only moderately. I am even-tempered and no longer have severe moods (my husband will attest to this). I formally, on a daily basis, had episodes of "spots before my eyes" and momentarily blurred vision - this has completely stopped. A most significant result is the absence of fatigue. It is simply something I remember from the past and no longer experience. The depression which had begun to make me question my overall sanity is also gone. My family and friends quite frankly think I'm a different person and are pleased with the new me. I feel like a new person. The primary benefit that I have gained from my treatment is complete absence of any physical ailments, symptoms, or complaints, and the general sense of overall well-being. I feel well physically and mentally. It feels almost miraculous. I can only, in understatement, say thank you Dr. Wilson for giving me my life back.

Linda B.

My problem began when I quit smoking 4 years ago. I started gaining weight. I tried to lose weight on my own, but to no avail. I went to a weight loss clinic and started their program. They kept telling me that I must be cheating because I wasn't losing weight and I was not in ketosis.

In August, 1988, I moved to Florida and tried another weight loss clinic. After 6 months of staying on their program of 800 calories a day, I lost 4 pounds. Discouraged and very depressed I went to an endocrinologist for help. My thyroid was under active and I was given Synthroid. A year later I was even more depressed, constantly tired, headaches every day and still overweight. I talked to my doctor. He told me I would just have to live with myself as I was, overweight and tired. I told him I refused to live the rest of my life the way I felt. He told me I needed to see a psychiatrist to help me accept the way I was. This caused me to feel even more hopeless, depressed and discouraged. I even felt I must be going crazy. Every night for months I cried myself to sleep, growing more and more despondent.

Fortunately, I was told about Dr. Wilson. He explained to me what could be causing my metabolism to be so sluggish and that the depression and fatigue could be related to Wilson's Syndrome. In just a few short weeks of beginning treatment, I was beginning to feel less fatigued and the depression was lifting. In just a couple of months, I lost 40 pounds, and even more important, the fatigue was gone. Depression, fatigue, and headaches are no longer a part of my day. I eagerly face each new day with energy and a positive outlook. I am so thankful to Dr. Wilson, his staff, and the many hours of research he has done to find help for me. I have truly been given a new lease on life.

Debbie W.

I am writing this letter to thank you for what you have done for me. Your diagnosis and treatment of me has changed my life!

Five years ago my life and my health seemed to take a turn for the worse. I was under an extreme amount of stress but it never occurred to me that the problems I was experiencing were also responsible for the changes taking place in my body. I had headaches, my skin was becoming dry and flaky, I had a loss of energy, and some accompanying depression. I also began to gain weight even though my food intake had actually **decreased**. Being a reasonably intelligent person and aware of my body and its reactions, I knew something was wrong. I began to retain fluids and my feet and ankles were so swollen and painful that, at times, it became uncomfortable to stand or walk.

At this point I decided to seek professional help. I went to two different doctors and got the same answers from them, answers that were to prove to be of no help whatsoever. Both said they could find nothing that was not within "normal" limits. In other words, they as much as said there was nothing that could be done to help me. I was beginning to think all of my problems were in my head rather than in my body.

When I found out about the Wilson's Syndrome Treatment Center, I made an appointment. As I filled out the patient information sheet and checked off all my symptoms, I became embarrassed at the number of symptoms I had that corresponded with your list. When my temperature was taken and registered below normal, I remember saying to the nurse, "That's O.K., It's always low." Little did I realize at the time how important that fact would prove to be.

Needless to say, you know the rest of the story. I began taking the medication and remarkably, within 3 days, I began to feel much better. All of my symptoms disappeared within the first week. My family and friends could not believe the immediate changes in me. I had almost forgotten what feeling good was all about. I know there must be many, many people who are in the same condition I was. If only they could know about your treatment. I refer everyone I meet who has the same symptoms I had.

Now that I understand Wilson's Syndrome and its symptoms, I believe that this condition attributed greatly to my mother's ill health. My life has changed completely thanks to you and your research. It's good to know that there are still doctors who are not content to rest on the knowledge they acquired in medical school or on the research of others. Thank you again for everything.

Sandra G. and Suzi G.

Sandra: I'm writing to thank you for the return of my good health! Since I began treatment for Wilson's Syndrome I have felt better than I have for over ten years.

After three days on your medication, my daughter said, "Mom, I can't believe it. You even look better." It's been a steady improvement ever since, and after only two months, all those years of ailments, lethargy, depression, bronchitis, and on and on, seem almost like a bad dream. I can actually walk up stairs without having to rest at the top, and I'm using only about a fourth of the bronchial medication. I have also slept better than I have in years. I would be too exhausted, sleep fitfully for one to three hours, then pace for a couple of hours and drag myself out of bed with the alarm. This has not happened once since my first day of your treatment. It's wonderful to wake up rested and looking forward to the new day. Again, thank you and God bless you.

Suzi: I felt the need to take a moment to write a letter of thanks to you. I have been following your treatment of my mother, Sandra, and I must tell you the results of your work are a miracle. As long as I can remember, she has struggled and fought with her health. The headaches she suffered would send her life into a downward spiral of pain from which she would take days to recover. She was in so much pain that she would be unable to perform even the smallest daily tasks, and her family suffered with her. Within three days of your treatment, my mother had more spirit, vigor, and love of life than I had seen in her for ten years. She has enjoyed each day as if it was her first and the joy on her face is a sight to behold. She shines with the same youthful glow that we have missed for so long.

Doctor, your work has given this family their mother back, and to you we are eternally grateful. May the Lord bless you and your work.

Sally S.

There are no words to describe the relief and difference I have felt since undergoing the treatment for Wilson's Syndrome. I not only feel better physically but also mentally.

Where do I begin with my story? When I first read of the treatment, I was more than skeptical, to say the least. When I read the list of symptoms, I thought, "Come on, be real—all these symptoms just from thyroid?" There were so many of my own symptoms listed there. But I had had good medical treatment and had been on Synthroid for years so surely I was just imagining these symptoms, wasn't I? This was what I had been led to believe for over 30 years.

Now since I feel so much better, I look back on the years when I was so very, very tired while raising my children and waking each morning more tired than when I went to bed; of wanting to just pull the covers over my head and cry; of aching all over and having to concentrate so hard just to remember how to rise from a chair and not wanting anyone to know because you think it must all be in your mind.

You are only 25 years old and look great except your feet and hands swell and you are a little bit overweight since the children were born. No one knows you eat very little and must go on a starvation diet to lose any weight at all. You are able to keep a reasonably clean house and are active with your children's school, and even take a full-time job so your husband can go back to college. Even though each day you must push yourself physically and just will yourself to keep going.

All the time you keep these things to yourself because you don't want to complain, and your doctors cannot find anything physically wrong with you other than a low thyroid and you are receiving Synthroid for that, so that ought to fix what ails you. In fact, to go back a little bit, before the doctors gave me Synthroid for my problem, they sent me to the hospital for treatment with radioactive iodine, twice.

I look at many people now and wonder if they could be suffering form the same condition as I had, excusing it as stress, getting old, every day life, and a host of other titles.

I believe my condition was not ordinary, due to the fact that neither Dr. Wilson nor anyone else could determine just how much thyroid tissue had been destroyed because of the radioactive iodine. However, after I finally figured, "What do I have to lose?" I called and made the appointment to see Dr. Wilson. Upon my consultation visit with him, he told me all the symptoms I had felt over the years. I was impressed. Remember now, I was real skeptical, and as I said before, I had had good medical treatment over the years, but simply received either blank stares when I related my problem or the feeling of "Quiet, woman, I'm the doctor, there is nothing wrong with you," or, "I'll determine what is wrong with you." Or as one very kind doctor admitted, he just couldn't figure women out. So with a shrug of the shoulder, I went on my way and felt, "What's the use, just live with it. Everyone must feel this way, they just don't mention it." And I wouldn't either.

My grandmother, who was a very intelligent person, but very cranky and at times seemingly uncaring, had her thyroid removed at Ford Hospital in Detroit around the turn of the century. She never received any medication for her condition.

Now I can see that perhaps her complaints were not unjustified, and her short temper was perhaps due to her physical condition of low thyroid or no thyroid. She is gone now. I wish I had been more understanding.

My normal body temperature has been 96.0 degrees for as long as I can remember. One doctor told me if my temperature went to 98.6 I should consider this as 2 degrees of fever and treat it that way.

I thought of myself as cool, calm, and collected, although I was on high blood pressure medicine. I guess I wasn't too cool, calm, and collected. Dr. Wilson took me off Synthroid and started me on T3 medicine for approximately 10 months. After that time, he weaned me off all thyroid medication. I have been off both Synthroid and T3 for six months now, and the thyroid blood test done last week shows that both my T4 and TSH are within normal limits. After 30 years my thyroid gland is functioning properly on its own, and I'm doing much better now than when I was on thyroid medicine. I have lost 40 pounds and reduced my blood pressure medicine by 1/2. I have kept the 40 pounds off for the last six months with little or no effect.

I hold the position of executive secretary for a very busy public figure and pride myself on being a good wife, a very efficient secretary, a great mom and grandmom, and very active in several volunteer organizations. What more can I say, Dr. Wilson, other than I wished you had been around 30 years ago.

Linda G.

I am a single mother, part-time student, and a full-time employee of an insurance agency. There was a time when I could not have possibly kept the daily schedule I have now, and absolutely could not have thought clearly, even if I could manage the hours. I recall very well a little over 2 years ago when I could not concentrate on instructions being given for a new job. I would record the information and go home and listen to it again. My goal through the day was to survive physically until I could sit down at home for the rest of the night until bedtime. I would be completely exhausted.

One spring day at work, I really panicked when I realized I could not add simple figures such as 6 + 4. Later that summer I became so sleepy while driving home one night from an all-day shopping trip that I had to let my teenage daughter drive us back to my mom's house where we were visiting. I was oblivious to the fact that she was lost and driving miles and miles out of our way. I was in a very deep sleep.

When I mentioned my symptoms to a doctor treating my daughter, he stated that I needed to increase my thyroid medication. This helped for a while, but only a short time later I was feeling as badly as ever. Added to my chronic yeast infections, allergies, and other strange symptoms such as fibromyalgia, I was also diagnosed with cytomegalovirus. My husband, also a medical doctor, was never able to help me find the cause of my symptoms.

Then one day a patient in the emergency room where my husband was working told him about the work of Dr. Wilson. Within a few short weeks, my daughter and I were both Dr. Wilson's patients. We finally had the answer for our bizarre symptoms.

The stress I am under at present would put many people in the hospital. I'm convinced of it. Yet, I am now able to continue, so far, without even one day being sick from the many viruses that have attacked many people I know this winter. When my best friend called from home in another state, she had a terrible disease and was not finding much help, although her husband is a doctor. As she described her symptoms, I realized she had Wilson's Syndrome. Her husband was convinced to call Dr. Wilson. Now my friend is also finding help from her "strange disease".

I will be forever thankful for the work of Dr. Wilson and his discovery that helped me and two of the most important people in the world to me. He has given to us, and I am sure to many others, a quality of life that before would not have been possible.

Joyce Carnefix

The first time I heard the TV information about Wilson's Syndrome, my ears perked up. They were all there, all the symptoms I had been complaining about for years. The only thing that was missing was my name. I was skeptical. The axiom, "If it sounds too good to be true, it probably is," came to mind. Still I couldn't help but wonder could it be true? Still I did nothing about it. Hadn't all the doctors I had been to for years told me that nothing was wrong with my thyroid? It always tested in normal range, to the low side but still normal. I was told I needed to lose the fat, be less sedentary, and my blood pressure would come down along with the cholesterol and triglycerides, and my constant fatigue would vanish. That was all well and good, but how was I to accomplish it when I was just too utterly exhausted to drag myself out of the chair?

The decision to see Dr. Wilson came after my daughter, Cathy, showed me a brochure about Wilson's Syndrome. She informed me that several women in her office, including a mutual friend, were getting this treatment and they were all having great results. I discussed with our mutual friend the results she was realizing from the treatment. She was very pleased and I was very impressed.

I made an appointment with Dr. Wilson. After a number of lab tests, filling out five pages of medical history, and having a physical, I was ready for an evaluation. Dr. Wilson said that my symptoms and my medical history certainly suggested a depressed metabolism. But because of my high blood pressure, he was reluctant to start me on the treatment. After insisting on close monitoring, he agreed to take me as a patient. One of the first benefits I noticed after beginning to take T3, was my improved sleep patterns. Instead of waking a dozen or more times during the night (even though going right back to sleep), I was sleeping through the night and awakening in the morning more rested and refreshed. Soon after, I became aware of a decrease in the chronic fatigue with which I had been beleaguered for years. It was so good not to feel totally exhausted all the time. For a decade or more, I felt as if there were heavy balls and chains attached to my arms and legs as I tried to move around. Finally, someone had found the key to unlock them. The next thing I became conscious of was a small budding and growing energy level. It had been so long since I had had any energy that it was hard to recognize at first.

Dr. Wilson had asked me on my first visit, "If this treatment could only accomplish one thing, what would you want it to be?" My answer, "To feel good and have the energy of a normal person." He asked me for an assessment of my perception of my energy level compared to a "normal person." I replied, "About 25 percent." At this writing I perceive my energy level to be about 90 percent of normal and still growing. What a blessing.

After several months of treatment when I began feeling much better, Dr. Wilson suggested that it was time to chose a good nutritional diet and begin an exercise program to promote weight loss. I had tried for years to diet, but even if a few pounds came off, they seemed to come right back with a few more for company. And when I tried to exercise, lethargy, that was my constant companion, soon canceled that out. But this time it worked. I had enough energy to a least begin exercising regularly and with the diet the weight began to come off. As the weight came off, I was able to increase my exercise. As I increased my exercise, more weight came off and my energy level continued to rise. It's amazing, but I have become hooked on exercise - me, the original couch potato. Three to five times a week, I walk 4 miles exercising my arms with 2 pound weights as I walk. Also I exercise 45 minutes or more every day. In addition, I have organized and run a weight control support group at my church once a week. Things are looking up. Friends and acquaintances, especially those who haven't seen me in several months keep remarking, "You look marvelous, you look 25 years younger." That's good to hear, but what is really great is that I feel 40 years younger. Oh I forgot to say, I'll be 62 in August and haven't felt this good since my early 20's.

Dr. Wilson suggested that I might enjoy decreased fatigue when I began treatment. There were some things though, that he forgot to mention. The improved elasticity and tone of my complexion, the loss of the "turkey waddle" from my neck, the addition of body to my hair (perms take better and last longer and sets last to the next shampoo).

My general health is much improved. There is more resistance to illness. Colds which have plagued me all my life come less often and are less severe. Also they are not progressing to sinus and ear infections or bronchitis as they have for the past several years. My blood pressure which was dangerously high (at one point 210 over 110) came down to the point where my medication for it had to be cut in half. Dr. Wilson suspects that I may be able to go off the blood pressure medicine completely.

When I realize just how much help I have received with this treatment and how much better I feel and look it seems almost miraculous and the solution was so simple. I keep trying to spread the news to others who are suffering as I did for so long; not sick, just half dead: there is help out there.

Donna D.

Since starting treatments I have finally been free from migraine headaches. I took Fiorinal on a daily basis whenever I got a headache so as not to go into a full blown migraine. When the Fiorinal didn't work I was given Darvon. I was also sent, on occasion, to the emergency room for a shot, because the pain was so intense. It was humiliating because they seemed to act as if I was faking just to get a shot of pain killer, as if I enjoyed waiting for hours to get stuck with a needle. I have had to take nothing for pain for the past two years, because I no longer have headaches, much less migraines. Thanks, Dr. Wilson.

Diane T.

I am a 40-year-old housewife. I have been seeing Dr. Wilson for one year and continue to go to him for treatment for Wilson's Syndrome. Prior to learning about Dr. Wilson I was suffering from the following symptoms: migraine headaches for over 20 years, constipation, fatigue, dry skin, fluid retention, dry hair, brittle, peeling and splitting soft nails, easy bruising, lack of sweating, allergies, frequent colds, heat and cold intolerance, itchiness, decreased hair and nail growth, cold hands and feet, slow wound healing, ringing of the ears, and a continuous low body temperature (97.1 degrees).

I consulted several different doctors: a family practitioner, an endocrinologist, an internal medicine specialist, a neurologist, and an ear-nose-throat specialist for all my symptoms listed above. I had to take blood test after blood test, complete physicals, upper and lower GI series, x-rays, EEG, EKG, CAT scan, RAST, pollen and food allergy testing. All the tests that were performed came back negative except for the allergy test. However, I was taking the allergy serum shots for pollen and food allergies for approximately 1 1/2 years when I discontinued the treatment because it was not helping me and the costs were very expensive. I had suffered for so long (20 years) with migraine headaches that I had the doctor admit me to the hospital and run the necessary tests and x-rays to be sure that I did not have a tumor or blood clot on the brain. I had gone to the neurologist in 1976 and 1977, and was admitted again to the hospital by a different neurologist in 1977 and had more tests done in 1978 by another neurologist. All the tests came back negative and the doctor could only prescribe Cafergot medication to take prior to the onset of the migraine headaches. The medication never worked and I continued to suffer until I went to Dr. Wilson for treatment in April of 1990.

I could not understand why none of the doctors could find anything wrong. I was angry with the medical profession because they could not help me from my suffering and pain. I did not know where to turn and it affected my life with my family and my work. I was constantly sick with migraines, colds, fatigue, and no energy to do anything or go anywhere with my family.

I missed a lot of time off work because of my migraines and being sick with colds. The job was very stressful and I started to have chest pains, stomach pains, and nausea. The more work that was put on me, the more stress I carried around with me, which, in turn, affected my health. Gradually my body's health went down and stayed down. I would continue to have new symptoms causing me to worry more, adding stress which only made the symptoms worse.

I can remember laying on the couch with a migraine headache in March of 1990 when I saw the information on television about Wilson's Syndrome. I took the number down, discussed it with my husband, then contacted Dr. Wilson's office for a consultation. At that time it was explained what Wilson's Syndrome is and how it affects your health, what the symptoms are, and how your nationality may be connected to Wilson's Syndrome. I was intrigued since it was pointed out at that time to me, before I ever mentioned my nationality, that the syndrome seems to be more common in patients whose ancestors survived famine (such as Irish, Russian, and Polish). They seem to get the syndrome more easily with the most prone combination being Irish, part Indian, and partly Polish. I had all the symptoms and the nationality Irish and Indian going for me. So I felt that he may be able to help me, and understood how much suffering and pain I was in and had been for practically all my life.

After starting treatment, I noticed some slight changes for the better and as my temperature continued to become normal, my migraines went completely away. (I had been to doctors for migraine headaches for 20 years and was put on Cafergot, pain pills, etc., but nothing helped.) I have less bruising, less fatigue, less constipation, and less fluid retention. I am still under Dr. Wilson's care and will remain so because his treatment is helping me to live my life again. What I found so amazing is that when the body temperature runs below 98.6 some of the symptoms that were gone, come back. When I am put under a lot stress that causes my temperature to become abnormal and drop below 98.6, it takes about a week to get the system back to normal again and then I notice my symptoms disappearing. I have never felt this good in my life. I recommend the treatment for just migraines alone.

Elizabeth W., Ed.D., RN

The most serious of my physical complaints were a general fatigue/depression, severe indigestion/dyspepsia/flatus, and night sweats. I also suffered from dry itchy skin, brittle hair and nails, constipation, frequent respiratory infections, frequent and severe migraine type headaches, debilitating pain in my feet, ankles, and finger joints, and occasionally, a tender abdomen "in the upper right quadrant." Frequently I found bruises on my extremities and could not relate them to any apparent injuries. I was also experiencing difficulty with memory, particularly when I was under job stress. Often I would read the same paragraph two to three times unable to concentrate. I was constantly making long lists to be certain not to forget a project of commitment. This was particularly disconcerting due to the high level of job functioning required in my position as vice president of operations of a 579 bed community hospital. In the past two years I also became irritated by happenings that previously were tolerated. It was noticed by my husband and especially my secretary.

When my mother was diagnosed with terminal cancer in early 1990, the stresses were exacerbated and I became less able to cope due to the additional responsibilities of her care. It seemed that my personal stress level at work, my general feeling of "ill health," and my mother's illness were too much. I resigned my job which I probably would not have done at **that** time if I had been better able to cope.

As I learn more about this disorder, I can recognize the beginning of the symptoms 20 years earlier. At age 30, after having 4 children in 6 1/2 years, relocating 5 times in 8 years, I was diagnosed by a rural doctor as having a mild thyroid condition. He did not use blood tests but took my oral temperature, blood pressure, and checked knee jerk reflex. My blood pressure/temperature were low and reflexes sluggish. At that time, I was placed on a small amount of thyroid even though I was about 10 to 15 pounds over normal desired weight, I quickly lost weight and felt good. We relocated, however, in 12 months and I was not able to have the prescription renewed. Each MD after that stated that I did not have a thyroid deficiency.

In 1976, I had a total hysterectomy with a traumatic post surgical wound infection. Within several weeks, I returned to my high pressure job, but it seemed that I began to feel progressively worse. Even though I was an excellent job performer, my heart was no longer in my work. My weight began to increase 5 to 6 pounds per year; I noticed that my oral temperature was about 1 degree below normal. On visits to the physician, I would explain my symptoms and state that I had previously taken thyroid. The physician would complete an EKG and blood chemistry profile and tell me that I was very healthy. Once I even visited a psychologist who also informed me that except for mild depression due to my job stress, I was very healthy even mentally.

Last fall was the first time I recognized that my symptoms were possibly related. I scheduled a visit with Dr. Wilson. I could hardly believe it. It became so obvious. I have been under treatment for 3 to 4 months. My body temperature is not yet totally stabilized, but I feel like a new person. The joint pains have completely disappeared. I started a 1,200 calorie diet 5 weeks ago and I'm losing about 2 1/2 pounds per week with no difficulty. The fatigue and depression have been eliminated. My nails and hair are growing back. My nails are also stronger. The chest pains, indigestion/ dyspepsia/flatus are gone. My quality of life has improved a 100 percent and my husband and I have even started playing golf and other recreational activities together that we have not done in years. How I wish that 20 years ago this had been diagnosed. Even 5 years ago would have been a blessing.

I have recognized that other members of my family may also be suffering from the same disorder. And I'm looking forward to sharing my changed life with them in hopes that they also can be helped. At age 51, I lost 15 to 20 years of quality of life. I hope that others will not have to do the same. It is my desire that physicians be able to recognize this disorder and aid the millions of people suffering from it.